Imperialism and R

CW00404408

Since the end of the Cold War, the United States has emerged as the hegemonic superpower with enormous military might and a strong but faltering economy. This unparalleled supremacy has been accompanied by an aggressive interventionist foreign policy which has been condemned by many as imperialist. *Imperialism and Resistance* offers a radical critique of this new imperialism of the US and its allies, including Britain.

The author explains how the US imperial turn has been underpinned by a number of significant factors such as US military spending, American economic power and the politics of oil. He also shows the terrible consequences of these policies in terms of deepening global inequality and injustice.

In the final sections of the book, the author explicitly addresses the thorny question of how best to resist the new imperialism, drawing upon his own experience as an activist in the anti-globalisation and anti-war movements.

John Rees is a founding member of the Stop the War Coalition in Britain and, as one of its current leaders, was central to the organisation on 15 February 2003, of the biggest demonstration in British political history. He has appeared widely in the media as a spokesman for the anti-war movement including on BBC2's *Newsnight* and Radio 4's *Today* programme. He is also vice-president of the International Campaign Against US Aggression founded in Cairo in December 2002. John Rees was previously a national executive member of the National Union of Students. He is a former editor of the quarterly journal *International Socialism* and a frequent visitor to the Middle East. His previous publications include *The Algebra of Revolution* (Routledge, 1998).

Imperialism and Resistance

John Rees

Routledge
Taylor & Francis Group

LONDON AND NEW YORK

First published 2006
by Routledge
2 Park Square, Milton Park, Abingdon, Oxon OX14 4RN

Simultaneously published in the USA and Canada
by Routledge
270 Madison Avenue, New York, NY 10016

Routledge is an Imprint of the Taylor and Francis Group, an informa business

© 2006 Routledge

Typeset in Joanna by Taylor & Francis Books
Printed and bound in Great Britain by MPG Books Ltd, Bodmin

British Library Cataloguing in Publication Data
A catalogue record for this book is available from the British Library

Library of Congress Cataloging-in-Publication Data
A catalog record for this book has been requested

ISBN10: 0-415-34675-4 (hbk)
ISBN10: 0-415-34676-2 (pbk)

ISBN13: 978-0-415-34675-7 (hbk)
ISBN13: 978-0-415-34676-4 (pbk)

I hate indifference. Living means taking sides . . . Indifference is the dead weight of history. It is a lead weight for those with new ideas, a ballast within which the most beautiful enthusiasms can drown, a swamp which defends the old order far better than any warriors or strong defences, because it sucks into its entrails the best activists, often stopping them from making history.

Indifference is a powerful force in history. It works passively but it works nevertheless . . . Generally events take place not because lots of people desire them, but because many people don't commit themselves, they let things happen . . . The apparent random nature of history is nothing but an illusion created by indifference, by absenteeism . . .

I take sides. I live. In the active consciousness of my side I already feel the future society being built. In this human chain nobody carries a heavy weight, everything which happens is not the result of luck or fate, but is the result of our conscious work. Nobody looks on at a minority making sacrifices . . .

I am alive, therefore I take sides. That's why I hate those who don't take sides, those who are indifferent.

Antonio Gramsci, 1917

Contents

Illustrations

Acknowledgements

It has been a privilege to be a part of the leadership of the Stop the War Coalition since it was founded in 2001, the week after the attack on the twin towers. All those I have worked with have enriched my understanding of imperialism and how to resist it, particularly Andrew Murray, Andrew Burgin, Chris Nineham, Jane Shallice, Kate Hudson, Tony Benn, and Jeremy Corbyn. George Galloway is simply the most implacable and eloquent opponent of imperialism that I know.

I am grateful to my editor at Routledge, Craig Fowlie, for encouraging me and to Simon Assaf for helping prepare the graphs and tables for publication. Some parts of this book appeared in a different form as articles in the quarterly journal *International Socialism*. Thanks are due to Sally Campbell who produced the journals in which they appeared.

My longest standing debts are to those who read and commented on the draft of this book – Alex Callinicos, Chris Bambery, and Chris Harman. I have lost two great friends and teachers, Tony Cliff and Paul Foot, while this book was being written but it bears the mark of their influence nevertheless.

Carmel Brown is the harshest critic of my writing and the most enthusiastic in encouraging me to do more of it. She edited chapter five, and kept an endless flow of articles, anecdotes and statistics heading towards me as I wrote. She read and commented on the final manuscript. I count myself lucky to have her friendship and that of my shop-steward, Seren Nolan, and her sister, Hope Nolan.

Lindsey German has been my constant companion through this time. She read many of the chapters as they were written and the whole book when it was complete. Her advice is better than most not only because she knows more about this subject than many but also because she has done more to resist the new imperialism than anyone.

I am grateful to those in Cairo with whom I have organised in recent years but whom it is still not safe to name. We will all celebrate together when imperialism and dictatorship no longer disfigure the great capitals of Cairo and Baghdad. Then, in every sense, we can build a new Jerusalem.

Introduction

In November 1989 I was in Berlin. For the three days before the Berlin Wall fell I passed back and forth through Checkpoint Charlie participating in the demonstrations in East Berlin and interviewing those who were organising them. Each night I would return to the West hiding the tapes of the interviews in my bag or entrusting them to others to bring through the checkpoint later. Going into East Berlin the day before the Wall fell the Stasi officer at the barrier found socialist papers in my bag. He called his superior who read the reports on the East German demonstrations with rare concentration. He called his superior, who did the same. Then he waved me through. I think I knew then that the old order was about to depart the scene.

So, in a way, I feel I was there when the Cold War ended and the new imperialism began. The people I talked to in Gethsemene Church, one of the organising centres of the movement, or secretly in their flats, wanted democracy. But they didn't want to be simply incorporated into the West. They wanted the job security and the welfare provision they knew and the democratic rights that they did not. But that was not what happened. So I saw first in Berlin a pattern much repeated since – the hope for democracy soon to be soured by neo-liberal 'shock therapy'.

Nearly a decade later, in a very different country, I saw a strikingly similar political process at work. In 1998 I was reporting on the movement that overthrew the Suharto dictatorship in Indonesia. Marching with and talking to the students who were the heart of that revolution the same paradox presented itself. We met in secret and marched under the guns of the notoriously brutal Indonesian army. The desire for democracy was fierce and all too easy to understand. But like the East Germans at the end of the previous decade they also hoped that democracy would not simply mean the same old elites presiding over the same poverty and inequality.

Today, once again, I find myself directly involved in a country facing the challenge that the East Germans and the Indonesians faced in 1989 and 1998. Parts of this book were written in Cairo. There is an old adage that says the world looks very different from the cottage and the castle. By the same token the world looks very different when you view it from Cairo than it does from London. And the view in Cairo does not reveal a loyal Egyptian government allied to the West in a noble 'war against terror'. It reveals a brutal authoritarianism that shoots, jails and tortures its opponents. In 2002 I was protesting at the deployment of US troops before the invasion of Iraq outside the Qatar embassy in Cairo. There were, at most, 1,000 of us. We were staring down the barrels of a couple of armoured cars and surrounded by armed police who were there in far greater numbers that the protesters. Yet by the following March, on the day of the invasion of Iraq, the protesters filled Cairo's Tahrir Square for two days in the largest demonstration in Egypt for a generation. Again, people are organising against tyranny. And again they want more than the right to vote. The outcome of their struggle still hangs in the balance.

In these experiences I have seen the double helix of the modern age reveal itself. Neo-liberal economics and neo-conservative military strategy intertwine. The fall of the Berlin Wall simultaneously opened the East to the western market and allowed the military might of the US and its allies to act as its security guard. But everywhere, including in the western heartlands, there has been renewed resistance to this virus. Huge movements on every continent have arisen in opposition to privatisation, deregulation and globalisation. Their scale was magnified as they also came to oppose the new imperial project launched by the neo-conservatives in the US.

Direct experience alone, however essential, is never enough. It is always individual and therefore must always be tested against general experience. And this can only be done by social analysis and historical investigation. In this book I have tried to take the spur of experience and derive from it an overall account of the new imperialism.

The three titans of the modern world

There are three great powers in the modern world. The power of nation-states, of the international economy and the power of working people on whom all states, armies and corporations, ultimately, must depend. Many of the most important events in the modern world take place at the intersection where these three forces collide.

All three forces arose at the same historical moment when feudal methods of government and production gave way to the modern centralised nation-state, the market economy and the 'free' labour force on which it rested. In Britain and Holland that historical moment was in the 17th century. In France, Italy, Germany and the United States, partly as a result of competition and example, the late 18th century and the 19th century were the critical period of war and revolution.

This global transformation created (i) an international system of competing nation-states each of which commanded the monopoly of force within their geographical boundaries, (ii) a world market in which both private firms and nation-states compete for commercial dominance and, (iii) in every country, though to differing degrees, a labour force dependent for waged employment on the new lords of the domestic and international market.

The first weak embodiments of this system on the fringes of 17th century Europe have long since been outgrown. And with each new generation these three titans have each grown in strength. The nation-states of the modern world dwarf their own predecessors in every attribute. Such states were the minority of regimes at the beginning, with small professional armies. Now every state is a centralised, bureaucratic apparatus with a huge military capacity. The numbers employed by the state are swarms compared to their early counterparts.

To an important degree the growth of the state is the result of the growth of the economic system. The early states were both a product of this system and helped it to develop. The world of the English and Dutch East India Companies, of the conquest of India and the 'New World', was an early prototype of a world market. However its trade pales into insignificance before a single day's transactions on the international markets of the modern world. The East India Company in all its long history is a mere market stall beside a single year's trading by a single modern multinational.

Less remarked upon but no less real is the growth of the third titan. The workforces drawn into mills and workshops in London, Manchester and the northern industrial towns in the late 18th and early 19th centuries were the first of their kind in a world still dominated by agricultural labour performed by peasants. Now billions in every corner of the globe have inherited their fate.

The interaction of these titans as well as their growth is what concerns us here. Not only are they bound together as three aspects of a single process, three facets of a single object. They exist, moreover, in an inherently unstable relationship. And it is this instability, recast in every generation but never eliminated, that determines how our world unfolds. It is in this three-cornered struggle that wars and revolutions are fermented.

Our titans fight for the same reason that scorpions sting – it is in their nature. Let's examine these natures and the conflict between them.

The state is in its nature geographically limited. It holds, as the oldest sociological definition tells us, the monopoly of physical force in a defined geographical area. It is, in short, a national entity.

The competition between corporations is in its nature geographically unlimited. The search for markets, raw materials and labour is in its essence international. Certainly particular firms originate and often remain based in particular nations. But they also often operate internationally and, even when they don't, they are subject to the prices set by the exchange of goods on an international scale. The older the system has become, the more this is the case. Globalisation is merely the latest term for this process.

Since the very beginnings of the system the nationally bounded state and the internationally unbounded market have been intertwined in a variety of unstable ways. Each nation-state, with its monopoly of armed force, has sought to enrich itself and those corporations most closely associated with it at the expense of other states and their associated companies. The corporations have, for their part, sought to engage the armed might of the state in order to gain commercial advantage, often playing one state off against others. The states seek to use their unique asset, military power, to make the economic power relations turn to their advantage. The corporations seek to use their economic power to mould the state to their advantage.

Neither can withdraw from this not-so-warm embrace. The state needs economic strength and the corporations need military force. Yet the international nature of market competition drives the state beyond its boundaries bringing it into conflict with other states who are likewise impelled beyond their borders. To stay within borders is to invite competitive defeat. To move beyond them intensifies economic competition and, over time, raises the certainty of military conflict between states. The rise of the first colonial empires, the conflict between them, the graduation of these imperial clashes to the level of world war twice in the last century are only the most destructive results of this process.

Working people, our third titan, bear a contradictory relationship to corporations and the states. Necessary for both, they are at home in neither. For the corporations working people are seen as a production cost that must be lowered where possible, thus assisting profit-maximisation. The historically brief period of welfare capitalism in the 30 years after the Second World War has long since given way to a period that has more in common with the 1920s and 1930s in its unbridled celebration of market forces by the economic directors of the system. The state itself is more nakedly and obviously the enforcer of business priorities at home as abroad. Working people depend on a job and have to accommodate to the system, but they rarely share all its values. And often the convulsions of both the economic system and the rivalry between states confront working people with the challenge of passing from relative political quietude to an active intervention in their society.

This final point needs some elaboration since it rarely receives the detailed attention routinely paid to the actions of states and corporations. Nevertheless the history of the last century alone would be incomprehensible if we did not take into proper account the effect of those moments when ordinary people have transformed history through collective action. Among the major revolutions that have transformed the state we can number those in Mexico and Russia before the First World War, those in Russia, Germany and Hungary during and immediately after the First World War. In China in the 1920s and Spain in the 1930s the whole course of both nations' history was altered by revolution. After the Second World War national liberation movements profoundly altered the global state system by ending the era of direct colonial rule. The real beginning of the end of the bi-polar Cold War world was inaugurated by the rise of Solidarity in Poland in the early 1980s and its final demise came in the Eastern European revolutions of 1989. Even more recently dictatorial regimes in South Africa, Indonesia and Serbia have fallen to popular movements.

Modern imperialism is defined by the conflict between these three titans. They are bound together as three facets of a single, contradictory totality. Without the competitive dynamic between the individual economic units of the system they would not find themselves constantly pitted against others in a battle for survival. Without the states and their armouries such economic competition would not ultimately also involve military competition. Without competitive economic expansion the working class would not grow. Nor would it find its livelihood under the constant economic and political pressure which is the initial spur to resistance.

The development of modern imperialism is the story of how this three-cornered struggle has been recast as the system has expanded. Of course there were empires before the rise of capitalism and the modern nation-state. Ancient Rome and the Ottoman Empire are two obvious examples. But the pre-modern empires did not have the same competitive economic dynamic, rested on a much more limited productive base and did not concentrate political and military force in such powerful state machines. Nor were society-transforming social revolutions the ever-present alter ego of the system.

In its initial infant form modern imperialism arose in England and Holland in the 17th century as the birth-partner of modern capitalism. As the new system grew it clashed with older empires, like the Spanish Empire. By a process of competition and emulation the old societies of Europe either became like the new powers or faced decline. As they transformed the first, colonial system of imperialist competition grew. The 19th century colonial system of the European powers faced its global crisis when the first industrialised total war began in 1914. The redrawing of power relations between the major powers lasted from the First World War to the end of the Second World War. The settlement of that conflict was institutionalised in a new pattern of great power rivalry, the Cold War. The shifts in economic power during the Cold War period ultimately undermined the international state structure. The revolutions of 1989 were the midwife of the new era. We now live in an age where economic accumulation, nation-states and the working people on whom they depend are, once again, contesting the future shape of our world.

So here are our three great titans: the state, the world economy and the international workforce it has created. The struggle between them is the history of our era.

This book is an attempt to explain how these three titans clash and how the result of their battles shapes our world. In chapter one, 'Arms and America', I trace the imperial profile of the

United States from the Cold War to the invasion of Iraq. The argument is that the military capacity of the US state relative to its rivals is greater now than at any point in its history. The chapter examines the rise of the neo-conservatives and the grand strategy that they have articulated for the US ruling class in the post-Cold War world. Chapter two, by contrast, examines the relative decline of the United States' economic weight in the world economy and assesses the strengths and weaknesses of its competitors. It is in this couplet – US relative military strength and economic decline – that much of the instability in the contemporary international order rests.

'Oil and empire', chapter three, examines why the Middle East has become such a crucial arena in which this new imperial rivalry is played out. It examines how important oil is to the world economy and to the US economy in particular. And it is in this chapter that we first examine the response of the third titan, popular resistance, to the dominant economic and imperial order. The long history of resistance to imperialism in the Middle East from the rise of Arab nationalism to the resurgence of Islam is charted.

Chapter four, 'Globalisation and inequality', examines the relationship between nation-states and international corporations, between the new imperialism and neo-liberal economic policy. Inequality between rich and poor nations and between the rich and poor within nations is one of the primary consequences of globalisation. This is the background both to the development of 'failed' states and to the growing gap between the political elite and the mass of the working people in the advanced economies. This chapter therefore highlights the common cause of both the economic and political attacks on poor countries internationally and poor people domestically. It shows that the new imperial state is a threat to democracy at home and abroad because it acts to reinforce the inequalities sustained and created by the deregulated global market.

One of the key justifications for modern wars is that they are fought to secure democracy. Chapter five looks at how democracy arose in Britain, America and France in the revolutions of the 17th and 18th centuries. But it examines these historical experiences so that we can compare what was possible then with what might be possible in the much more advanced conditions of modern democratic revolutions. The analysis looks at how the class forces and political leaderships of the revolutions interact. And it compares the revolutions of modern times in Eastern Europe, South Africa, and Indonesia with their forerunners in Europe and Russia. It also examines how the imperial powers seek to intervene in these popular processes to attain their own preferred outcomes. These revolutions are revealed as the central moments when the economic and imperial titans meet face to face with popular resistance in its most dynamic form.

Chapters six and seven, 'War and ideology' and 'Resisting imperialism', recount the intellectual case for resisting imperialism and neo-liberalism and the strategies that are likely to be most effective in so doing. It draws on the history of the anti-globalisation and anti-war movement internationally to chart a course that can lead us away from the brink of continued economic insecurity and the threat of war.

I hope that the analysis contained in this book will contribute to our understanding of the new imperial age. But every set of ideas contains an imperative to action. This is especially true of an analysis which describes an unstable and contradictory social system since such contradictions can only be resolved by political action. The real purpose of *Imperialism and Resistance* is to assist in making sure that such contradictions are solved by, and to the benefit of, the mass of people, not in the interests of the masters of war.

1 Arms and America

The shock to the international state system caused by the collapse of the Eastern bloc in 1989 is a root cause of the instability now endemic in global politics. The bi-polar architecture of the Cold War world fixed all power relations in their place from the Second World War until the East European revolutions. The US is now attempting to create a new imperial order, but the process is contested and dangerous.

This is a seismic shift in the landscape of world politics. If we were to reach for historical parallels then only the rise of European colonialism up to the First World War or the fall of the Iron Curtain across Europe after the Second World War would be appropriate in scale and consequence. To fully grasp this enormity a review of Cold War imperial rivalry is necessary.

The Cold War

The United States emerged from the Second World War as the only major power whose civilian economy had grown at the same time as its military economy. In every other combatant nation, Allied or Axis, the civilian economy had been ravaged for the sake of waging war. The US penetration of the global market advanced at the cost of enemies and allies alike everywhere from the Far East to the European heartlands of capitalism. As direct European colonial administration gave way to the wave of national liberation struggles and the emergence of independent states in the Third World, so US-led military alliances, client states and economic domination replaced them in many parts of the globe.

The exception, and it was a huge exception, was in Russia itself and those areas of Eastern Europe where the Nazis had been driven out by force of Russian arms. At Yalta and subsequent conferences this military reality became an agreed division of Europe by the major powers. After the 1949 revolution China also fell beyond the direct reach of the western military and western corporations.

For the entirety of the Cold War period the kind of struggle between the major powers that had given the 20th century two world wars was transformed into a different kind of battle for superiority. In the first instance the superpowers battled it out in hot wars in every corner of the Third World. From South-East Asia, through Africa and Cuba, all the way to Chile every battle was fought under the banners of West and East, Capitalism and Communism.

The main form of direct conflict between the US and Russian superpowers was the arms race. The arms race was not only about the sheer military might of the contending armed forces. It was about economic muscle. In a nuclear arms race, in an arms race that was also a space race, in a race where weapons superiority means technological superiority, the scale and sophistication of the contending *economies* was the decisive factor.

A rough military parity between the superpowers emerged that would deter either side from beginning a conventional war in Europe. However there was never an economic parity. Russia industrialised later and its economy was always smaller than that of the United States. The Russian and some of the Eastern European economies were for a considerable period faster growing than most of their western competitors. State control insulated them from the vagaries of the world market and allowed them to concentrate resources on building or rebuilding their industrial strength. Over the longer term, however, the reconstruction of the world market and the pressure of the arms race undermined the viability of the state dominated economies in Eastern Europe.

By the time Ronald Reagan embarked on the Star Wars project in the 1980s the explicit goal was as much to exert economic pressure on Russia as it was to develop a weapon the Russians could not match. The economic resources expended in research and manufacture were as important as the efficacy of the weapons produced.

The arms race also took its toll on the US economy. The cost of winning the arms race was borne overwhelmingly by the US, but the benefits were felt not just by the US but by all those western economies who participated in the long post-war economic boom underpinned by arms spending. At the height of the Reagan arms boom the US was spending 7 percent of GNP on the military but the other NATO countries were spending half that figure.[1] This kind of disparity, which existed throughout the Cold War, meant that German and Japanese capital, for instance, grew in the world market at the expense of the US.

Moreover, as the size of the world economy grew so the scale of arms spending necessary to underpin the boom grew as well. The US was reaching the limit of what it could afford to spend on arms not just relative to its competitors but also relative to the total amount needed to sustain global growth. These fissures in the world system were apparent from the 1970s when global growth rates began to fall to half what they had been at the height of the post-war boom. From this moment on boom and bust cycles assumed greater severity than at any time in the post-war years.

By the end of the Cold War the US had economically undermined the East European economic structure by means of the arms race, but the scale of arms spending needed to do this had also eroded its own economic advantage over its western rivals.

At the start of the 21st century the US certainly remains the most powerful economy in the world but it no longer so exceeds its rivals that it can determine the course of events by the use of its economic weight, as it did through the Marshall Plan at the end of the Second World War. Multilateral economic institutions like the IMF, the World Bank and the WTO, enjoy US support in a way that their political and military counterparts no longer do. This is not because the US is somehow more naturally collaborative in the economic field but simply because the relative decline of the US economy obliges it to be so.

There is no similar decline in the relative power of the US military. In fact, quite the reverse: US military power emerged from the Cold War more overwhelmingly dominant on a global scale than it has ever been.

It is in this contradictory couplet – relative economic decline and absolute military superiority – that much of the meaning of US strategy in the 21st century is to be found.

The United States and the post-Cold War world

The end of the Cold War was supposed to herald a new world order of peace and prosperity. The rationale for high arms expenditure, the nuclear stand-off between the superpowers, was over. Indeed there was a fall in the proportion of national wealth devoted to arms spending.

The global proportion of Gross National Product (GNP) spent on arms declined from 5.2 percent in 1985 to 2.8 percent in 1995. Over the same decade the percentage of GNP spent by the US on arms fell from 6.1 percent to 3.8 percent. In the same years NATO countries cut arms spending from 3.5 percent to 2.4 percent. In Britain the figure fell from 5.1 percent to 3 percent.[2] But the fall in the percentage of GNP spent on arms is not the whole story.

The fall in US arms spending was not as sharp as in other states. So the proportion of US spending as a total of all nations' arms expenditure rose dramatically at the end of the Cold War.

The result was a massive shift in the military balance of power in favour of the United States. Nowhere was this shift more decisive than in the relationship between the US and the so-called 'threat states'.

The general shift in the military balance can be seen in Table 1.1 on page 16, again highlighting the especially dramatic advantage that the US now enjoys over the 'threat states'.

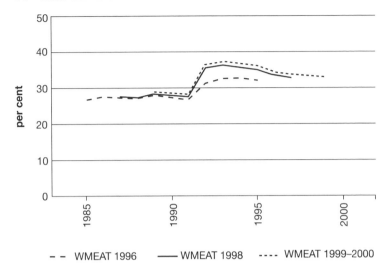

Figure 1.1   US military spending as a percentage of world military spending, 1985–1999[3]

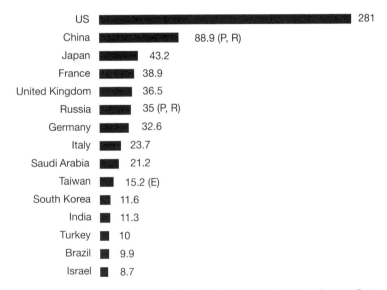

Figure 1.2   Top 15 nations, as ranked by military spending in billions of US dollars in 1999.[4]
(E): Estimate based on partial or uncertain data; **(P)**: Value data converted from national currency at estimated purchasing power

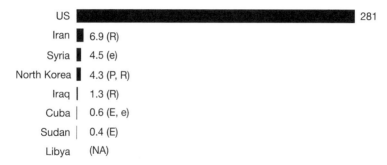

US ▬▬▬▬▬▬▬▬▬▬▬▬▬▬▬ 281
Iran ▮ 6.9 (R)
Syria ▮ 4.5 (e)
North Korea ▮ 4.3 (P, R)
Iraq | 1.3 (R)
Cuba | 0.6 (E, e)
Sudan | 0.4 (E)
Libya (NA)

Figure 1.3 US and some potential enemy nations, as ranked by military spending in billions of US dollars in 1999.[5]
(**e**): Major share of total military expenditures believed omitted, probably including most expenditures on arms procurement; (**E**): Estimate based on partial or uncertain data; (**NA**): Data not available; (**P**): Value data converted from national currency at estimated purchasing power parity; (**R**): Rough estimate

The study from which Table 1.1 is drawn concludes 'Despite post-Cold War spending reductions, the United States and its friends and allies today have a spending edge over potential adversaries that is far greater than existed during the Cold War'.[6] Moreover, 'the burden of defense borne by the United States, its allies, and close friends is today more equitably distributed among the members of this group – even though the United States continues to devote more of its GNP to defense than is the average for the group.'

As the full reality of this situation emerged during the 1990s sections of the US ruling class began to formulate a strategy adequate to the new balance of power. This was no incidental matter. It was clear to US policy makers that they possessed overwhelming military might. Clear too that the collapse of the East European bloc meant that a third of the globe that had been closed to western corporations and military strategists since the Second World War was now, literally, open for business. However, it was by no means clear how to go about exploiting this situation nor was it clear how dangerous, both internationally and domestically, the new world order would be for US rulers.

Table 1.1 US military spending as a fraction of spending by selected groups of states, 1986 and 1994

| | Ratio of US spending to group spending | | | | Change in relative US spending |
	1986		1994		1986–1994
	United States	Group	United States	Group	
1. Non US world	0.39	1	0.53	1	+35%
2. Non NATO world	0.50	1	0.78	1	+56%
3. Non OECD world	0.54	1	0.96	1	+77%
4. Potential threat states	0.67	1	1.72	1	+157%

The first Gulf War in 1991, for instance, demonstrated the power of US arms – but it also revealed that those directing US foreign policy were keen to stress multilateralism, including the involvement of the United Nations. Indeed, the US entered the first Gulf War on a programme very much borrowed from the Cold War. The US air-land battle plan was drawn from existing NATO strategy in Europe. The US had long realised that it would face a Warsaw Pact army in Europe that outnumbered NATO forces. In order to compensate for this imbalance it had developed the idea of carpet-bombing the rear echelons of the enemy, destroying reserves, cutting off the front line troops and disrupting supplies.

A similar plan already existed to meet a Russian thrust into Iran, should one materialize. Norman Schwarzkopf, the US commander in the Gulf War, simply took this strategy over for use against the Iraqi army. But in the transition there were some important alterations in plan and circumstance. Firstly, the air-war component was massively enlarged until it became the largest and most devastating air assault ever conducted. The US flew 88,000 sorties against Iraq in six weeks. They dropped more munitions in that time than were dropped on Germany in the whole of the Second World War.[7]

Secondly, the targets were not the rear of the army of another superpower, but the cities of a third world country. Stephen

Pelletiere, the CIA's senior political analyst during the Iran-Iraq war concludes: 'In the Iraqi case, the strategy was massaged, so to speak, by the air-war theorists ... into a strategy of bombing the Iraqi homefront into submission ... the Americans took a style of war meant to be used against the army of a fellow superpower (Russia) and turned it against a third-rate power, shifting the focus to the Iraqis' homefront.'[8]

Similarly, the ideological justifications for war in 1991 and throughout the rest of the decade presented an incoherent admixture of elements drawn from the Cold War world and the post-Cold War world. Already in 1991 Saddam Hussein was a 'new Hitler', just as Nasser had been in 1956. In the United States' Latin American adventures the 'war against drugs' emerged as a contender for the role of the leading ideological justification for war. The 'war on terror' was periodically in use as well. Before the attack on the twin towers of New York's World Trade Center on 11 September 2001 none of these notions had the general ideological force that anti-communism had provided during the Cold War.

Indeed, the major difference between the Gulf War and the Cold War era lay not on the side of the United States but on the side of Iraq. It may or may not be the case that Saddam believed he had the acquiescence of the United States for the attack on Kuwait. But what he knew for certain was that there was no longer a Russian veto on his actions in the way that there would have been throughout the Cold War period. The Cold War bi-polar world held 'rogue states' in check by agreement between the superpowers. Now that dangerous stability was gone. The US fought the first Gulf War because it wanted no post-Cold War challenges to its power. This was immediately true in the Middle East but in the wider frame the US wanted the war to send a message to European and other ruling classes that it was still the world's effective policeman. Ever since the rulers of the United States have been grappling with the question of how to contain future challenges to its power, hence its obsession with rogue states.

So through the first attack on Iraq and long before the attack on the twin towers the neo-conservatives in the American foreign policy elite were formulating a strategy for the US in the post-Cold War world.

The roots of US strategy

Henry Kissinger surveyed the post-Cold War world from the point of view of the US ruling elite and came to this conclusion: 'Geopolitically, America is an island off the shores of the large landmass of Eurasia, whose resources and population far exceed those of the United States. The domination by a single power of either of Eurasia's two principal spheres – Europe or Asia – remains a good definition of strategic danger for America, Cold War or no Cold War. For such a grouping would have the capacity to outstrip America economically and, in the end, militarily'.[9]

Increasingly throughout the 1990s voices were raised within the US establishment that argued for the US to find a way of dominating the 'Eurasian landmass'. The right of the US foreign policy establishment had immediately recognized that the Middle East was strategically, economically, ideologically, not to mention geographically, at the heart of the Eurasian problem. Although 'getting Eurasia right' might not resolve all the US's problems in other important parts of the world like Latin America or South-East Asia it was, nevertheless, disproportionately important. The first Gulf War was fought to demonstrate that no matter what else might be changing in the midst of the turbulent events of recent years in Eastern Europe and Russia, there was to be no change in US domination of the Middle East.

The first Gulf War had all but destroyed Saddam Hussein's regime. Indeed it took the active connivance of the US, encouraging and then deserting a popular Iraqi insurrection in favour of the devil they knew, to keep Saddam in power. The subsequent UN sanctions regime, as we now know beyond all doubt, not only inflicted untold misery on the Iraqi people but also kept the Iraqi regime from developing any effective weapons of mass destruction. In a way the first Gulf War was won too well for the good of the US. Stephen Pelletiere explains:

'With the collapse of the Soviet Union, the great threat to the Gulf (which allegedly the Russians had posed) was no more. Further, Iraq had been defeated ... and even before that – in the Iran-Iraq War – Baghdad had succeeded in laying low the Iranians. So, effectively, *there was no threat to the Gulf* any longer and consequently no reason for the Americans to keep up a military presence there.'[10]

Yet the first Gulf War became increasingly regarded as a failure because it did not advance the cause which Henry Kissinger espoused, wider domination of the Eurasian landmass. For Washington hawks the first Gulf War was too 'multilateral' and too limited in its consequences both in Iraq and in the rest of the Middle East. In short, it was over too soon – a fact for which the hawks never forgave Colin Powell, the then Chairman of the Joint Chiefs of Staff who had halted the pursuit of the retreating Iraqi army after the massacre on the Basra road for fear it would inflame anti-war opinion in the US.

The hawks' wider aims and the narrower compelling goal of continued domination of the Middle East came closer together in the years of the Clinton presidency. The evolution of this policy was part of a wider shift in the Clinton administration's foreign policy profile led by Secretary of State Madeleine Albright and her mentor Zbigniew Brzezinski.

Polish born Brzezinski is a central figure in the American foreign policy elite and to follow his career is to see the evolution of a central strand in US policy. Brzezinski was Jimmy Carter's National Security Advisor and he had considerable influence on the first Clinton administration through his ally and Clinton's National Security Advisor Anthony Lake. Brzezinski was an early advocate of NATO expansion and through Lake, was instrumental in getting Clinton to commit himself to this course as early as 1994. Brzezinski's influence continued in Clinton's second administration when his former pupil at Columbia University, Madeleine Albright, was made Secretary of State. Albright had also worked under Brzezinski in the Carter administration.[11]

Brzezinski's 'three grand imperatives of imperial geostrategy' are 'to prevent collusion and maintain security among the vassals, to keep tributaries pliant and protected, and to keep the barbarians from coming together'. And the most pressing task is to 'consolidate and perpetuate the prevailing geopolitical pluralism on the map of Eurasia' by 'manoeuvre and manipulation in order to prevent the emergence of a hostile coalition that could eventually seek to challenge America's primacy'. Those that must be divided and ruled are Germany, Russia and Iran as well as Japan and China.[12] It was Brzezinski who infamously defended US support for the Taliban thus: 'What is more important in the world view of history? The Taliban or the fall of the Soviet Empire? A few stirred up Muslims or the liberation of Central Europe and the end of the Cold War?'[13]

The Brzezinski strategy has not gone unopposed among America's rulers. Some, like Clinton's Secretary of State Warren Christopher, were ambivalent about NATO expansion. Some have seen Islam as a threat rather than a useful counter in the game of geopolitical realpolitik. Some, like Strobe Talbott, started out the 1990s with a more benign and inclusive attitude towards Russia, hoping that it could be brought into the Western camp as more of an ally than a competitor. But a combination of the catastrophic performance of the Russian and former Soviet Republics' economies, deeply authoritarian governments throughout the region, and the logic of two wars in three years gave the 'expansionists' ascendancy.

The Kosovo war in 1999 can now be seen as a step towards the kind of war policy the US far-right were developing. It was carried out by NATO and the UN was only called in to sanctify the resulting colonial set-up. It was justified by reference to the plight of the Kosovans, developing the 'humanitarian imperialist' discourse to new heights. And it was fought in a geographical area that forms a critical intersection of the Eurasian landmass, opening paths to the former Russian republics on the shores of the Caspian and the energy sources they control. In all these ways it was the true precursor of the invasion of Iraq.

Brzezinski became a firm advocate of war in the Balkans. This was, in part, because he saw the Balkan war as a testing ground for US policy throughout the whole Caspian and Central Asian area: 'In the Brzezinski scheme of things ... "Serbia" is Russia, and Croatia, Bosnia, Kosovo etc., are the Ukraine, the Baltic States, Georgia and the former Soviet Republics of "the Eurasian Balkans"'.[14] And, of course, 'having become an advocate for American oil companies wishing to establish themselves in the former Soviet Republics of the Caucasus and Central Asia, Brzezinski regards American predominance in this region ... as a prime objective. With this in mind, apart from alliances with China and Turkey, our champion of democracy takes a positive view both of the strengthening of relations between Pakistan and Afghanistan (with the Taliban acting as cement) and of the Islamic resurgence in Saudi Arabia as well as Iran (with which he favours an alliance).'[15]

It does not take great perspicacity to see in this scenario the outlines of US diplomacy in the Afghan conflict, notwithstanding the small alteration that the 'few stirred up Muslims' are giving the US elite more trouble than Brzezinski foresaw.

In the very month that the Balkan War broke out, NATO integrated Poland, the Czech Republic and Hungary into the alliance. The southern flank of NATO between Hungary and Greece was then pierced only by the states of the former Yugoslavia. This alone gave NATO a considerable strategic interest in controlling the Balkans.

But there was more at stake. The effect of NATO enlargement was to swing the Iron Curtain to the east. Where once it divided Germany, it came in 1999 to run down the eastern borders of Poland, the Czech Republic and Hungary, ending at the borders of the former Yugoslavia. Thus the whole ten year long process of NATO's eastward push became caught up with the fate of the Balkans in general and the former Yugoslav states in particular. The US, not a newly united Germany, needed to lead NATO to the new frontier.

President Clinton expressed NATO's war aims clearly enough in the *International Herald Tribune* article where he insisted that 'lasting stability' in the Balkans could only come if 'the European Union and the United States ... do for southeastern Europe what it did for Europe after World War II and for Central Europe after the Cold War ... We can do that by rebuilding struggling economies, encouraging trade and investment and helping the nations of the region to join NATO and the European Union'. The nations of the area, Clinton continued, were already responding to 'the pull of integration' by sticking with their pro-market reforms and 'supporting NATO's campaign'.

The new Iron Curtain between western and eastern Europe was not the end of the Balkans' strategic importance for NATO. The fate of the southern flank of NATO, through Greece and Turkey, is tied to another crucial area of post-Cold War instability – the arc of oil states running up from the traditional spheres of western interest in Iran and Iraq to the Caspian Sea and the newly independent states on Russia's southern rim.

US and NATO plans for military co-operation with these states were hugely accelerated by the Balkan war. *The Economist* reported that during the Balkan war the nations of the Caspian area have 'plainly divided into pro-Russian and pro-NATO camps'. One of the main tasks of the alliance with the Caspian states is, according to the *Financial Times*, 'to develop the area's rich oil and gas deposits to the exclusion of Russia'.

There was and is a rich prize at stake in the Caspian Sea region. Its proven oil reserves are estimated at between 16 and 32 billion barrels, comparable to the US's reserves of 22 billion barrels and more than the North Sea's 17 billion barrels. Chevron's Tengiz field is the largest oil reservoir discovered in the last 25 years and contains 6 billion barrels. A 1 billion barrel field is now considered to be a 'big, world class find' according to the *Financial Times*. The Offshore Kazakhstan International Operating Company (OKIOC), whose shareholders include Mobil, Total, Britain's BG, Statoil of Norway and America's Philips Corporation, is investigating a field in the north Caspian said to be three times the size of Tengiz. No wonder the *Financial Times* reports 'the political implications of a discovery could be more far-reaching than the potential commercial rewards.'

These reserves are all a long way from the Balkans, but the routes by which the oil must come west are not. As the Balkan war began a new pipeline was opened carrying Caspian Sea oil through Azerbaijan and Georgia. The oil will continue its journey by tanker through the Black Sea, the Bosporus and on past the Turkish and Greek coast. Since the Balkan war a big export pipeline from Baku in Azerbaijan to Ceyhan on Turkey's Mediterranean coast has gone ahead. Such a pipeline is a US foreign policy priority, as it would help wean the former Soviet republics along the Caspian away from Russia while undermining growing commercial interests in using Iran as an oil export route.

US Energy Secretary Bill Richardson explained at the time, 'This is about America's energy security ... It's also about preventing strategic inroads by those who don't share our values. We are trying to move these newly independent countries toward the west. We would like to see them reliant on western commercial and political interests. We've made a substantial political investment in the Caspian and it's important that both the pipeline map and the politics come out right.'

It is the 'pipeline map' to which Richardson refers that connects the Caspian Sea oil reserves to the security of the area between Turkey, Greece and the other Balkan states. There are, as the *International Herald Tribune* points out, 'profound economic and geopolitical consequences' stemming from the decisions about the routes by which the oil will come west: 'Rivalries played out here will have a decisive impact in shaping the post-Communist world, and in determining how much influence the United States will have over its development.'

Commentators who claimed a link between Caspian oil and the Kosovo war were ridiculed at the time, not least by then Labour Foreign Secretary Robin Cook who thought he had a conclusive argument in the statement that 'there is no oil in Kosovo.' Yet there were already plans for a Trans-Balkan pipeline bringing oil from the Caspian to the Mediterranean, in addition to the Baku-Ceyhan route, in the 1990s. At a meeting to discuss the project in Sofia in 1998 the Albanian president made it clear that his consent for the project would rest on Kosovan autonomy because 'no solution within Serbian borders will bring lasting peace.'[16]

The deal to build the pipeline was finally signed in December 2004 between US corporation AMBO and Balkan governments, again in Sofia. One report insisted that although the Balkan war had 'left investors jittery ... the situation seems to have stabilized (and) the future looks bright for AMBO.' The report continued, 'This week's gala event in Sofia brought together the major leaders of the countries involved: the Macedonian, Bulgarian and Albanian Prime Ministers, Vlado Buckovski, Simeon Saxe-Coburg-Gotha and Fatos Nano respectively. On Monday they signed a political declaration confirming their countries' support for the pipeline.

'AMBO president Ted Ferguson claims that his project has received $900 million of investor funds " ... from the Overseas Private Investment Corporation (OPIC) – a US development agency – the Eximbank and Credit Suisse First Boston, among others." ... The construction of the pipeline should take three or four years and when finished will transport 750,000 barrels of oil per day ... crossing the Balkan Peninsula overland and terminating at the Adriatic port of Vlore.'[17]

The Balkans became a contested area once again because the tectonic plates of the major powers now grind against each other in this area, just as they did before the accident of Cold War imperial geography and the long post-war boom gave them temporary respite.

The Balkan war changed the thinking of the US and its allies, redefining what was possible and acceptable in the post-Cold War world. NATO explicitly redefined its 'strategic concepts' so that it was no longer simply a defensive alliance, as it claimed throughout the Cold War. All the old Cold War NATO practices remain, including its commitment to 'first use' of nuclear weapons if it deems such use to be necessary. But immediately after the fall of the East European states in 1991, NATO redefined its aims so that 'out of area' operations became part of a new 'strategic concept'. At first this was seen as primarily a 'peacekeeping' role. But, reports the International Institute for Strategic Studies, 'NATO's exclusive command of the Implementation Force (IFOR) operations in Bosnia completely changed this view.' Thus the collapse of the East European regimes and NATO's expansionism fuelled its concern with the Balkans; and its experience in the Balkans fuelled its determination to use military weight beyond its borders. None of this was lost on the neo-conservatives waiting in the wings for the American elections that were just two years away.

The ascendancy of the neo-conservatives

The Balkan war helped to redraw the imperial project on the ground. But even before it broke out the neo-conservatives were making their case for a renewed US imperial offensive.

In the aftermath of the first Gulf War Paul Wolfowitz's draft of the Pentagon's Defense Planning Guidance was leaked to the press in 1992. It argued the now familiar case for active US military intervention to prevent the rise of competitor powers. The US, said Wolfowitz, must use any and all means to prevent the emergence of rival states. Opposition from US allies forced the first President Bush to remove the offending passages before the document re-emerged as the Pentagon's Defense Planning Guidance 1994–99.

But throughout the 1990s the neo-conservatives were bolstering their case. In January 1998 a letter was sent to President Clinton signed by 18 foreign policy experts, 11 of whom were to be members of the Bush administration. They included Donald Rumsfeld, Paul Wolfowitz, John Bolton, Richard Perle, James Woolsey, William Kristol, Francis Fukuyama, and Richard Armitage – all key propagandists for the invasion of Iraq five years later. The letter was a blueprint for the 'war on terror' long before the twin towers were attacked and articulated many of the key themes of the Project for the New American Century, a non-profit making organisation formed the previous year to 'promote American global leadership'.

'American policy towards Iraq is not succeeding' because the policy of containment is failing, argued the authors, and President Clinton should use the upcoming State of the Union Address to call for 'the removal of Saddam Hussein's regime from power.'

Saddam's regime was avoiding UN searches for weapons of mass destruction and as a consequence 'in the not-too-distant future we will be unable to determine with any reasonable level of confidence whether Iraq does or does not possess such weapons'. If Saddam is allowed to pose a threat then 'a significant portion of the world's supply of oil will be put at hazard.' To achieve the overthrow of Saddam the US should act unilaterally because 'we can no longer rely on our partners in the Gulf War coalition' and 'American policy cannot continue to be crippled by a misguided insistence on unanimity in the UN Security Council'.[18]

When George W Bush became president of the United States at the start of the new millennium he brought to the helm of government the very people most committed to this course of action. Vice President Dick Cheney was an oil executive and the former Secretary of Defense. Then National Security Advisor Condoleezza Rice was the director of a transnational oil corporation and a Russia scholar. Secretary of State Colin Powell had no diplomatic training but was, of course, Chair of the Joint Chiefs of Staff during the Gulf War. Donald Rumsfeld, appointed Secretary of Defense, is a former chief executive officer of Searle Pharmaceuticals and was, with Dick Cheney, the featured speaker at the Russian-American Business Leaders Forum in May 2000. It is safe to say that the central concerns of this group have always been oil, Russia and the military.

Events in the Middle East, as well as wider post-Cold War imperatives, were conspiring to make this neo-conservative agenda an increasingly attractive, indeed necessary, policy for the US ruling class as a whole. Critically, the US relationship with Saudi Arabia was under intense pressure.

Saudi Arabia was essential to US influence in the Middle East for a number of reasons. Militarily the US depended on Saudi Arabia for its largest bases in the region. Furthermore, the Saudis were big customers for the US arms industry. Even more importantly the Saudi regime was the US's chosen partner in stabilising oil prices. As the biggest oil producer in the world the Saudis had, since a four day visit paid to them by George

Bush senior in 1986, been raising or lowering their production to keep oil prices in a band acceptable to the US.

Immediately after the first Iraq war the Gulf States were spending more on US armaments than the Pentagon was paying to equip its own forces. Difficulties with this level of arms payments by the Saudis to the US began in 1992 when the Saudis began to have cash flow problems. Eventually a deal was struck with McDonnell-Douglas, Hughes Aircraft, General Dynamics, FMC and Raytheon to stretch repayment over a longer period. But President Clinton then also insisted on a Saudi commitment to buy civilian aircraft from Boeing and McDonnell-Douglas. The Saudis agreed but by 1999 they were forced to announce a cut in arms spending of between $7 and $9 billion dollars.[19]

The presence of US forces in Saudi Arabia was becoming increasingly domestically unpopular. Indeed if there is one issue most identifiable as that which motivated Osama Bin Laden and other radical Saudi Islamicists then US troops on Saudi soil might well qualify. In 1995 a bomb in Riyadh killed five Americans, one a US army sergeant. The following year the Khobar Towers was blown up killing 17 US military personnel. The Saudi royal family made it clear to the US that it wanted its troops to leave the Kingdom.

As importantly, Saudi Arabia was proving unreliable as an oil price stabiliser. In late 1997 the great crash in the Asian economies hit the world market. Global economic contraction hit the oil market just at the moment when Saudi Arabia was producing a glut of oil in order to help the US keep the price of oil down. In the midst of this price turmoil the right wing Venezuelan government decided to try and solve some of its problems by offering its nationalised oil fields up for sale to private corporations. Kuwait followed suit. The Saudis were tempted to do likewise until the protests of Saddam Hussein convinced them that this was an unwise move.

Then Hugo Chavez won the Venezuelan elections, cancelled the oil privatisation, and formed a bloc with Mexico and Saudi Arabia to drive the price of oil back up by cutting production. It worked. Oil prices rose from $14 to $27 a barrel in a matter of months. The US economy took a hit as the oil price rise helped to prick the dot.com bubble and undermine the long bull market.

The US was especially vulnerable because of its ever growing dependence on overseas oil sources. In the 1990s US oil companies spent more money looking for oil abroad than at home and most of their production and reserves were abroad. Moreover, at the beginning of the Clinton years the US was importing 46 percent of its oil, most of it from the Gulf States and most of that from Saudi Arabia. In the later Clinton years only 19 percent of oil imports were from the Gulf, the rest was from Mexico, Venezuela and Canada.[20]

Little wonder then that a Chavez-Saudi oil agreement should cause alarm in the US government, nor that during the 1990s 'diversification of sources' became the watchword of US energy policy, including those resources in the Caspian region. In this situation the prospect of gaining control over Iraq's oil in a second Gulf War was clearly an attractive possibility for the US elite.

So for all these reasons – military bases, arms purchases and oil – it is clear that by the time the planes hit the twin towers on 11 September 2001 the US was seeking ways to redraw the map of the Middle East. As an unnamed US diplomat told Scotland's *Sunday Herald* before the war: 'a rehabilitated Iraq is the only sound long-term strategic alternative to Saudi Arabia. It's not just a case of swapping horses in mid-stream, the impending US regime change in Baghdad is strategic necessity.'[21]

'The great opportunity': 11 September 2001

'How do you capitalise on these opportunities?', then National Security Advisor Condoleezza Rice asked her staff in the wake of the attacks on the World Trade Center and the Pentagon. The attack on the twin towers was not the cause of the transformation in the war policy of the US that followed, any more than the assassination of Archduke Ferdinand was the cause of the First World War. Neither was 'Islamic terrorism' the cause of the attacks on Afghanistan and Iraq any more than 'Serbian terrorism' was the cause of the First World War. But the attack on the twin towers was the occasion, the opportunity, for other plans with deeper causes to be enacted.

The US was in any case in need of transforming its imperial stance in the post-Cold War world in general, in Eurasia specifically and in the Middle East particularly. Despite the urgings of the ascendant neo-conservatives and for all that had happened in the course of the Balkan war, as of September 2001, these were only partly achieved goals. But cometh the hour, cometh the cabal.

The neo-conservative perspective was enabled by the attack on the twin towers. The target was always Iraq, despite the fact that most of the attackers were Saudis and none of them Iraqis. But a direct and immediate assault on Iraq was put aside since no link between the nationalist and secular Ba'ath regime and the Islamic radicalism of Osama Bin Laden could credibly be established. Moreover, the military, diplomatic and ideological preparation for an invasion of Iraq would take time. Not so with the Taliban regime in Afghanistan where Bin Laden was living. Afghanistan was, for the Bush administration, a preparatory phase through which the war in Iraq had to pass before it could begin in earnest.

It was all over quickly. By the end of 2001 and with only one military engagement of any significance, outside Mazur e Sharif, the tiny and fragile Taliban regime was scattered. Thousands of Afghans died in the carpet bombing. The US lost 52 soldiers. Now behind a cosmetic election the warlords run most of the country, opium production has increased exponentially, women still wear the burka and promised aid donations from the west have never materialised. Furthermore, as time passed the Taliban re-established themselves in parts of Afghanistan. Troop casualties have risen to the same levels as those in Iraq. More British and European troops have had to be deployed to try and stabilise the situation – all this years after victory was declared.

As James Risen, the *New York Times* national security correspondent, reports, 'As drug-fuelled violence worsened and

American casualties increased in Afghanistan in 2005, the tragedy was that it was still just a sideshow. Nearly four years after 9/11, American military operations in Afghanistan had more to do with maintaining the stability of the Karzai government than with fighting global terrorism.'[22]

The Afghan war, however, gave the Bush administration the momentum it needed to settle the new imperial design in stone and thus pave the way for the attack on Iraq. It was all finally set out in governmental black and white in the National Security Strategy of the United States in September 2002.[23]

The dominating themes of the NSS are these: the post-Cold War world has given the US an unparalleled opportunity to reshape the global economic environment to its advantage. This strategic goal is realisable because US military might, used pre-emptively, is available as the means and the post-9/11 ideological environment provides the justification.

The NSS is remarkable for the amount of space it devotes to promoting the idea of free market capitalism. Whole sections are devoted to the argument that no other economic system is possible or desirable. In unequivocal terms the NSS states that there is 'a single sustainable model for national success: freedom, democracy, and free enterprise'. This messianic message is repeated throughout the document: 'The lessons of history are clear: market economies, not command-and-control economies with the heavy hand of government, are the best way to promote prosperity and reduce poverty. Policies that further strengthen market incentives and market institutions are relevant for all economies – industrialized countries, emerging markets, and the developing world.' In short, the NSS is openly committed to the global advancement of the US model of capitalism, by military means if necessary.

The military strategy supporting this goal abandons multilateralism and embraces pre-emptive action as official policy. 'While the United States will constantly strive to enlist the support of the international community, we will not hesitate to act alone, if necessary, to exercise our right of self-defense by acting preemptively ... our best defense is a good offense'.

Leaving aside the illogicality of asserting that you can act in self-defence when you act pre-emptively, the NSS goes on to explain this change in policy as a result of the post-Cold War situation. 'The nature of the Cold War threat required the United States – with our allies and friends – to emphasize deterrence of the enemy's use of force, producing a grim strategy of mutual assured destruction. With the collapse of the Soviet Union and the end of the Cold War, our security environment has undergone profound transformation. But new deadly challenges have emerged from rogue states and terrorists'.

The NSS goes on to list the attributes that rogue states have in common. The remarkable fact about this list is that it is at least as much about the internal behaviour of the regimes as it is about the threat they pose to the US. These attributes, according to the NSS, include the fact that rogue states 'brutalize their own people and squander their national resources for the personal gain of the rulers', 'display no regard for international law', 'violate international treaties', 'are determined to acquire weapons of mass destruction', 'sponsor terrorism and hate the United States and everything for which it stands'.

This series of strongly ideological and subjective arguments is then used to justify the recurring theme of pre-emptive military action: 'In the Cold War, especially following the Cuban missile crisis, we faced a generally status quo, risk-averse adversary. Deterrence was an effective defense'. This is not, of course, what we were told during the existence of the 'evil empire'. Nevertheless the NSS continues, 'But deterrence based only upon the threat of retaliation is less likely to work against leaders of rogue states more willing to take risks, gambling with the lives of their people, and the wealth of their nations … The United States has long maintained the option of preemptive actions to counter a sufficient threat to our national security. The greater the threat, the greater is the risk of inaction – and the more compelling the case for taking anticipatory action … To forestall or prevent such hostile acts by our adversaries, the United States will, if necessary, act preemptively.'

The NSS does not however limit its scope to the consideration of relations with rogue states. It is a truly global blueprint for US grand strategy on the neo-conservative model. Unlike those commentators who can envisage no circumstances in which a modern conflict could involve a struggle between the major powers, the NSS is fully aware of such possibilities: 'The events of September 11, 2001, fundamentally changed the context for relations between the United States and other main centers of global power, and opened vast, new opportunities'. The US would prefer that these possibilities are exploited pacifically under US tutelage. But it actively contemplates the possibility that this will not be the case: 'We will strongly resist aggression from other great powers – even as we welcome their peaceful pursuit of prosperity, trade, and cultural advancement ... We are attentive to the possible renewal of old patterns of great power competition. Several potential great powers are now in the midst of internal transition – most importantly Russia, India, and China.'

The NSS then goes on to analyse the ways in which these potential rivals are either co-operating or otherwise with the US vision of the world. In the case of Russia, for instance, the NSS argues, 'Russia's top leaders ... understand, increasingly, that Cold War approaches do not serve their national interests and that Russian and American strategic interests overlap in many areas. United States policy seeks to use this turn in Russian thinking to refocus our relationship on emerging and potential common interests and challenges.' But this commitment sits uneasily with the following insistence on expanding US influence in the former Soviet Central Asian republics, still regarded by Russia as part of its legitimate sphere of influence. 'We will continue to bolster the independence and stability of the states of the former Soviet Union in the belief that a prosperous and stable neighborhood will reinforce Russia's growing commitment to integration into the Euro-Atlantic community.'

The document then reaffirms that 'we are realistic about the differences that still divide us from Russia and about the time and effort it will take to build an enduring strategic partnership.

Lingering distrust of our motives and policies by key Russian elites slows improvement in our relations. Russia's uneven commitment to the basic values of free-market democracy and dubious record in combating the proliferation of weapons of mass destruction remain matters of great concern. Russia's very weakness limits the opportunities for cooperation.'

India receives less attention but a slightly higher mark on the NSS's end of term report card: 'Differences remain, including over the development of India's nuclear and missile programs, and the pace of India's economic reforms. But while in the past these concerns may have dominated our thinking about India, today we start with a view of India as a growing world power with which we have common strategic interests ... '

The NSS's imperial tone is at its most wary in the case of China, carefully noting that 'China is our fourth largest trading partner, with over $100 billion in annual two-way trade'. But the NSS nevertheless goes on to warn the Chinese that 'a quarter century after beginning the process of shedding the worst features of the Communist legacy, China's leaders have not yet made the next series of fundamental choices about the character of their state. In pursuing advanced military capabilities that can threaten its neighbors in the Asia-Pacific region, China is following an outdated path that, in the end, will hamper its own pursuit of national greatness. In time, China will find that social and political freedom is the only source of that greatness.' The neo-conservatives are now obsessed with the Chinese economic powerhouse. They see growing economic strength harnessed to a militarized, nuclear armed state and predict a future great power rivalry to the US.

In all this plethora of economic and political strategy there is only one industrial commodity that receives specific mention in the NSS. It is not cars, steel or even computers. It is energy, specifically the aim to 'enhance energy security'. The NSS states: 'We will strengthen our own energy security and the shared prosperity of the global economy by working with our allies, trading partners, and energy producers to expand the sources and types of global energy supplied, especially in the Western Hemisphere, Africa, Central Asia, and the Caspian region.'

This is a simple codification of US policy as it emerged through the Balkan war under Clinton's presidency. As Michael Klare has written, 'It was President Clinton who initiated US military ties with Kazakhstan, Uzbekistan, Georgia and Azerbaijan, and who built up the US capacity to intervene in the Persian Gulf/Caspian Sea area.' Nevertheless, 'September 11 quickened the process and gave it a popular mandate'.[24] More than this, it gave the Bush administration the occasion to use those forces and to develop an explicit doctrine resting on the possibility of the repeated and unilateral use of military force. As the NSS concludes, 'It is time to reaffirm the essential role of American military strength. We must build and maintain our defenses beyond challenge.' The list of aims that follows is straight out of the Kissinger/Brzezinski school of imperial strategy. In this view the US military must 'assure our allies, dissuade future military competition, deter threats against U.S. interests, and decisively defeat any adversary if deterrence fails'.

The NSS concludes its review of the 'unparalleled strength of the United States armed forces' with a renewed statement of 'full spectrum dominance' in the post-Cold War struggle to reshape the global imperial architecture. 'Massive Cold War-era armies must be transformed to focus more on how an adversary might fight rather than where and when a war might occur.' And along with a transformation of the weaponry and strategy comes a transformation in the geography of deployment. 'The United States will require bases and stations within and beyond Western Europe and Northeast Asia, as well as temporary access arrangements for the long-distance deployment of U.S. forces. Before the war in Afghanistan, that area was low on the list of major planning contingencies ... We must prepare for more such deployments ... by developing assets such as advanced remote sensing, long-range precision strike capabilities, and transformed maneuver and expeditionary forces. This broad portfolio of military capabilities must also include the ability to defend the homeland, conduct information operations, ensure U.S. access to distant theaters, and protect critical U.S. infrastructure and assets in outer space.'

This reconfiguration of US military force is vital to under-standing the outcome of invasion of Iraq. In the 1990s the overwhelming military superiority of the US came to be understood in a very particular way by the US foreign policy elite. Firstly, the post-Cold War environment allowed for, and the relative economic decline of the US economy made necessary, an overall decline in defence spending. Secondly, the long shadow of the 'Vietnam syndrome' made US politicians wary of incurring high US casualties. In the first Gulf War these two elements were not as incompatible as they were later to become. The Cold War was barely over and so Colin Powell and Norman Schwarzkopf's doctrine of 'overwhelming force', a modification of Cold War battle plans, was adopted for the task of throwing the Iraqis out of Kuwait.

The invasion of Iraq itself in 2003 was a much more difficult task. But military doctrine in the US had changed, as the NSS shows. Now the emphasis was on the technical superiority of the US military rather than on superiority of numbers. This was a change driven partly by the end of the Cold War, partly by long term economic changes and partly by the neo-conservatives in the Bush administration who had to stitch together a ruling class consensus with cost conscious 'fiscal Republicans'. The result was the Rumsfeld-Wolfowitz plan to invade Iraq with 100,000 fewer troops than were used for the first Gulf War. The Iraqi army was easily defeated with such numbers but the resistance that met the US occupation could not be contained with the same ease.

Meanwhile, and with all the menace of the NSS notwith-standing, the most difficult battle to win for the Bush adminis-tration and its allies was the political battle. It had to convince multiple domestic and international audiences of a series of propositions that were simply untrue. These were (i) that Iraq possessed weapons of mass destruction, (ii) that there was a link between Iraq and Islamic terrorism, (iii) that Iraq was a uniquely evil regime in a way that, say, China was not, and (iv) that unilateral military action by the US and its allies was the only way to deal with Iraq.

It is fair to say of this political project (i) that it failed to convince a majority of governments around the world, (ii) that it failed to convince either the majority of the United Nations General Assembly or the majority of United Nations Security Council, and, most importantly, (iii) that it failed to convince a majority of the people of the world in countries both allied to and opposed to the United States. The cost of this failure can be measured by the opposition to the Iraq war by France and Germany, the most serious division among the western powers since before the Cold War. And beyond the divisions at a governmental level there has been a catastrophic decline in international popular support for US foreign policy.

The Iraq war was not, however, about the force of opinion. It was about the force of arms. Iraq was invaded and its army easily defeated. But as Napoleon first observed, there are many things you can do with bayonets but sitting on them is not one. The US and British armies in Iraq now have to face the consequences of failing to win the political argument about the war and subsequent occupation of Iraq. In the first instance this is an argument that they have failed to win with the Iraqi people, but it is also and importantly an argument that they have failed to win with their own people.

In this sense the Project for the New American Century though victorious in arms is in deep political trouble. Its ability to redraw the global map in the interests of the US corporations and military is now compromised. Whether it can recover its momentum or whether it will be halted in the sands of Iraq depends on how this political battle now progresses.

Conclusion

The end of the Cold War has left the US in a position of unparalleled military predominance. In the 1990s the US ruling elite immediately began using this strategic asset to redraw the imperial map of the world, first in the Gulf War and then in the Kosovo war. The full realisation of a new imperial design did not become clear until the rise of the neo-conservatives and the victory of George W Bush in the presidential election of 2000. Even then this scheme awaited the conditions in which it could be implemented. The attack on the World Trade Center in 2001 created those conditions.

The invasion of Iraq in 2003 has, however, also served to underline the limits of US power in a more general sense. These limits are in part the result of the resistance to the US government's colonial occupation both in Iraq and across the globe. But the limits are also imposed by the relative economic weakness of the US that has become apparent in the half-century or so since the end of the Second World War. The next chapter analyses the fate of the US economy during this period and assesses the strengths and weaknesses of its competitors. This critical meeting point between overwhelming military strength and relative economic decline is where we can best see the motivation of the US to rely increasingly rely on its military capacity to discipline both its allies and its competitors on the world stage.

2 US economic power in the age of globalisation

The world economy is made up of the totality of economic activity by competing states and corporations. This totality of economic activity has its own patterns of development that are characterised by certain general trends. The period from the Second World War to the 1970s was, for example, a period of high growth and limited recessions. The period since the 1970s has seen growth rates halve and the return of the boom–bust cycle. Again, the middle decades of the 20th century were dominated by certain state-led forms of development not just in the Eastern bloc but also in the welfare-state/nationalisation economies of the West and in the developmental models of the Third World. In the period since the 1970s, the neo-liberal era, the role of the state has not been reduced but it has been altered so that it is now much more the facilitator of global corporations. These kind of general characteristics of the world economy as a whole will be examined in chapter four.

This chapter is concerned with the relationships between the competing parts of the economy, predominantly with the economic strengths and weaknesses of the different states that compose the system. This competition is the origin of the general patterns in the world economy, patterns produced by blind interaction rather than conscious intention. But the weight and position of the competing states within this wider pattern is often the element that drives the system beyond economic competition towards military conflict.

The scene at the end of the Second World War

When the victors of the Second World War – Britain, Russia and America – met at the Yalta and Potsdam conferences in 1945 they set about constructing a new world order. Churchill had set the tone on an earlier visit to Moscow. He wrote down how he saw the post-war world on a sheet of paper. Russia would have 90 percent of the say in Romania, Britain 90 percent of the say in Greece and they would share Hungary and Yugoslavia. Churchill records, 'I pushed this across to Stalin. Then he took his blue pencil and made a large tick upon it, and passed it back to us. It was all settled in no more time than it takes to set down.'

This precise deal never got further than a piece of paper but it was exactly this spirit that dominated the Yalta and Potsdam conferences. US President Truman went to Potsdam convinced that America's unrivalled military *and* economic supremacy could get him '85 percent of what we want' as he told one of his aides. What Truman wanted was free markets throughout the world, open to American domination. He thought that American economic might plus the atom bomb, first successfully tested during the Potsdam conference, would get it for him.

Truman was wrong. Russian troops occupied Eastern Europe and Stalin correctly judged that Truman would not launch another war to try to dislodge them. Stalin's economic and political needs were diametrically opposed to Truman's. The Russian economy was stretched to breaking point by the war. Russians had suffered 20 million dead. Stalin needed security and reparations. In an open market Russia's weakened economy was bound to come off worse. Security demanded that Stalin exercise tight political control, economic needs demanded that he use it to plunder the Eastern bloc economies.

These are the economic realities behind the competition between state controlled East and 'free market' West during the Cold War. These were simply the best way of exploiting the fruits of victory given the different capabilities of Russia and America at the time. This was the root of the division of Europe.

It was also the origin of the two competing military alliances, NATO and the Warsaw Pact.

The rivalry shaped the world between 1945 and 1989. It brought military conflict close when Stalin blockaded Berlin in 1948, it resulted in war in Korea in 1950 and it brought the world to the edge of nuclear war over the Cuban missile crisis in 1962. Throughout the postwar period the superpowers jostled for influence, fought wars and backed allies across Asia, Latin America and Africa causing untold misery to their victims.

US economic power at the end of the Second World War

The settlement that concluded the Second World War ultimately rested on the economic power of the victors. This economic strength explains the emergence of the two superpowers and the division of Europe. The victors, however, were far from equal. The war cost Britain and France dear. Britain was severely weakened, France even more so. Russia and the US emerged as dominant powers. Of these two the US was very much the stronger.

The US ended the war in a position of unparalleled economic superiority. Its economic growth during the war years had been phenomenal. In 1945 the US economy's industrial production was more than double its annual production between 1935 and 1939. The US was producing more steel than Britain and Russia combined.[1] The US economy was producing half the world's coal, two thirds of the world's oil and over half the world's electricity.[2]

It was this economic superiority that was vital in delivering Allied victory. US aircraft production rose from nearly 6,000 in 1939 to over 96,000 in 1944, more than Germany and Japan together *and* more than Russia and Britain's combined aircraft production. It was the same story with shipping. By mid 1942 US shipyards were already launching merchant ships more quickly than German submarines could sink them. Small wonder that it was only the US that had the economic power to fight both a European and a Pacific war *and* spend some $2 billion on developing the atomic bomb.[3]

In other countries, be they victors or vanquished, war production had damaged the civilian economy. But in the US economic growth had been so great – over 15 percent a year – that the civilian economy expanded as well.[4] Even in 1952 nearly 60 percent of the total production of the top seven capitalist countries took place in the US. In 1953 the US was exporting five times as many manufactures as Germany and 17 times as many as Japan.[5]

The US ruling class used this enormous power to shape the world in its own image. The US had already moved to make the dollar the keystone of the world financial order. The 1944 Bretton Woods agreement fixed currency exchange rates in relation to gold. Since the US held 80 percent of world gold reserves this made the dollar 'as good as gold'.[6] This ensured that the dollar, and to a lesser extent sterling, were the international means of payment, forcing other countries to hold dollars in their reserves. So 'every dollar or pound held abroad … means that a similar amount of imports need not be met by exports – the rest of the world simply finance [the US and British] trade gap.' It also meant that other countries financed the erosion of their markets by more advanced US products.[7]

At the end of the war US exports were still restricted from getting into Europe and Japan by trade and monetary laws. US policy, enshrined in the International Monetary Fund and the General Agreement on Tariffs and Trade, aimed to push these aside.[8] The European powers had to allow their currencies to be devalued and their markets to be taken over if they wanted to grasp the economic lifeline America threw to the European powers – the European Recovery Programme, or Marshall Aid.

The European economies were devastated. There was famine in parts of Germany, bread rationing in France and a tightening of rationing in Britain. The European powers' imperial pretensions had largely been reduced to rubble alongside many of their cities. But economic aid was dependent on political docility. As General George Marshall himself put it, 'Benefits under the European Recovery Programme will come to an abrupt end in any country that votes Communism to power'. Looking at Europe, one US Congressman put it even more succinctly: 'too damned much socialism at home, and too damned much imperialism abroad'.[9]

The US was now in a position to use its economic might to oblige the European powers to get rid of socialism at home – the Communist Parties were mostly marginalised in the late 1940s – and to use its military might to take over the imperial duties that Britain, Germany and France were no longer in a position to perform.

America's military might was as great as its economic power. In 1949, even after demobilisation had begun, US forces were stationed in 56 countries and had the use of 400 bases world-wide. But perhaps the clearest demonstration of the US's growing imperial reach is the list of military alliances and treaties that it agreed in the decade after the war. The most important of these was NATO. Ernest Bevin, Labour's Foreign Secretary and NATO's initiator, called the day in 1949 when the pact was signed 'the finest in my life'. A year earlier Stafford Cripps had told the US Secretary of Defense, 'Britain must be regarded as the main base for the deployment of American power'.[10] NATO was consciously designed to counter internal as well as external threats to its member states. As the US Secretary of State, Dean Acheson, put it, 'revolutionary activity in a member country inspired and assisted from outside as in Greece would be considered an armed attack'.[11]

But it was not only in Europe that the US had military interests. The Rio Pact and the special defence arrangements with Canada meant that the US was militarily committed to the 'defence' of the entire western hemisphere. The ANZUS treaty added military commitments in the southwestern Pacific. The1950s saw the addition of bilateral treaties with Japan, South Korea, Taiwan and the Philippines. In 1954 the US, Britain, France and Australia joined the Philippines, Thailand and Pakistan to form the Southeast Asian Treaty Organisation (SEATO). The Middle East was given its version, the Central Treaty Organisation

(CENTO, originally the 1955 Baghdad Pact) in which Britain, Turkey, Iraq, Iran and Pakistan stood against 'subversion and attack'. Dean Rusk was speaking for the US ruling class when, in 1965, he said: 'This has become a very small planet and we have to be concerned with all of it – with all its land, waters, atmosphere, and with surrounding space'.[12] But, even as Rusk spoke, the US was losing that economic predominance on which the post-war political and military order was founded.

The period 1945–70 is, of course, the story of the greatest boom in capitalism's history – world manufacturing production grew threefold in the 20 years after 1953.[13] But within that boom some economies grew faster than others. In the race for growth, the US was one of the losers. From 1955 to 1970 capital stock in the US grew by 57 percent – but in the major European countries it grew by 116 percent and in Japan it grew by 500 percent.[14] West Germany's industrial output grew five-fold and Japan's grew thirteenfold between 1949 and 1970. Even if we look at the years 1965–80, which include the slump of the 1970s, the US Gross Domestic Product grew by only 2.7 percent per year while West Germany's grew by 3.3 percent, France's by 4.3 percent and Japan's by 6.3 percent. The figures for manufacturing industry, generally the most dynamic part of the industrial sector, are even worse for the US: America 2.5 percent, West Germany 3.3 percent, France 5.2 percent and Japan 9.4 percent.[15] In 1957 some 74 of the top 100 firms were American; in 1972 the figure was 53.[16]

Overall the US share of world manufacturing production sank from over 50 percent in 1945 to 31 percent in 1980 and is now at about 25 percent.[17] In 1956 the US accounted for 42 of the largest 50 corporations in the world. By 1989 it accounted for only 17 of the largest 50 firms. In the same time-span Europe rose from eight to 21 of the largest 50 corporations. Ten of these were German. Japan, which had none of the top 50 firms until 1968, accounted for 10 by 1989.[18]

Car production highlights the problem. In 1962 the US accounted for 52 percent of world production, by 1983 that figure was 23 percent, overtaken by both Japan (24 percent) and joint European car production (34 percent). Even in high technology goods, where the US has long been a leader, it is losing ground.[19] A Congressional study reported a slide in the trading surplus on high technology goods from $27 billion in 1980 to $4 billion in 1985. The dollar has long since ceased to be as good as gold – Europe is now the major holder of both currency reserves and gold.[20] It is ultimately this economic decline which underlies the US's dramatic slide from being the world's largest creditor nation to being the world's greatest debtor nation in just a few years.

The US is, of course, still the world's largest economy. It retains an important advantage over say the European Union (EU) which is often portrayed as an economic rival: the US is a single integrated state relatively free of centrifugal forces and capable of both international and domestic economic and military control over its destiny. In addition, the US ruling class has developed an important economic advantage in recent years: it has cut workers' real wages and it has reduced the percentage of US workers in unions to below 20 percent.

The decline the US has suffered is serious, but relative. However it is on just such relative decline that the fates of empires turn. Moreover the world order established after 1945 was predicated on the existence of *overwhelming* American economic and military predominance.

The US economy during the Cold War, from the long boom to the crisis of the 1970s

Cold War brinkmanship was supported by the highest level of military spending the world has ever seen. It is this spending which prevented the world economy from sinking back into the slump of the 1930s and produced the 25 year long post-war economic boom. Whilst every economy grew during the boom, some grew more than others. As we have seen the economies that grew most were those that did not have to foot the arms bill – notably Japan and West Germany. While America built missiles and bombers, West Germany and Japan built cars and electronics plants. As Immanuel Wallerstein argues 'The United

States ran into difficulties somewhere between 1967 and 1973 because ... it lost its economic edge. Western Europe and Japan became sufficiently strong to defend their own markets. They even began to invade US markets. They were then about as strong and competitive as the United States economically and that, of course, had political implications.'[21]

This problem was compounded, as Wallerstein says, by two others. One was the rise of third world nationalism. The Cold War architecture agreed at Yalta was challenged by four significant anti-colonial revolutions. In 1949 China passed out of the western sphere of control. The British left India. Arab nationalism altered the map of the Middle East. The successful Algerian revolution set the pattern and threw out the French. Then, in America's backyard the liberation of Cuba provided an ideological pole of attraction for rebels throughout Latin America, indeed throughout the world. Finally the US defeat in Vietnam was so great that only the end of the Cold War itself and the advent of the neo-conservative imperial project could even begin to repair the damage.

The third problem confronting US imperialism was the international mass movement that broke out in 1968 and continued well into the 1970s. In places, particularly in France, Italy, Britain and Portugal, this movement fused with a renewed wave of industrial unrest to mount a serious challenge to the ruling order. The revolt reached Chile and Argentina. Ideologically this challenged not only the US imperial part of the Yalta deal, it also created a New Left that was more sceptical of the social democratic, Labour and Communist components of the post-war status quo. In doing so it provided a root-and-branch critique of the Cold War settlement.

As Wallerstein summarises, 'the threefold fact of the rise of economic rivals, the world revolution of 1968 and its impact of mentalities across the world, and Vietnam's defeat of the United States, all taken together, mark the beginning of the decline of the United States'.[22]

The eventual defeat of this new wave of struggle and the containment and incorporation of the anti-colonial struggles and the regimes that arose from them was well underway by the end of the 1970s. The Reagan-Thatcher era was the revenge of a frightened ruling elite for the defeats imposed on them in the struggles of the previous 15 years. But while the Reagan-Thatcher years began to roll back the advances gained by working people across the whole post-war period of welfare state consensus it could not so easily deal with the economic problems in the US economy. Indeed, Reagan's renewed arms spending in the early 1980s exacerbated the problem. As military spending rocketed, the US went from being the world's greatest creditor to being the world's biggest debtor.

In a way the US was rescued from having to confront the full force of this problem by the simple fact that the pressures of the arms race on the new Gorbachev regime in Russia were greater still. Indeed, the Reagan arms boom was a gamble based on exactly this fact. Reagan's strategy was retro-nostalgia, an attempt to recoup the losses of the 1960s and 1970s by returning to the ideology and arms spending of the 1950s. The Russian economy was vulnerable to this attack because although it grew quickly after the Second World War it was still only half the size of the US economy at the end of the 1970s. Russia still had to match the Americans bomb for bomb, tank for tank. The burden was twice as great because the Russian economy was half the size of the US economy.

The situation was worsened because while western capitalists scoured the growing world market for sources of cheap labour, cheap raw materials and new markets, the state capitalists in the east were largely cut off from great swathes of the world economy. One result, for instance, was that when East Germany developed a new computer chip it cost, according to a *Financial Times* survey, 'more than 20 percent of total annual investments' when it could have been bought more cheaply on the world market. It was this lack of competitiveness that glasnost, the arms cuts and the introduction of the market in Eastern Europe, were meant to overcome.

The revolutions in Eastern Europe, particularly in the strategically vital East Germany, cut short this process, ending the bi-polar world. This left the US still carrying an enormous military burden and facing the prospect of European enlargement with a newly unified Germany at its heart.

The US economy and its competitors in the era of the new imperialism

The neo-liberal social and economic offensive of the last 25 years is the domestic counterpart to the renewed US imperial drive. But they are chronologically discontinuous. The neo-liberal offensive began in the late 1970s and was, at first, the counterpart of Reagan's Second Cold War. During this period the neo-liberal strategy was essentially a domestic response to economic decline, welfare spending and labour militancy. Only with the collapse of the state-led economic model in 1989 did the neo-liberal offensive join with the neo-conservative foreign policy offensive to form a unified global economic and military programme for US imperialism.

In its first phase neo-liberalism had three aims. The first was to reduce wages. The second was to reduce other costs, including the cost of protecting the environment, by allowing corporations to transfer these to public bodies. The third was to cut the welfare state by reducing funding, privatising services and lowering standards of provision. The conservative regimes of the 1980s managed to achieve some of these goals, particularly in the United States, to a degree in Britain, less so in other industrialised countries. But even in the US costs were not lowered to anything like their 1945 levels.

There was, for a relatively brief period in the 1990s, a much exaggerated spurt in the US economy but it was not matched by the performance of the world economy as a whole. Robert Brenner explains why the US boom made so little difference to the world economy:

'before the mid-1990s the US profitability revival not only imparted little increased dynamism to the world economy, but also came to a large extent at the expense of the economies of its leading competitors and trading partners, especially Japan and Germany. This was because, right up to the end of 1993, US producers secured their gains primarily by means of the falling dollar and essentially flat real wages, as well as reduced corporate taxation, but with the benefit of little increase in investment. They therefore raised their rates of return by attacking their rivals' markets, but generated in the process relatively little increase in demand, either investment demand or consumer demand, for their rivals' products. When the US government moved in 1993 to balance the budget, the growth of US-generated demand in the world market received an additional negative shock.'[23]

Moreover, as Peter Gowan notes, 'the boom has turned out to be a bubble, and the American bubble has turned out to have involved a great deal of parasitic and predatory activity, actually undermining the American productive base, as in the paradigmatic case of Enron. This marks a very substantial setback for the drive to reorganise American and international capitalism to assure US capitalist dominance through the first half of the twenty-first century.'[24]

The scale of this collapse was in direct proportion to the hype promoting the 'New Economy' at the height of the bubble. The US economy decelerated faster than it had done at any time since the Second World War. Growth in GDP slumped from 5 percent in the year ending in mid-2000 to minus 0.1 percent the following year. Real wages which had been growing at 3.5 percent were cut in real terms by 0.1 percent.

The short-lived boom had pulled up the international economy, but now 'under the impact of plummeting US imports, the economies of Japan, Europe, and East Asia lost steam as fast as the US, while much of the developing world, notably Latin America, was plunged, after a brief honeymoon, back into crisis. A mutually reinforcing international recessionary process was unleashed ...' [25]

There is an important point to be made here. Even in those comparatively short periods where US capitalism has managed to slow its decline relative to its competitors it has not done so in a way which sustains the global economy. This marks a very important difference between the post-Second World War moment of US dominance and the current situation. Then US growth, or more precisely US arms spending, was a rising tide that lifted all ships. Now the reverse is true. Then US-led growth helped to oil the wheels of US strategic dominance. Now the inability of the US economy to underwrite global growth stokes international resentment at US imperial designs. On an ebb tide there is greater conflict over who will occupy the deeper channels.

The economic heart of Europe

The most dynamic economy in post-war Europe was the West German economy. Limited in arms spending by the post-war settlement, it reconstructed its manufacturing sector and oriented on export growth. From the late 1940s to the late 1960s it achieved impressive growth rates and it did so not only through exploiting the extraordinary growth of the world market that took place during the long post war boom, but by taking an ever-increasing share of that market. The deficit spending by the US during the Vietnam war sucked in German and Japanese imports to the further competitive disadvantage of the US economy.

Towards the end of the long boom other European economies, notably the Italian and French, as well as the Japanese, were beginning to compete with German growth. And as the various industrialised economies began to catch up with the US, and as the world market itself grew, the effect of US arms spending had a decreasing effect in warding off recessions. So although US deficit spending again pulled the German economy out of the deep oil-crisis recession of 1974–75 it could not do so before it had lost 20 percent of its manufacturing work-force.[26] And the other side of the US deficit was a rise in the value of the German mark and therefore a tougher market for German exports.

By the 1990s the long post-war boom was two decades in the past and the competitive advantage the German economy had been able to create was long gone. German unification may have given the German state strategic advantages but it had considerable economic costs. By the early 1990s 'the German economy once again came face to face with the problem of relatively high costs in international terms, under conditions of system-wide manufacturing over-capacity, and, like Japan, entered its longest recession since 1950. Between 1991 and 1995, GDP grew at an annual rate of just 0.9 percent'.[27]

While the fading of the German economic miracle diminished one specific challenge to the US a more general European challenge emerged to replace it. The halting progress of the European Union towards effective economic union is a story almost as complex as the Brussels bureaucracy itself. But the gradual convergence of the German, French and Italian economies did provide, by the early 21st century, a platform for a unified currency capable of operating as an alternative to the dollar. This is the first time such a thing has happened since the decline of sterling.

The main advantage that the German state now has derives as much from its strategic position as it does from its recent economic performance, although it remains the world's largest exporter. The German economic miracle re-established Germany in the major league of industrial powers. But it is the re-unification of Germany that places it at the heart of both the further integration of the European Union and the extension of the EU into Eastern Europe. It is also, as we shall see, a major force in deciding the future development of Russia.

West Germany forged ahead with unification itself when the US government was cautioning a slower pace. Germany's initial post-unification insistence on recognising Slovenia against US wishes was one of the prime causes of the unravelling of Yugoslavia. It was this move that encouraged the US to take the lead in the Kosovo war for fear of an emerging German challenge to its hegemony in NATO. In the case of the Iraq war Germany was second only to France in creating the greatest fracture in the western alliance since the Second World War.

There is little that suggests that these conflicts will immediately result in armed clashes between these powers, but there is equally little to suggest that we have not entered a period where such disputes will both increase in severity and govern the military conflicts that happen in other parts of the globe.

Japan: from miracle to crisis

The Japanese economy became the second largest economy in the world during the post-war boom. Japanese firms took a greater share of the expanding world market at the expense of US producers. They also began to take markets from US producers in the US itself.

This huge surge was in part based on a semi-state directed economy. The alliance between the huge city banks, the major employers and the Japanese state meant that the Japanese economy had more than a little in common with the wholly state directed economies of the Eastern bloc. The government suppressed consumer demand, encouraged saving and directed the accumulated funds into capital investment by means of low interest rates for corporate borrowing. Exports were encouraged and imports discouraged by ensuring that the huge Japanese corporations, the keiretsu, bought their inputs from each other. This meant that throughout the long boom Japan maintained the lowest ratio of manufacturing imports to manufacturing output of any advanced economy. The result of all this was that Japan enjoyed the greatest investment growth of any industrialised economy.

This Japanese advance in the world market at the expense of the US economy was sustained by the impact of the Vietnam War. Robert Brenner records that,

'Throughout the whole post-war boom – and indeed throughout much of the long downturn that followed it – Japanese manufacturing had relied heavily on its ability to penetrate the huge American market, as well as to appropriate an ever greater share of world export markets from US producers. As growing Vietnam-induced federal deficits both extended the US boom in the years after 1965 and gave rise to accelerating inflation, Japanese export growth, driven upward by the red-hot US market and the reduced competitiveness of US producers, reached its post-war zenith, and Japanese profit rates, investment growth, productivity growth, and wage growth all reached their post-war peaks. The apex of the "Japanese Miracle" was attained around 1970'.[28]

The effects of the Vietnam War were, however, ultimately contradictory for the Japanese economy as well as for the US economy. The 'equalisation' of the major economies during the long boom and the exacerbation of the US economy's competitive difficulties by the Vietnam war led to the eventual abandonment of the Bretton Woods agreement and the inauguration of floating exchange rates in 1973. But the decline of the dollar meant the rise of the yen and so a rise in the cost of Japanese imports, making them less competitive. Japanese export growth fell by 75 percent between 1971 and 1973.

The Japanese government responded by giving the economy more of what had helped sustain growth in the first place, cheap credit, although in the changed world economy of the 1970s this only produced a weak boom and substantial inflation. In any case the bottom fell out of the world market with the 1974–75 'oil crisis' recession. Japanese industry was hit again. Overall, in the years 1969–75 the previously ever-expanding manufacturing labour force fell by nearly 15 percent.

The early 1970s were the turning point. After this the Japanese economy was thrust back into a cycle of boom and bust. Repeated and sometimes successful attempts to meet each new slump with more cheap credit could never overcome the structural change that was afflicting the world economy. The long arms spending boom was over and even the most miraculous industrialised economies were having to run to stand still.

At this point too, Japanese spurts of growth became underwritten by US deficits. Record US federal and current account deficits significantly helped the Japanese economy out of the world recession of the early 1980s. Japanese exports to the US were once again enjoying a spectacular rise. This symbiotic relationship meant that because Japan had become the US's largest and most reliable creditor the US had an interest in the continued growth of the Japanese economy. Equally, the Japanese were happy to lend to the US so that it could cover the gap between imports and exports because in doing so they were protecting their own sales to the US market.

Such interdependence, however, always has its limits since no state is happy to go on borrowing indefinitely to sustain other nations' exports. In 1985 the Japanese were forced to accept the Plaza Accord in the face of a rising clamour for protectionist policies in the US. Rather than risk being excluded from US markets altogether, the Japanese accepted a rise in the value of the yen which would curtail exports to the US. In fact the yen rose far further than anyone predicted, producing an unprecedented crisis in Japanese manufacturing. Now the Japanese were having a crisis exported to their manufacturing sector, just as they had exported one to the US in the early 1980s.

Once again the Japanese state poured cheap money into the economy to stimulate investment. Once again, it worked for a while. In the boom of the second half of the 1980s gross capital stock in Japan rose by 6.7 percent a year, two thirds faster than in the US. Labour productivity rose more than twice as fast in Japan as it did in the US. But the price of the boom, when it arrived, was higher than ever before. Rocketing land prices, share values and consumer spending resting on low interest rates could not be sustained. In 1989 and 1990 the Japanese state raised interest rates to curtail rising stock market and land values. The Japanese economy tilted into a 32 month long recession, the second longest in the post-war period. GDP growth averaged just 0.8 percent between 1991 and 1995. Imports surged into the Japanese economy. In 1994 and 1995 manufacturing product prices suffered by far their greatest decline since the Second World War.

The Japanese economy still maintains a high rate of accumulation and remains a serious competitor for the US, especially in relation to China. But it has struggled to retain this position amid the gale of deregulated world competition.

Russia: the dangers of decline

If the new economic instability arises from the relative strength of the Japanese, German and, as we shall see below, Chinese economies in the post-war period then the destabilisation that may arise from Russia has a very different profile. It is the rise and precipitate fall of the Russian economy that is the source of concern here.

It is not the case, as some Cold War ideologues would have it, that the Russian economy has always failed because it was state directed. Indeed, for the majority of what we may call the state-led phase of world economic development that took place in the middle decades of the last century the Russian economy industrialised and continued to grow at a rate faster than its western competitors. There was nothing inherently socialist about this, despite the ideology that the Russian state inherited from the 1917 revolution. State direction of resources has been a feature of every industrialising economy and the later the industrialisation takes place, the more competitive the economic environment, the more centralised the state direction of economic growth tended to be – whichever side of the Cold War divide it occurred.

Moreover, the key characteristics of the Russian form of state capitalist development took shape during the isolationist, slump and war dominated decades of the 1930s, 1940s and 1950s. The result was a particularly sealed or autarkic form of state dominated development, in contrast to some later but similarly state dominated models in South-East Asia where the orientation was on breaking into the world market. But for a sustained period this strategy, however brutal, worked: on CIA figures the output of the Russian economy grew from 33 percent of US output in 1950 to just under 60 percent by the mid-1970s. Industrial output per head in Russia rose from 25 percent of the European average in 1929 to 90 percent in 1980.[29]

The crisis of Russian state led industrialisation came about for three reasons. Firstly, despite its faster rate of growth, the total size of the Russian economy never caught up with the US and so the competitive pressure mediated through the arms race could never be successfully countered. Secondly and as importantly the post-war recovery and growth of the world market gradually made the 'autarkic' state-led model of development increasingly ineffective. Internationalised resourcing, production and sales trumped the internalised model of Russia and Eastern Europe. This was not a crisis of all forms of state intervention, merely a crisis of those forms of state direction that concentrated on domestic development rather than on breaking into some section of the world market. Thirdly, these pressures became magnified by the slow-down in the world economy in the mid-1970s.

The final cracking open of the Russian and East European economies came with the fall of the Berlin Wall in 1989. But the 'shock therapy' of exposure to the world market has only made a bad situation into a calamity. In the early 1990s Russia experienced a 40 to 50 percent contraction of its economy, the greatest ever decline for an advanced economy during peacetime. The collapse of industrial production was even greater. Inflation soared as prices were liberalised. Savings were wiped out. Capital investment fell by 75 percent. The United Nations Development Programme argued that the 'transition to the market' was a euphemism for 'what in reality has been a Great Depression'.[30]

By the mid-1990s some financial stability was achieved but one of the leading figures of post-Soviet liberalism, Grigorii Yavlinsky, explained the cost: 'we have low inflation, a low budget deficit, but we have almost no economic activity.' In so far as there was any other progress in the 1990s it rested on raw material and oil sales and financial manipulation. When the already catastrophically weakened Russian economy was hit by the East Asian crisis in 1998 there was financial panic, the devaluation of the rouble and the collapse of the banking system. For ordinary Russians greater poverty and a further decline in living standards were the result.[31]

The destruction of the Russian empire in Eastern Europe, the independence of the former Soviet republics in the 'near abroad', and the ruination of the economy have reduced Russia from the status of superpower to that of a weakened regional power. Russian military bases in Vietnam and Cuba have been closed while Moscow has agreed to the opening of US military bases across the newly independent states in Central Asia. Petrodollars earned as a result of high oil prices are being recycled, Japanese and Saudi-style, into the purchase of US government bonds. Rather than solve Russia's economic problems, this helps stem the tide of recession in the US. The accession of Russia has turned the G7 club of industrialised states into the G8.

The critical fact about Russian decline has been, as we have seen, to open up the entire Eurasian landmass to a 'goldrush' by the western governments and corporations on a scale that dwarfs the original in the Klondike. The effect of this on the strategic position of Russia creates a wholly new instability in the world system.

The initial post-Cold War position of the Russian governing and business elites to this transformation was a more or less uncritical pro-Americanism. But the subsequent economic disaster and the inability of the US to underpin the reconstruction of the Russian economy have forced a change. One consequence is that Germany has become more important for the Russian economy. This has produced a kind of schizophrenia in Russian policy. 'Over the past decade Russia has been politically dependent on the United States, and economically dependent of Germany', writes Boris Kagarlitsky, 'The United States dictated Russia's political agenda while Germany gradually became its most important business partner and source of foreign investment'.[32]

This schizophrenia is worsened by the bitterness that economic failure and the collapse of empire has created among the Russian people, a bitterness that finds a nationalist expression. Some 80 percent of Russians now regard Mikhail Gorbachev as a 'traitor' personally responsible for all the disasters of that have befallen them since 1989. Furthermore, 60 percent of Russians regard the US as a 'hostile country'.

All this could have been contained more securely, if not more happily, if it were not taking place in the world where the US is driving a renewed global imperial project. As Kagarlitsky argues, 'This system worked quite well so long as Germany kept a low profile in international affairs and at least made a show of solidarity with the United States. When disagreements between the United States and Germany came to the surface, however, the Russian leadership was at a loss.'[33]

The attack on Iraq produced precisely this circumstance. Russia may no longer have been a superpower but it was a nuclear power with a seat on the UN Security Council and large outstanding debts owed to it by Iraq. As Franco-German opposition to US policy grew, so Russia became strategically important for both camps. Moreover, the 'euro-core countries' have their own oil and raw material needs and in this respect their ties with the Russian economy are different, and an alternative, to US domination of oil supplies in the Arab world. This is why, as Kagarlitsky notes, the struggle around the Iraq war at the UN was very much a struggle between Washington and Berlin for Moscow's vote. Strategic and diplomatic struggles had turned Russia 'into a real battlefield' on which 'the Russian elites are already visibly divided into pro-American and pro-German factions'.[34]

This situation is likely to endure. Putin likes the US war on terror since it licenses both domestic repression and the continued war in Chechnya, Russia's foothold in the oil rich Caucasus. But the price of US encirclement, unpaid for by any great US led economic assistance, is proving very high for Russia's government. Russia will remain subordinate, its loyalties divided. But it is now the object as well as the subject of great power rivalry. As such it greatly adds to the instability of the world system.

China industrialises

The challenge of the Chinese economy is qualitatively different to the challenge of the German or Japanese economies. It is potentially far greater in scale. Unlike the European Union the Chinese state is unified and possesses a pronounced nationalist ideology. Most importantly the Chinese economy is not just 'another' competing industrialised economy. It is a massive and swiftly *industrialising* economy that is bound to upset the regional and ultimately the global balance of power.

The Chinese economy is also industrialising in a manner distinct from the Russian economy. The Chinese economy, like the Russian economy in the Stalinist period, went through a phase of state-led primitive accumulation of capital. It has now, more successfully than Russia, managed a reorientation on the world market. Moreover, it has sustained this transition under a fiercely authoritarian government still capable of directing economic resources. This Stalinism-with-Coke may be an unstable mixture not least because the human cost is so high. But while it lasts it is a combination of market-orientation, state economic direction and domestic repression that fits the neo-liberal moment.

Any parallels with US fears in the 1980s about growing competition with Japan are unhelpful. Those concerns in some sections of the US governing elite arose from the ground gained by the Japanese economy in the long post-war boom. They subsided as the Japanese competitive threat receded during the long stagnation of the Japanese economy in the 1990s. The industrialisation of China is of a wholly different order. There will no doubt be severe economic crises in China. And Chinese industrialisation will be affected by the boom-bust cycle in the world economy. Nevertheless Chinese industrialisation is a much deeper economic process that will continue through a number of booms and slumps. This is the pattern in all industrialising economies.

If we look at the proportion of the world economy that China has historically commanded, excepting the period since Europe-wide industrialisation, it amounts to about one-quarter of global production. If industrialisation were to return the Chinese economy to that kind of weight in the world economy it could not help but significantly alter the relations between the world's most powerful nation-states. There is already concern in the US that this process is well underway, as one account notes: 'Chinese power is on the rise, and the US, although the world's only superpower, is in danger of losing its grip as the unchallenged arbiter of Asian security.' With US policy focusing on

Iraq, 'Beijing, its influence enhanced by a fast growing economy that has fuelled an export-led recovery across Asia, has not hesitated to fill the vacuum left by US inattention'.[35]

South Korea's trade with China is so great that the US is having difficulty getting its normally compliant ally to toe the line in its ongoing conflict with North Korea. One diplomat working on the North Korean issue reported: 'China is using its economic power in the region. The US is trying to maintain its traditional role, and others – while recognising that role – are not prepared to accept the degree of US dominance they had before'.[36] It is a sign of the times that China has now replaced Japan as the main destination for Asia's exports and that, in 2004, Japanese trade with China exceeded Japanese trade with the US for the first time.

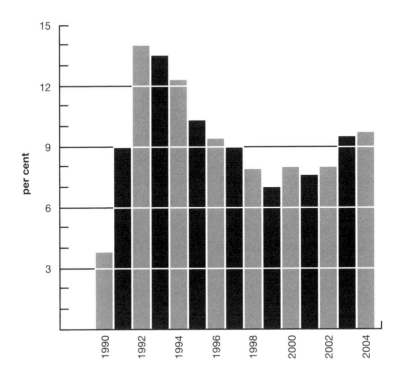

Figure 2.1 China's GDP, % growth on a year earlier

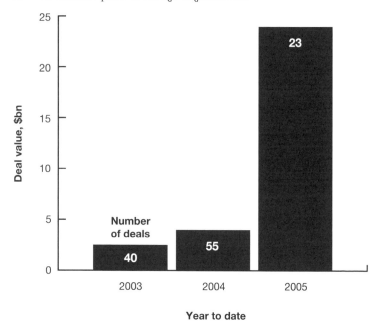

Figure 2.2 Announced mergers and acquisitions by Chinese companies abroad

China's increasing economic weight is also having its effect beyond Asia, as can be seen from Figure 2.2 showing the increase in Chinese mergers and acquisitions overseas. China is, after the US, the greatest recipient of global investment but its wage levels are one-fiftieth of those in the US and Japan. China's growth rate has been averaging a huge 8 to 10 percent and its share of the world economy has doubled in the past decade, albeit only to 4 percent. It is consuming 7 percent of the world's oil supply, 25 percent of its aluminium, 30 percent of iron-ore, 31 percent of coal and 27 percent of steel output.[37]

Little surprise that 'China has made friends in places as far apart as south-east Asia, India, Latin America and Africa, often in the quest for oil and other natural resources to fuel the Chinese industrial revolution'. Again such economic relationships inevitably have the capacity to result in conflict at a diplomatic and military level: 'China's energy driven relationship with Iran – a

Chinese state oil company recently struck a $70 billion deal to buy oil and gas over three decades – is also complicating EU-US efforts to put pressure on the Islamic government to give up its nuclear programme'.[38] In September 2004 China blocked US-proposed UN action against Sudan as a result of its oil contracts. There are already calls from the US foreign policy elite for a tougher stance towards China. William Clark Jr., President Clinton's Secretary of State for East Asian affairs, says 'The US must be more aggressive with China in discussing with China its oil needs ... ensuring that the oil available is shared equitably.'[39]

China's integration into the world market is seen by some as a guarantor that US-Chinese relations could not deteriorate beyond a certain point. And it is certainly true that any US attempt to limit China's economic growth would be opposed by those US multinationals which already have too much to lose from investments and markets in China were such attempts to succeed. And it is also true that there has been an implicit bargain in US-Chinese economic relations – the US looks benignly on China's surging exports and the consequent Chinese trade surplus with the US as long as China recycles its wealth to finance the US budget deficit. In other words the US is repeating the relationship that it has already developed with oil producers in the Middle East, the Japanese and others. Nevertheless, this understanding has limits. In March 2006 the *Financial Times* reported that 'the US administration warned ... it was heading for confrontation with China over bilateral economic relations if Beijing did not move immediately to open its markets to American imports. Carlos Gutierrez, commerce secretary, ... said that the US had almost run out of patience waiting for China to take significant steps to reduce its ballooning $200 billion trade surplus with the US.'[40]

The question remains, however, whether such economic interdependence precludes diplomatic and, ultimately, military conflict. The historical evidence is that it does not. The economies of the industrialised world were becoming increasingly interdependent before the First World War. Indeed international trade was developing more quickly before the First World War than it was to do in the wake of that war and for much of the isolationist 1920s and 1930s. But it was precisely this inter-dependence, which always involves economic competition as well as economic co-operation, that meant that even purely economic rivalry could not be contained within the economic sphere. Such stresses, at a certain point, graduate to the sphere of relations between states. In the case of the First World War military action to redraw the basis of economic relations was the weapon of choice for enough of the world's states to cause a global conflict.

The world environment in which China is industrialising makes for a greater likelihood of such conflict in the longer run. The more the US depends on investments in China and on the Chinese financing the US deficit the more it will need to exer-cise its military might to protect these economic lifelines. Fur-ther, as Peter Gowan notes, 'the fundamental geopolitical problem inherent in the turns of Russia and China towards capitalism ... [was that it] undermined their usefulness as potential threats to Western Europe and Japan in need of US military services for protection. They also set up competitive pressures within the core countries to gain privileged relations with these two states and privileged access to their labour and product markets and resources and assets. The obvious danger from an American point of view was that in the West a Ger-many anchored within a more cohesive EU could establish a privileged partnership with Russia, while some or all of the East Asian capitalisms could link up with China in a strong regional network that could weaken American leverage and economic penetration.'[41]

Latin America: losing control of the backyard

The threat to US hegemony posed by Latin America is mainly political rather than economic. If there is one area of the globe in which the US has been more exercised about sustaining its influence than the Middle East it is Latin America. In Latin America US counter-revolutionary policy has its longest and most intense history. But in recent years the old authoritarian regimes have given way in the face of a continent-wide mass mobilisation against neo-liberal economic policy and dictatorship. As one Argentinean writer records:

'Neo-liberalism did not reduce social struggle, and the ruling classes were not able to achieve the kind of victories they had won in previous decades: on the contrary, they have had to face risings which have brought down several presidents in the Andean region and the southern cone. Direct action on the land (Peru), an indigenous rising (Ecuador), pressure from the streets (Argentina), in insurrectionary climate (Bolivia), land occupations (Brazil), anti-imperialist protests (Chile), and a new political movement (Uruguay) and resistance to military coups (Venezuela) have inspired a new cycle of resistance throughout the region.'[42]

The extent of the transformation in the political landscape is hard to overstate: 'The ruling classes have lost the confidence they displayed in the 1990s and many of their principal representatives have withdrawn form the scene (Menem in Argentina, Fujimori in Peru, Salinas in Mexico, Perez in Venezuela, Lozada in Bolivia).'[43]

The most obvious and immediate cause of this transformation is the failure of neo-liberal economic policies. Crises, low growth and bankruptcy have been as endemic as growing inequality, elite profiteering and political corruption. The waves of struggle in Latin America have been predominantly social struggles which have grown over into, or combined with, political struggles against the domestic regimes. But there has, since 9/11, been an important international dimension. The US administration's obsession with Iraq has created a space in which the Latin American revolt has developed. The quicksand in 'post-war' Iraq is so deep that the US has partially lost its grip on its own backyard.

The most serious threat to the US comes from the government of Hugo Chavez in Venezuela. We have already seen, in the previous chapter, the impact on US policy of Chavez's control over Venezuela's oil industry. Claudio Katz underlines this point and also highlights the wider context:

> 'The US pulls the strings of any coup attempt or terrorist provocation from Colombia, but Washington has no Pinochet to turn to and has to rely on its 'friends in the Organisation of American States' to undermine Chavez. Bush cannot act in too barefaced a way while he is stuck in the Middle East quagmire. He does not dare compare Chavez to Saddam – and Chavez cannot be tamed like Gaddafi. The US needs Venezuelan oil and it needs to combat Venezuela's active involvement in OPEC and its attempts to redirect crude oil to new clients in China and Latin America.'[44]

Of course the challenge to the US by other Latin American governments is by no means the same as that represented by Chavez. Elsewhere, despite the replacement of the previous authoritarian leaders, the new 'democratic' order is largely proving all too compatible with neo-liberal economic policy. Interestingly many of the recent mobilisations against neo-liberalism have had the new 'democratic' governments in their sights. For now it suffices to say that the declared US aim of being able to fight more than one major conflict at the same time looks as if it is being sorely tried in Latin America. It is simply beyond belief that in any era before the declaration of the 'war on terror' the US would have allowed events in Latin America to carry on as far as they have now done without more serious covert or overt intervention.

The world economy and competition between national economies

The structural relationships in the world economy changed with the onset of the crisis of the 1970s. The high tide of growth which lifted all ships began to ebb. Those economies which had risen furthest fastest, like the German and Japanese economies, saw the end of their unique period of expansion. The interests of the major economies were still intimately linked but they now had to try and ensure that their overall slow growth did not turn into a catastrophic failure in any one country, thus dragging down the whole system. As each economy tried to advance at the expense of the others they were confronted at every turn with the fact that this sort of competitive relationship is easier to sustain in a rapidly expanding global economy than it is in a stagnating or slowly growing economy. The relations between the major economies over the last 15 years illustrate this point.

In the early 1990s the US economy had led the way in pulling up the Japanese and German economies from their longest slump since the 1950s. But by the mid-1990s the German and Japanese economies were aiding US recovery from difficulties that were, in part, a product of the US's determination not to allow the Japanese economy to cause the kind of damage to the world system that the earlier Mexican collapse had caused.

> 'The fact remains that, while the US economic revival took place largely at the expense of its leading rivals, that it had to do so was ultimately at the cost of the US economy itself. The US recovery of the early 1990s was thus itself limited by the ever slower growth of world demand, and in particular the related intensification of international competition in manufacturing, which placed intense downward pressure on prices throughout the world economy. Perhaps most directly to the point, in an interdependent world economy, the US economy could not easily sustain a truly serious crisis of its leading partners and rivals. Just as Japan and Germany had to ... rescue US manufacturing from its crisis of the first half of the 1980s, at great cost to themselves, so the US [was] obliged to accept a quite similar bailout of Japan's crisis bound manufacturing sector.'[45]

The end of the Japanese and German economic miracles at the conclusion of the long boom left them more equal with the US.

It ended the immediate post-war dispersion of economic power in which the US had been overwhelmingly powerful. But the world that resulted was one of systematic failure, not simply competitive failure. Now everyone was in the mire. They were more equal but less capable of extracting themselves from the mud. The advanced economies might compete to shift the burden among themselves, might even co-operate in shifting the burden among themselves, but none of them, not even the US, could cure their common distress.

Consequently, no-one could prevent the South-East Asian crash at the end of the 1990s. The inescapable conclusion, notwithstanding frequent proclamations by establishment commentators of an escape from boom and bust, is that 'there is little evidence that either the world economy, or its US component has succeeded in transcending the long downturn, the very extended period of slowed growth that began around 1973 ... Successive attempts by governments and corporations to restore profitability, especially by way of elevated interest rates and reduced wage and social spending growth have failed ... '[46]

The evidence of this global stagnation is now so strong as to be irrefutable. Work done for the Organisation for Economic Co-operation and Development shows that the rate of growth in real global GDP fell from 4.9 percent between 1950 and 1973, to 3 percent between 1973 and 1989, a drop of 39 percent. The UN figures show GDP growing at 5.4 percent in the 1960s, 4.1 percent in the 1970s, 3 percent in the 1980s and 2.3 percent in the 1990s.[47]

In these circumstances competitive pressures that arise in the economic sphere can only ultimately be resolved in the political sphere – that is at the level of the relations between states. States ultimately decide the fate of the corporations in general precisely because, although competing corporations have needs and interests, they do not have the capacity, other than through the state, to articulate a 'general will' of their own. Capital can only exist as many capitals, noted Karl Marx. This is simply the logical corollary of accepting that capitalism is a system based on competition between different units of capital, be they corner shops or multi-national corporations. And the logical corollary of this is that only the state can form 'the executive committee for the management of the common affairs of the bourgeoisie'. The state becomes the arbiter, ultimately by means of force, of disputes arising in the field of economic competition.

Moreover, the state must also evaluate its own strategic and military needs and enact these as it sees fit. These may, at particular conjunctures, only partially coincide with the economic imperatives of even the most powerful corporations. We have already seen in the case of the Balkan pipelines how the economic needs of the corporations, which favoured the cheapest pipeline route through Iran, were overridden by the US state in favour of a more expensive but more strategically desirable route through Turkey. Such disputes, and disputes of much greater importance, will continue to be generated by the uncontrolled dynamic of economic competition. And in an environment of deregulated but sclerotic growth this competition cannot help but generate disputes between states and coalitions of states.

Conclusion

The US may still be the most powerful economy in the world but it is no longer so powerful that it is capable of sustaining a long period of stable capitalist development in the way that it did for a generation after the Second World War. The end of the long boom and the rise of other advanced economies make the world market a much more competitive environment than before. This economic condition has now combined with renewed instability in the state system following the end of the Cold War to create an environment more volatile than any since the 1920s and 1930s.

This new instability is nowhere more obvious than in the Middle East. The next chapter examines the struggle of western imperialism to control the region and its most valuable commodity, oil. In this long conflict the interrelation of the military power of states, the economic interest of corporations and popular resistance has determined the history of the last century.

3   Oil and empire

Oil is not just another commodity. It supplies the bulk of the world's energy. It provides power for the train, the plane and the automobile. It is also the basis of all types of plastics from food wrapping to the windows on airliners. Perhaps even more importantly it provides the fertilizer and pesticide on which a huge amount of modern agriculture depends. Oil is food, light, heat and transport. No other single commodity can make the same claim. It really doesn't get much more important than this.

The corporations that produce this oil are the largest in the world, richer and more powerful than many governments. In 2001 the biggest oil company, Exxon Mobil, earned 187 billion dollars, BP, the second largest oil firm, made 174 billion dollars and Royal Dutch Shell came third with 135 billion dollars. Saudi Arabia itself, home to the largest and most profitable oil reserves in the world, only made 58 billion dollars from oil.[1] In many of the world's most troubled regions oil corporations not only perform their commercial functions but also act as an arm of their home government in discussions with other states.

There is little prospect of oil becoming any less central to modern capitalism in the near future. In 2004 global oil consumption was the largest for almost 30 years.[2] On current projections oil and gas use will rise by 2 percent a year until 2025. In that year oil and gas use will be 50 percent higher than in 2001 and six times the amount used in 1960.[3] This rise will in part be a result of a surge in oil use caused by industrial growth in China, Russia and India, where it will more than double. China alone accounts for a third of the increase in demand for oil since 2000.[4]

Some of the wars of the 20th century were about oil and in all the wars of the 20th century access to oil and the use of oil was an important part of victory. From Churchill's decision before the First World War, as First Lord of the Admiralty, to fuel British battleships with oil making them faster than their German coal-fired counter-parts to US forces burning 2 million barrels of oil a week as they invaded Iraq, oil has been crucial.

Have we reached peak oil production?

Oil is a commodity so central to modern society that it would create a huge social crisis if it were running out. Many experts argue that we are at, or are approaching, the peak of oil production and that, in the near future, oil production is set to decline. Table 3.1 shows the most important oil producers, how much oil it is estimated they have left and the year of peak production.

If these figures are correct then only the oil extraction in Middle East states and the small amount of oil in Kazakhstan is still to reach its peak production. What seems clear is that according to current levels of technology and geological knowledge many oil fields are past or approaching their peak of production. Given the rapidly rising global demand for oil there is therefore an important structural element in the gathering crisis surrounding oil production.

There are however some important qualifications to be made. Firstly, accurate figures about oil reserves are very hard to find. The estimates given by corporations and states are not independently verified. It may be the case that companies and countries more often exaggerate their reserves than underestimate them – in which case the peak oil crisis is even nearer than we think. In 1997, for instance, some 59 countries claimed their reserves had not changed at all from the previous year despite being constantly drained in the preceding 12 months. In

Table 3.1 Where is the world's oil and how much is left?[5]

Country	Remaining oil reserves[a] (billions of barrels)	Amount of oil drained[b] (billions of barrels)	Peak year of oil production[c]
Saudi Arabia	262	97	2008
Iraq	112	28	2017
Abu Dhabi	98	19	2011
Kuwait	96	32	2015
Iran	90	56	1974
Venezuela	78	47	1970
Russia	60	127	1987
United States	30	172	1971
Libya	29	23	1970
Nigeria	24	23	2006
China	18	30	2003
Qatar	15	7	2000
Mexico	13	31	2003
Norway	10	17	2001
Kazakhstan	9	6	2033
Algeria	9	13	1978
Brazil	8	5	1986
Canada	7	19	1973

[a] BP *statistical review of world energy* 2003. Does not include shale oil and tar sands.

[b] Association for Study of Peak Oil, "World Summary, Regular Oil Production", 15 May 2004. Does not include shale oil, tar sands, oil from polar regions, bitumen, extra heavy oil, liquid extracted from gasfields, or oil under more than 500 meters of water.

[c] Association for Study of Peak Oil, "World Summary, Regular Oil Production", 15 May 2004.

1985 Kuwait announced that its reserves were 50 percent higher than previously claimed. And in 2005 it was still claiming exactly the same reserves after 20 years of extraction – a claim that seems to have more to do with the fact that OPEC production quotas are based on claimed reserves than it does with geology.[6] And in 2004 Shell admitted it had overestimated its oil and gas reserves by a massive 3.9 million barrels. But it is also the case that oil fields sometimes hold more than was initially estimated. For instance, between 1946 and 1989 the estimates of the amount of oil in US fields were constantly revised upwards.

Trying to gauge accurately the real global reserves of oil is therefore an extremely inexact science. Indeed, it's difficult not to agree with George Monbiot: 'I have now read 4,000 pages of reports on global oil supply, and I know less about it now than when I started. The only firm conclusion I have reached is that the people sitting on the world's reserves are liars.'[7]

There is however a second reason for caution about the argument that global oil supplies have peaked. New technology is making it possible to get more oil out of the ground. Increasingly sophisticated '3D' geological surveys mean that oil deposits, even relatively small ones, can be more easily identified and extracted. Horizontal drilling techniques mean that oil is more easily accessible than it was before. And, paradoxically, the high price of oil makes previously uneconomic prospects capable of being developed at a profit. The tar sands of Alberta, Canada, for instance, could provide more proven reserves than Saudi Arabia. The cost of extracting the oil from the tar sand ran to about 30 dollars a barrel in the 1980s when the price of a barrel was between 20 and 25 dollars. But the massive hike in oil prices since then makes the prospect altogether more attractive for oil companies. And a new 'steam assisted gravity drainage' system, which shoots steam down the drill hole and pushes the tar sand out, has sent the cost of producing oil this way down to between five and seven dollars a barrel. The oil industry in Alberta is burning 20 percent of the national gas supply and using 25 percent of Alberta's water supply while causing widespread environmental damage – but these considerations have never been uppermost in the minds of oil executives.

Thirdly, new discoveries of oil cannot be ruled out. From the North Sea a generation ago to the Tengiz field in the Caspian Sea more recently, new fields have been brought online. None have been on the scale of the fields in the Middle East and none produce oil as cheaply. Neither do they, even collectively, produce oil on such a scale as to compensate for the rapidly rising demand for oil. But they, and other future discoveries, may slow the pace at which a crisis of oil supply develops.

For all these reasons it is best to see the coming crisis of oil supply not simply as a once and for all natural limit although, of course, such a limit must be reached at some point. It is better to formulate the natural resource side of the crisis in this way: at the current level of technology and on the basis of what is currently known about global oil reserves demand is outstripping supply, driving up prices and forcing the pace of both state and corporate efforts to secure existing supplies.

The danger in the current situation lies as much in the relationship between the power structure of the state system and the oil supply as it does in the absolute amount of oil left in the crust of the earth. Critical in this regard is the fact that oil is running out *in the United States* at a time when US dependence upon it is greater than ever.

Rising demand for oil in other states with limited domestic supplies, like India and China, will force these states 'to jostle with the United States, Europe and Japan in seeking access to the few producing zones with surplus petroleum, greatly exacerbating the already competitive pressures in these highly volatile areas'. Moreover, oil scarcity, whether absolute or relative to a particular country's resource, will produce greater emphasis on the military side of oil security.[8]

Oil in the USA

Oil is at the heart of modern US capitalism. The oil consumption of the US is 25 percent of the global total. Oil powers 97 percent of transportation in the US. That alone accounts for one barrel in every seven consumed in the world. On top of that oil provides for 40 percent of total energy used in the US.[9] It's the same story in the US military which consumes 85 million barrels of oil a year making it the biggest single consumer of oil in the country, possibly in the world. No wonder when the Abrams tank uses a gallon of fuel every half-mile and burns 12 gallons of gas an hour when it's standing still with the motor idling. It

has been calculated that 70 percent of the weight of all the soldiers, vehicles, and weapons of the entire US army is pure
fuel.[10]

Oil was discovered first in the US. The huge corporations that
grew around its production entered into a symbiotic relationship
with the huge automobile corporations that depend on it. Until
the 1940s oil was mainly an internal and domestic issue for the
United States because the domestic demand for oil was met by
domestic supply. But by the end of the Second World War it was
apparent that the domestic demand for oil would outstrip the
declining production of oil within the United States. Oil became
a foreign policy and national security issue from the moment
that the US economy became dependent on imported oil.

In the Second World War US oil wells provided six out of
every seven barrels used by all the Allied powers during the
conflict. But by the 1950s the US was importing 10 percent of
its oil, in the 1960s that figure rose to 18 percent and, by the
1970s it rose to over 40 percent. In April 1988 the previously
unthinkable happened: US dependence on imported oil passed
the 50 percent barrier. If current trends continue, by 2025 US
oil consumption will rise by half as much again as it currently
consumes. Domestic production is set to stay the same and so
the entire increase will come from imported oil.[11]

As part of the US's rise to superpower status its political and
military leaders repeatedly stressed the centrality of oil supply to
its national security strategy. During the Second World War
President Roosevelt made a remarkable extension of the Lend-
Lease programme, designed to aid wartime Allied powers, to
Saudi Arabia. In order to bring Saudi Arabia within the terms of
the Lend-Lease Act he had to declare that 'the defense of Saudi
Arabia is vital to the defense of the United States'. By 1945 the
State Department was informing President Truman that 'in Saudi
Arabia the oil resources constitute a stupendous source of stra-
tegic power, and one of the greatest material prizes in human
history'. And in the same year the State Department observed,
'The oil resources of Saudi Arabia ... must remain under
American control for the dual purpose of supplementing and

replacing our dwindling reserves, and preventing this power potential falling into unfriendly hands'.

The continuity in US policy on this issue is remarkable, a point made by Secretary of Defense Dick Cheney to the Senate Armed Services Committee in 1990 when he recalled that the ties between the US and Saudi Arabia 'hark back ... to 1945, when President Franklin Delano Roosevelt met with King Abdul Aziz on the USS *Quincy*, at the end of World War II, and affirmed at that time that the United States had a lasting and continuing interest in the security of that kingdom'.[12] But for all the continuity in the aim of US strategy there have been very great changes in the conditions under which it has had to pursue that strategy.

Challenges to US oil strategy in the Middle East

The fate of the Middle East has been bound up with the oil industry since the early 20th century. The collapse of the Ottoman Empire after the First World War gave the imperial powers, mainly France and Britain, and the oil corporations an invaluable chance to divide the oil wealth of the region among themselves. The discoverer of Iraq's oil wealth, Armenian prospector and creator of the Turkish Petroleum Company, Calouste Gulbenkian, brought together a consortium which eventually combined Anglo-Persian (forerunner of BP), Shell, Standard Oil New Jersey (Exxon to be), Socony (Mobil) and others to exploit the region's reserves under the name of the Iraq Petroleum Company. No one was quite sure where the Ottoman lands began and ended so Gulbenkian took a red pencil and drew a line on the map that ran around the whole of Saudi Arabia and Iraq as well as much else. See Map 3.1. The Red Line Agreement established a de facto oil cartel in much of the Middle East.

In the same period, and also as a result of the decline of the Ottoman Empire, the beginnings of the Israeli state took shape on Palestinian land. The Balfour Declaration in November 1917 committed the British state to 'the establishment in Palestine of a national home for the Jewish people ...' The Balfour

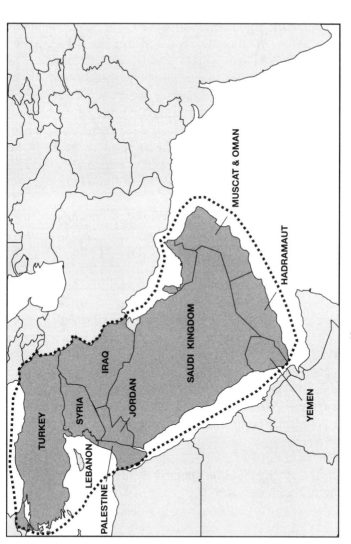

Map 3.1 The Red Line Agreement 1928[13]

Declaration heralded the increase of Jewish settlers on Palestinian land. This Zionist movement had gained such strength during the inter-war period that when Richard Crossman reported for the 1946 Anglo-American Committee of Inquiry into the future of Palestine he wrote that the Jewish Agency there was 'really a state within a state, with its own budget, secret cabinet, army, and above all, intelligence service. It is the most efficient, dynamic, toughest organisation I have ever seen and it is not afraid of us (the British)'.[14] And so it transpired. With the establishment of the state of Israel the imperial powers, above all the US, worked to create a force in the Middle East capable of assisting in the control of its Arab neighbours and standing against the anti-colonial impulses of the post-Second World War world.

The Israeli newspaper *Ha'aretz* described the situation perfectly in 1951: 'The feudal regimes of the Middle East have had to make such concessions to the nationalist movements . . . that they become more reluctant to supply Britain and the United States with their natural resources and military bases . . . Strengthening Israel helps the Western powers . . . Israel is to become the watchdog. There is no fear that Israel will undertake any aggressive policy towards the Arab states when this would contradict the wishes of the US and Britain. But if for any reason the Western powers should sometimes prefer to close their eyes, Israel could be relied upon to punish one or several neighbouring states whose discourtesy to the West went beyond the bounds of the permissible'.

As President Ronald Reagan characteristically bluntly expressed the same point in 1980, Israel has a 'combat experienced military . . . a force in the Middle East that is actually of benefit to the US. If there was no Israel with that force we'd have to supply that with our own'.[15]

In the very year that Israel's role in the Middle East was predicted by *Ha'aretz* the US and Britain were grappling with one of the most momentous revolts against oil imperialism in the post-Second World War period.

The Anglo-Iranian oil company was doing very well from Iranian oil. But Iran was not. Anglo-Iranian registered £250 million profit between 1945 and 1950. The Iranian government received £90 million in royalties. Indeed, the British government received more in taxes from Iranian oil than the Iranian government received in royalties.[16] The Iranian state, headed by the Shah, was unstable, dominated by the British oil interest which engendered widespread anti-colonial sentiments. As similar anti-colonial feelings forced other oil corporations across the Middle East to renegotiate more favourable contracts with their hosts, Anglo-Iranian held firm. But when their rival Aramco signed a new deal in Saudi Arabia, Anglo-Iranian's position became untenable. They offered their own improved deal to the Iranian parliament. But it was too late.

The elderly radical who headed the Iranian parliament's oil committee was Mohammed Mossedegh. He declared, 'the source of all the misfortunes of this tortured nation is the oil company'. But the Prime Minister and Army Chief of Staff, General Razmara, rejected the motion for nationalisation of Anglo-Iranian. Four days later he was assassinated entering Tehran's central mosque, by an Islamic militant. Mossedegh became the new prime minister and the nationalisation law was passed and went into effect on 1 May 1951.

The nationalisation of the Anglo-Iranian company was a crisis with global implications. The US Petroleum Administration for Defense estimated that without Iranian oil, which at this time accounted for 40 percent of Middle East production, global demand would exceed supply by the end of 1951.

For the British the loss was a traumatic illustration of imperial decline as the band played out the last of the British nationals from the giant Abadan refinery. Britain made ready for military intervention. But on the brink of action it pulled back.

One reason for this hesitation was the attitude of the US. The Korean War had just begun and the US now saw world politics through the Cold War lens. Churchill, who had purchased the British government's share in Anglo-Iranian 37 years earlier, raged at the US attitude. He told Clement Attlee that he was 'rather shocked at the attitude of the United States, who did not seem to appreciate fully the importance of the great area extending from the Caspian to the Persian Gulf: it was more important than Korea.'[17] Yet it was exactly this that the US did appreciate. They worried that an armed intervention would raise anti-colonial feeling further and give the Russians the excuse to intervene from the north. So British armed intervention was ruled out.

Negotiations to get Iran back into the Western fold got nowhere. All of them ultimately foundered on the intense anti-British feeling in Iran. Mossedegh was always, and not surprisingly given the fate of his predecessor, most concerned to ride the tiger of the anti-colonial movement. In the US, Secretary of State Dulles told the National Security Council that Mossedegh was a precursor of Communism and that this would mean, 'Not only would the free world be deprived of the enormous assets represented by Iranian oil . . . but the Russians would secure these assets . . . Worse still . . . if Iran succumbed to the Communists there was little doubt that in short order so would the other areas of the Middle East, with some 60 percent of the world's oil reserves . . . '[18]

Overt military action was ruled out. But covert action was not. The US and British jointly approved an operation to over-throw Mossedegh. The resulting coup was a close run thing but it was ultimately successful. Iran was made safe for the Shah, and for Western, mostly US, oil companies.

It is not hard to discern in these events the original of the pattern that was to recur in the Middle East many times, albeit with varying results. Only a handful of years passed before, in 1956, another nationalisation, this time of the Suez Canal, again brought Britain to the point of military action. At that time two-thirds of canal traffic was carrying oil and two-thirds of Europe's oil supply came through the canal. Britain and France's long imperial history in Egypt left the majority of canal tolls going to European shareholders of which the largest was the British government.

Nasser's nationalisation occasioned something like panic among Britain's ruling elite. Just months before the seizure of the canal Prime Minister Anthony Eden told a visiting Russian delegation, 'I must be absolutely blunt about the oil because we would fight for it'. And he continued, 'We could not live with-out oil and ... we had no intention of being strangled to death.'[19]

So this time the British went ahead with military action, aided by France and, notably, Israel. That which Iran had proved behind the scenes, Suez proved in full view of the world. The US was opposed to the invasion for the same reasons it had opposed military action in Iran– it would inflame Arab nation-alism and raise the prospect of allowing the Russians further influence in the Middle East. So when Nasser blocked the canal, the US refused to make good European oil supplies. The British Chancellor of the Exchequer exclaimed, 'Oil sanctions! That finishes it.'[20] He spoke more than he knew. It was obvious to anyone who cared to look that US, not European, imperialism now held the whip hand. And, in part because these inter-imperialist divisions were greater in Suez than in Iran, Nasser fared better than Mossedegh, inflicting a great defeat on his enemies. The Suez adventure was over and the British were out of the Middle East.

After Suez nothing was ever the same again. The British were never to return as a major power in the Middle East. Henceforth their presence could only be as US camp followers. The US model of post-colonial economic imperialism was now domi-nant. The direct rule of the European empires fell before the tide of anti-colonialism. But it was replaced by US imperial power exercised thorough economic coercion, client ruling classes and, in *extremis*, covert or overt military intervention.

The impact of Suez can also be seen in the rise of Arab nationalism. Two years after Suez Nasser helped engineer a coup against the British-backed Hashemite royal family in Iraq. The new nationalist regime revoked concessions to the oil compa-nies in 1960, drastically reducing their stake in the Iraqi oil fields. In the same year Saudi Arabia, Venezuela, Kuwait, Iran and Iraq formed the Organisation of Petroleum Exporting Countries. A series of price cuts by oil majors like BP and Standard Oil of New Jersey had hit the revenue of oil exporting countries. OPEC was their response.

The rising tide of Arab nationalism continued to put pressure on the oil majors throughout the 1960s. Syria nationalised its oil fields in 1964 and, two years later, increased charges paid by Western oil companies for the use of pipelines. But when Syria raised the loading tax and demanded payment of arrears the oil companies' cartel agreed the rate increase but refused to pay the arrears. Syria stopped the flow of oil.

The US and Britain responded by pouring arms into Saudi Arabia. The Israeli prime minister threatened that if raids on Israel continued the army would invade Syria. Egypt led the Arab response declaring a 'jihad' and amassing the army in Sinai. The 1967 war was a quick and absolute victory for Israel.[21]

The 1967 war was a dramatic defeat for Arab nationalism. But the shifting economics of oil supply gave OPEC greater power with the passage of time. As we have seen, domestic US oil supply was in decline. In the decade after OPEC was formed there was a 21 million barrel increase in Western demand for oil. Two-thirds of that was being met by Middle Eastern oil. OPEC producers could see that it was their oil, not that of the United States, which mattered most to the world economy. By 1973 the market price of crude oil had doubled over the preceding three years. That year Saudi oil minister Sheik Ahmed Yamani declared, 'The moment has come. We are masters of our own commodity.'[22]

But 1973 turned out to be a decisive year for other reasons. Just as OPEC were discussing oil price rises, Egypt and Syria, with Russian support, attacked Israel and began the Yom Kippur War. The US supported Israel, at first air-lifting supplies and then agreeing 2.2 billion dollars of military aid. OPEC raised the price of oil by 70 percent sending it over 5 dollars a barrel. Saudi Arabia announced that it would cut off oil supplies to any nation that supported Israel. Other Arab states did the same. Oil prices jumped again, to 16 dollars a barrel.

The US was no longer able to increase domestic oil production to make good the shortfall and the Nixon administration drew up plans for US troops to seize the oil fields of the Middle East. It didn't come to that because the Arab states lifted the embargo on a promise that Western European governments would support the Arab position, although oil shipments to the US were not resumed until 1974.

Finally a traumatic decade for imperialism in the Middle East ended worse than it had begun: in 1979 the Iranian revolution threw out the Shah. Driven forward by strikes and occupations in the oil fields and massive demonstrations on the streets, the revolution's first institutional expression was the *shoras*, popular councils with strong echoes of the soviets that grew from the Russian revolutions of 1905 and 1917. To develop such institutions of popular power would have taken a left possessing greater political clarity than the Iranian left. Ultimately the power vacuum created by the incapacity of the left was filled by Ayatollah Khomeini. In the final phase of the revolution a US defence attaché summarised the situation in an unimpeachably brief but accurate message to Washington: 'Army surrenders; Khomeini wins. Destroy all classifieds'.[23]

All the foreign oil companies were thrown out of Iran. Crude oil hit 30 dollars a barrel and the crisis was only mitigated because Saudi Arabia agreed to increase its production. The major oil companies were now frozen out of direct access to Saudi Arabia, Iraq and Iran. Western oil supply was clearly in the hands of Middle Eastern governments.

From the Carter Doctrine to the invasion of Iraq

The consequences of this post-war series of reverses for imperialism in the Middle East, and particularly of the Iranian revolution, were widespread and long-lasting. First it meant a renewed insistence by President Carter and his successors that any threat to Middle East oil would be taken as a direct threat to US national interests. Second, for oil supply and military bases the US came to place much greater reliance on the region's main oil producer, a conservative state seemingly immune from the tide of revolution, Saudi Arabia. Third, the war that broke out between Iran and Iraq led eventually to the fatal Washington 'tilt' towards Saddam Hussein's regime. Lastly, but by no means of least importance, Islamic radicalism was greatly fuelled by the Iranian revolution.

The immediate result of these changes was but more humiliation for the United States. President Carter was already beset by an energy crisis at home as a result of the Iranian revolution when, in response to the entry to the US of the former Shah, Iranian demonstrators overran the US embassy and took its staff hostage. The following month, December 1979, Russian troops invaded Afghanistan. The US, like the British before them, had long feared a Russian push into the Persian Gulf. Now, with Iran in turmoil and her neighbour invaded, the worst seemed to be happening.

The Carter Doctrine was the US policy response. In his State of the Union address Carter insisted, 'An attempt by any outside force to gain control of the Persian Gulf region will be regarded as an assault on the vital interests of the United States of America and will be repelled by any means necessary, including military force.'[24] In a general sense this was no more than a forceful restatement of Presidential doctrine since Truman. But in the conditions of 1980 it also meant that the US would rest less on local surrogates and more on its own direct military intervention.

The first attempt to act on the Carter Doctrine was not, however, a happy one for the president. The hostage crisis and the invasion of Afghanistan had probably already doomed Carter's presidency before he decided to launch military action to rescue the hostages. But the fate of the mission sealed the president's fate as well. As the helicopters sent to deliver the rescue teams to the US embassy in Tehran failed through mechanical breakdown or crashed into their supply planes in a desert sandstorm, Carter himself ordered the mission aborted. It was the single most humiliating reverse for US imperialism since its staff clambered from the roof of its embassy in Vietnam.

The loss of Iran bequeathed Carter's successors a two-pronged policy: (i) arm US allies, especially Saudi Arabia, to the hilt and (ii) rely, where they dared, on direct US military intervention. The second of these was much the more difficult and so Saudi Arabia became a key recipient of US arms as well as a much-favoured 'swing producer' on whom stability in the oil market depended. This policy was to have fateful consequences as it intertwined with another consequence of the events of 1979, the arming of the Taliban to counter the Russian invasion of Afghanistan.

In a remarkable turn of fate, a development detested by the US, the Iranian revolution, and two developments in which it conspired, its alliance with the Saudi regime and the victory of the Taliban, all contributed to the growth of Islamic radicalism. And in dealing with the Iranian revolution the US gave this vicious spiral another twist. The outbreak of the Iran-Iraq war was initially greeted by the US with a cautious pro-Iraq stance. But as the Iranians gained the upper hand Washington began to 'tilt' further towards Saddam Hussein's Iraq. Military and other aid flowed to Iraq. Human rights abuses in Iraq were ignored or excused by the US. Saddam Hussein's miscalculation, just two years after the end of the Iran-Iraq war, that the US would acquiesce in the invasion of Kuwait seems more rational when viewed in the light of these events.

Had Saddam been a little less driven by the debt and destruction caused by the war with Iran or a little more attentive to US policy towards Saudi Arabia perhaps he would have been more easily convinced that the US would never let the invasion of Kuwait stand. The first President Bush put it in unequivocal terms in a TV broadcast on 8 August 1990, 'Our country now imports nearly half the oil it consumes and could face a major threat to its economic independence ... the sovereign independence of Saudi Arabia is of vital interest to the United States.'[25]

US and allied troops poured into the Middle East, especially into bases in Saudi Arabia. The Saudis agreed to this so long as the bases were withdrawn when Saddam was defeated. It was not to be. This was to further infuriate Osama Bin Laden. The rejection of his offer to the Saudi elite, whose head of security he knew well through the Afghan campaign, to deploy his Arab-Afghan fighters, now veterans of Kashmir and Bosnia as well as Afghanistan, rather than the US troops to rid Kuwait of Saddam had already led to a breach with his previous patrons.

The gross military imbalance of the first Gulf War ensured the easy defeat of Iraq, a spectacle all too grimly summarised in what one US pilot described as 'the turkey-shoot' on the Basra road when retreating Iraqi soldiers and civilians were gunned down. The policy of 'containment' by no-fly zones, military incursions and sanctions left Iraq a broken society over the following decade. But the US also paid a price for the war – the decline of its relationship with Saudi Arabia. As we have seen in previous chapters the 1990s were the decade in which the main prop of US policy in the Middle East fell away. Saudi Arabia, the last untouched bastion of pro-US stability, became 'unreliable'.

Part of the change was to do with Saudi Arabia's domestic politics. A high birth-rate gave Saudi a population in which 75 percent were under 30 years old and 50 percent were under 18 years. Per capita income which was the same as the United States in 1981 (28,600 dollars) had collapsed to just 6,800 dollars by 2001. Unemployment had risen, particularly among young, educated Saudi men where it had gone from zero to 30 percent in a decade. This situation generated a layer of disaffected and educated radicals, just the group who, as we shall see in chapter five, had been crucial to the development of so many revolutionary situations internationally in the anti-colonial era. As Michael Klare notes, the Saudi economic situation 'produced a surplus of well-educated, ambitious, and often alienated young men with high expectations and few economic opportunities – perfect fodder for political or religious extremists'.[26]

This domestic situation could not however fail to interact with international politics. The presence of US bases became a lightning conductor. The Saudi royal family tried to buy off discontent, but they could not quell the torrent of disaffection. For the US this left a huge dilemma, as we have seen in previous chapters. Having lost Iran, lost Iraq and with Saudi Arabia becoming less hospitable the US needed to dramatically redraw the map of the Middle East. Leaving Saudi would possibly stabilise the royal regime, but it could only be done if some other source of oil and bases could be secured. From this point on the policy of 'containing' Saddam Hussein was a wasting asset. Regime change in Iraq was, sooner or later, going to come. The attack on the twin towers ensured that the moment arrived sooner rather than later.

The drive to diversify

A few months before the attack on the twin towers, in May 2001, George W Bush announced 'diversity is important not only for energy security, but also for national security. Over-dependence on any one source of energy, especially a foreign source, leaves us vulnerable to price shocks, supply interruptions and, in the worst case, blackmail'.[27] The Bush administration was not the first to make this case. It had been made by every one of its predecessors since it became clear that US oil production was in decline.

There are a number of areas that the US looks to as alternative oil suppliers to the Middle East. 'The Caspian Sea can ... be a rapidly growing new area of supply', argued the US National Energy Policy issued in 2001.[28] The drive to diversify has led to greater US military involvement in the Caspian area. In 1999 the US Central Command, created by President Carter to implement his doctrine of increased military intervention in the Middle East, had its area of operations enlarged to cover the Central Asian states of the Caspian Sea basin. This drive, made possible by the fall of the Berlin Wall and facilitated by the Kosovo war, was greatly assisted by the aftermath of 9/11. As Assistant Secretary of State A Elizabeth Jones told the Senate Foreign Relations Committee, 'Our country is now linked with this region in ways we could never have imagined before September 11.' US assistance to the greater Caspian Sea area in the period 2002–4 increased by 50 percent over the previous three year period.[29]

The difficulty for the US diversification strategy in the Caspian region is that diversity does not mean stability. The US is now, through the search for oil and as a result of conflicts in the former Yugoslavia and Afghanistan, drawn into an inherently unstable part of the world which is part of the former empire of one of its great power rivals. Meanwhile Russia is still struggling to assert its influence on its newly independent neighbours. 'It hasn't been left unnoticed in Russia that certain outside interests are trying to weaken our position in the Caspian basin' the Russian Foreign Ministry argued in May 2000, 'no one should be perplexed that Russia is determined to resist the attempts to encroach on her interests.'[30] Perhaps nothing indicates the dangers better than the fact that in December 2002 Russia installed a squadron of fighter planes and 700 support troops near Bishkek in Kyrgyzstan – very close to the existing US base at Kyrgyzstan's Manas International Airport.[31]

Other potential sources of oil imports for the US may not be as unstable as the Caspian region but for the US they are difficult in their own way. Venezuela's recent political turmoil is at least as threatening to the US as anything that has happened in the Middle East. Hugo Chavez has already played a role in the unfolding crisis of US oil policy by cancelling the proposed privatisation of the oil industry when he came to power. Venezuela is, of course, one of the non-Arab members of OPEC. And the Chavez regime's radical politics means that it is one of the new centres of anti-imperialist sentiment in Latin America. Next door Colombia is an oil producer that is reckoned to have considerable untapped oil reserves. But US supplies from Colombia have actually declined from 468,000 barrels in 1999 to 256,000 in 2002 because oil corporations fear that the country cannot sustain political stability.

So in some of the important areas where the US is looking for oil to supplement or replace Middle Eastern supplies it faces other forms of instability which, in turn, encourage it to use its military might to ensure 'energy security'. But there is another problem.

The US is currently scouring the globe for alternative sources of oil. From Alberta in Canada to the opening of Alaska's Arctic National Wildlife Refuge prospecting, from Russia's oil fields to Angola and Nigeria the most powerful corporations in the world are now roaming the globalised economy looking for more reserves of black gold. But for all this frenetic activity the US remains faced with a huge problem which the debate over the Arctic National Wildlife Refuge illustrates. Even if this great natural wilderness contains the 10 billion barrels of oil that the Bush administration and the oil industry claim, it will only reduce US dependency on imports by about 3 percent a year during the next 20 years. The US is faced with the simple fact that the supplies of oil available will not eradicate its dependence on the Middle East.

So after all the great drive to diversify, the picture in 2002 looked like this: Canada led the world in US sources of imports, at 17 percent, followed by Saudi Arabia on 13.7 percent, Mexico on 13.5 percent, and Venezuela on 12 percent. The year before the figures were Canada 15.4 percent, Saudi Arabia 14 percent, Venezuela 13 percent, and Mexico 12.1 percent. Canada has been the leader since at least 2001. In 2002, US imports from the Persian Gulf region amounted to 19.8 percent of US total oil imports. The same year, a total of 40 percent came from OPEC member nations, which include countries such as Venezuela and Indonesia that are outside the Persian Gulf. In a wider international context the picture is as follows: in 2003 the leading oil consumers were the US (20 million barrels per day), China (5.6), and Japan (5.5). The leading oil importers were the US (11.1 million barrels a day), Japan (5.3) and Germany (2.5).[32]

The truth is that no source of oil in the world is as plentiful, as easy to extract, and therefore as profitable as the oil in the Middle East. Even after its long hymn to diversity the US National Energy Policy was forced to conclude 'Middle East oil production will remain central to world oil security ... the Gulf will be a primary focus of US international energy policy'.[33] This drive to diversity has added to geopolitical instability by taking the guns and tanks where the prospectors go. Energy security and national security are co-joined in US strategic planning.

Finally, and most importantly, the domestic oil needs of the US are far from the only reason it is concerned to dominate Middle East oil production. It may be true that both Europe and China are now more dependent on Middle East oil than the US. But this is precisely the reason why the US is centrally concerned not to lose its imperial writ in the region. Control over the Middle East is not just about securing the US domestic oil needs, it's about exercising control over the oil needs of the US's allies and competitors. And since the US's overwhelming strength is now more military than economic there is a logic in the militarization of the Middle East – it plays to the strength of the US and allows its corporations to follow through the door kicked open by the military. This goes some way to explain the division over the Iraq war between Russia, France and Germany on the one hand and the US on the other. The imperial configuration of European powers is the reverse of US – their economic power is greater than their military profile. Hence their preference for a non-military solution to the Iraq crisis. Their preference has been fully vindicated by the manner in which US corporations were favoured in the economic carve-up of post-war Iraq.

From Arab nationalism to Islamic revival

Since the countries of the Middle East were carved out of the remnants of the Ottoman Empire by the great powers at the end of the First World War there has always been resistance to this oil-fuelled imperialism. It continues today in Iraq, in Palestine, in Lebanon and among Iranians, Syrians and Egyptians. It is not now, nor has it ever been, far from the surface in any country in the Middle East. However, the form it has taken, its dominant ideological expression, has changed.

Nationalism of various hues has always been a pervading ethos. And for most of the period since the Second World War this nationalism was often associated with Communism. This was for two main reasons. Firstly, the indigenous Communist Parties both had some real roots among workers, peasants and the poor and were genuinely opposed to imperialism. But they were also, out of a theoretical predisposition, inclined to conflate the national struggle and the class struggle. They imagined that a section of the indigenous capitalist class was opposed to the imperialist structure and therefore tended to subordinate their politics to the need, as they saw it, to create a cross-class Popular Front. Secondly, in a globe divided by the Cold War, Moscow often found advantage in sustaining the opponents of US imperialism. The aid might be limited and always dependent of the realpolitik judgements of the Russian state, but it carried weight in the international anti-imperialist movements.

Over time this orientation by the Communist Parties of the Middle East almost universally ended in their destruction in the most important countries. In Iraq the history of the Communist Party is of a series of betrayals by their nationalist allies. In Iran the errors of the Communists in relation to Mossedegh's nationalist movement led to the virtual disappearance of the movement until the revolution of 1979. In Egypt the subordination of the Communists to the Nasserite current led to its destruction at the hands of the military leaders of the nationalist movement.

The eventual fate of the nationalist wave has been equally unhappy. The independent Arab regimes of the 1950s have all made their peace with the new imperial order. The great radicalising charge of Nasserism, the most powerful of all the Arab nationalist movements, ended in the brutal, farcical Mubarak regime. The heroic notion of a pan-Arab state, proclaimed by the Communist International in the 1920s, reduced itself to the Ba'ath tyranny in Iraq and Syria.

The rise of Islamic militancy cannot be explained without this context. The exhaustion of the nationalist project and the elimination of the Communist alternative resulted in the anti-imperialist impulse taking another form. The Iranian revolution of 1979 was the most important single episode in this transition.

The core of the revolution in Iran was the oil workers' strike action but by February 1979 every corner of Iranian society was in ferment. 'The "riot of democracy" was in full swing, with workers', women's, peasants' and national minority movements setting the pace. Fevered debates were taking place in every area of Iranian society and potentially the left had a huge audience'.[34] The political leadership of the revolution was contested by Ayatollah Khomeini's Islamic current and the left.

For the left to provide successful leadership in this context it would have needed to combine unity with all those struggling against the Shah with political independence, specifically on the central issue of workers' organisations providing the basis for a successful challenge to the existing state. But the main left party, the Tudeh, shared the old Stalinist approach which regarded talk of independent working class leadership as premature because of the 'undeveloped' nature of Iranian capitalism. Rather, they thought, the revolution would first go through a democratic stage and so they gave unconditional support to the provisional government and liquidated their supporters into the movement around Khomeini.

The Fedayeen had broken from the Tudeh party in the wake of the coup against Mossedegh. At that time the Tudeh, in a rehearsal of their error in 1979, failed to act independently of the nationalist government. But although the leaders of the Fedayeen identified the political failure of the Tudeh their solution to this was armed guerrilla struggle. In 1979 this strategy was as incapable as that of the Tudeh of providing independent leadership from within the working class.

It was this absence of an independent organisation on the left that allowed the Khomeini movement to politically dominate the revolution. Similar developments also rooted in the wider failure of the left assisted the rise of Islamic currents elsewhere, notably among the Palestinians and in Lebanon. More broadly, as we shall see in chapter five, the relationship between spontaneous revolutionary development, imperialism and political organisation has recurred in new forms since 1979. Crucially, a decade after the Iranian revolution, these debates were alive again as the 'velvet revolutions' swept across Eastern Europe.

Conclusion

The Middle East is crucial to western imperialism for both economic reasons and for strategic reasons. Oil is not only at the heart of all modern economies in the immediate sense that without it they would not function. It is also highly profitable. Even a state that does not need it for its own purposes can use control over oil to exercise power over other states. In fact, the US has all three reasons for wanting as much control as it can obtain over the oil of the Middle East. Moreover, the Middle East is a crucial strategic area in the new imperial geography of the post-Cold War world. It stands at the heart of the Eurasian landmass with Europe to its west, Russia and the Central Asian states to its north and India, Afghanistan and, further, China to its north east. Popular resistance in this part of the world has never been long tolerated by imperial powers.

The effects of end of the long post-war boom and the rise of the new imperialism are not limited to the Middle East. Globalisation has reshaped relations between the state, the economy and the people in every corner of the globe, including in the advanced countries. Chapter four looks at this process and the effect it has had on traditional political organisation and resistance in the heartlands of the system.

4 Globalisation and inequality

The huge extension of international trade, finance and production by multinational corporations is at the core of most people's understanding of the term 'globalisation'. This meaning does indeed capture an important part of what has been happening to the world economy. However, it is worth being more precise about the different pace of development in each of these three areas.

Capitalism has always been an international trading system. As the system has grown the volume and extent of trade has grown with it. International trade tripled between 1870 and 1913 as Europe and America industrialised. Protectionism in the inter-war period curtailed international trade, but US hegemony of the post-Second World War global economy led to renewed growth. The value of world exports grew from 315 billion dollars in 1950 to 3,447 billion dollars in 1990. Post-war trade has been much more a trade in manufactured goods, and much more between industrialised nations, than the earlier period of exchange of manufactured goods from industrialised countries for the raw materials of less developed, peripheral economies.[1]

The growth in international financial transactions has been even more spectacular. The ratio of foreign exchange transactions to world trade was nine to one in 1973. By 1992 it had risen to 90 to one. International bank lending has also grown dramatically. As a proportion of world trade it was 7.8 percent in 1965 but by 1991 it had risen to 104.6 percent. There has also been a massive growth in the market for government debt. This has led to huge expansion of government bonds held in the hands of 'foreigners'.[2]

International production has been slower to develop than international trade and finance. Much of what is commonly thought to be new about globalisation refers to this process of creating international networks of production by means of foreign direct investment (FDI). The stock of FDI in the world economy increased from 68 billion dollars in 1960 to 1,948 billion dollars in 1992. This marked a percentage increase of FDI in world production from 4.4 percent to 8.4 percent over the same period. But over 90 percent of FDI is concentrated in 10 developed countries and about 66 percent originates in the US, Germany, Britain and Japan.[3]

This international extension of the capitalist system has undoubtedly enhanced the power of major multinational corporations. On one estimate the top 300 transnational corporations account for 70 percent of FDI and 25 percent of the world's capital. The sales of the largest 350 corporations account for one-third of the combined gross national product of the advanced capitalist countries.[4] Transnational corporations accounted for 75 percent of trade in services. They also control 80 percent of all land under export crops.[5]

We should be careful about attributing all the enhanced powers of these corporations to the growth of the world market, as the more economistic accounts of globalisation suggest. There have been some crucial 'political magnifiers' that have enhanced the impression of an unstoppable growth in the power of multinational corporations.

The great cycle of defeats for the working class which began in the mid-1970s are at least as important in explaining the growing power of big business in the last 25 years. These defeats were central in undermining the welfare state consensus that had prevailed among governing elites since the 1950s. This in turn paved the way for the neo-liberal economic orthodoxy that has done so much to facilitate and legitimise globalisation. In particular this process helped transform the notion of the state from one in which government acted as a balance and corrective to market forces into a notion of government as the handmaiden and advocate of big business.

And without the fall of the Berlin Wall and the advance of western-style capitalism in Russia and Eastern Europe the ideology of globalisation simply would not have had the purchase that it achieved in the last 10 years. After all, what would 'globalisation' be if half the industrial world had still been beyond its reach? But the Berlin Wall did fall and the economies of Eastern Europe suffered the full force of the gale of 'creative destruction'. The triumph of the market was short-lived, its consequences hard felt and the instability it brought is a major factor in the drive to war.

The state and globalisation

The role of the state has certainly been significantly altered by globalisation, but it has not necessarily been weakened. Even in the area of direct economic 'interference' in the economy, the devil supposedly banished by the Reagan-Thatcher years, the facts are at variance with the ideology. From the Savings and Loans rescue by the American Federal Reserve during the recession in the 1990s to the handouts given to the ailing airline industry in the last recession, there is a lot more 'Keynesianism' around than the free market boosters would like to admit.

Neither have the international and domestic police functions of the state been at all diminished by the growth in international production. To give only one pertinent domestic example: the growth of international production has created, as it must, an international working class and therefore a global labour market. This in turn creates an international migration of labour, just as early industrialisation sucked labour from the land into the mill-towns, northern cities and metropolis of 19th century Britain. The attempt to control this process to their own advantage has enormously increased the police powers of states over immigration and asylum issues.

Internationally the state remains indispensable in underpinning the activities of multinationals. There are no proposals, even from the most hysterical free marketers, to return to the infancy of the capitalist system when corporations like the East India Company would employ their own troops. Armed action or the threat of armed action by the state remains the last resort for every capitalist corporation whose markets or production facilities are endangered by international rivals, be they states, other corporations or restive foreign populations unconvinced of the virtues of the free market.

These then are the senses in which the role of the state remains consistent with its past. But globalisation has also set in train some contradictory trends. Crucially globalisation has accelerated the trend for states to attempt to control the development of the system through international and intergovernmental organisations.

The World Trade Organisation, the International Monetary Fund, the World Bank, the European Union, NATO and a host of other similar bodies were mostly set up to underwrite the US-led post-1945 system, but they have gained renewed prominence because of globalisation. None of these institutions can override the authority of the nation-states that compose them. They are as much the site of conflict and paralysis as they are the embryo of 'international government', but they do mark an attempt, particularly by the major states, to co-ordinate a response to the unruly powers unleashed by the growth of market forces. This then is the supra-national trend enhanced by globalisation.

In reaction to this process a renewed nationalism is also being fuelled. This can take a number of forms. Those nations impoverished by globalisation and excluded from the elite clubs of the major powers can react by refurbishing a nationalist identity. This has been a constant motif in Russian politics and in the politics of the Balkan successor states ever since 1989. The same process can be seen in China, in Iraq, and in Indonesia after the fall of Suharto. Even at the core of the system the fear and insecurity, the sense of powerlessness induced in ordinary people when they are confronted by private and state bureaucracies of international dimensions, finds expression in the reactionary nationalism of, for instance, Austrian leader Jorge Haider or former Italian prime minister Silvio Berlusconi.

The search for a stable cultural identity in the midst of a changing and unpredictable world also fuels many nationalist movements that seek to break apart current nation-states. Scottish nationalism and Basque separatism have their more or less muscular, more or less progressive counterparts around the globe. The rise of political Islam must also be seen in this context. No simple formula about the progressive or regressive nature of Islamic movements is appropriate. Clearly, the Islam of the Hamas fighters in Palestine, or the FIS militants in Algeria is not the same as that propagated by the reactionary Saudi royal family. But the social root, which is the level at which we are discussing the issue here, has some similarities – a desperation to find some personal and meaningful pattern in a social world increasingly dominated by huge and distant monoliths whose power over the livelihood of millions seems absolute.

In the industrialized democracies the changing function of the state – less 'welfare provider' more 'pro-business facilitator' – has hollowed out the democratic aspects of the state machine.

The ideology that came to embody this change was neo-liberalism. But Margaret Thatcher did not invent it when she came to power in 1979. The preceding Labour administration under James Callaghan deserves that credit. It was the Labour government that accepted the terms of the austerity package proposed by the IMF in 1976. The main condition of the IMF loan, insisted on by the US Treasury, was that the government deficit must be reduced by cutting demand. Interest rates were raised and government spending reduced. Wage, job and welfare cuts were the hallmark of the 'social contract' agreed by the unions to bail out the government. As Colin Leys notes,

'From 1976 onwards Labour accordingly became "monetarist". Its leaders accepted that full employment could no longer be achieved by government spending but must be sought through private sector growth. For the necessary private investment to take place, prices must reflect real values, and this in turn required "squeezing" inflation out of the system and permitting the free movement of capital. In 1978 Treasury officials began preparing to abolish capital controls.'[6]

Margaret Thatcher came to power in the aftermath of the bitter rearguard strikes of the Winter of Discontent. She immediately removed controls on the international movement of capital and dramatically increased interest rates. She used both the law and mass unemployment as weapons in a series of titanic battles aimed at breaking the power of the unions. In the course of this offensive she also marginalised the old 'one nation' grandees of her own party. The result was the destruction of the liberal, welfare state consensus of the preceding decades.

The actions of the Callaghan and Thatcher administrations were fundamentally a response to the collapse of the long post-war boom. Their policies, and their American equivalents during the Reagan years, also helped bring into being the deregulated world of globalisation. As Colin Leys argues, 'The global economy was thus the creation of states, led – or pushed – by the US and the UK, but as soon as it took shape and gathered weight the market forces developing in it had greater and greater impact on the economies of those states . . .'[7]

These changes were political as well as economic and social. When the work of the Thatcher and Major administrations was complete there had been an important change in the British political system. The adaptation of the British state to the work of promoting a deregulated economy required a considerable alteration in its structures. Power was more centralised, the democratic space within the state reduced and direct role of major corporations in the running of society significantly increased.

This change is not just to do with the extensive privatisation of nationalised industries. Nor is it only to do with the massive deregulation of markets that has reduced the degree of state control over the economy. It also reached into the core operations of the state proper:

'In 1975 the civil service was still ... led by a small corps
of patrician public servants dedicated to prudent socio-
economic management and the gradual adaptation of
policy to evolutionary social change. By 2000 it had been
broken up into a set of small, central, policy making
ministries, led by civil servants promoted for their entre-
preneurial style; and a huge range of national and local
executive agencies, whether hived off from ministries, like
the Prison Service, or the oddly named "quasi-autonomous
non-governmental organisations" ("quangos") such as the
Office for Standards in Education ("Ofsted") or the regional health authorities, organised on business lines with
chief executives on performance-related pay.'[8]

Moreover, in 1975 local government had considerable discre-
tionary tax-raising and spending powers, ran the schools, social
services and long term residential and nursing care. By 2000
these responsibilities had been removed from local elected
representatives.

Those wanting to protest such changes not only faced the
most restrictive trade union laws in western Europe but a bar-
rage of new legislation restricting civil liberties: the Public
Order Act 1986, the Criminal Justice Act 1994, the Security
Service Act 1996, the Police Act 1997 and the Terrorism Act
2000. A new avalanche of anti-terror laws followed the attack
on the World Trade Center and the London bombings of 2005.

This centralisation of the state and restriction of its already
limited democratic aspects is not just a function of the impact of
neo-liberal economic policy and of globalisation. These have
certainly required a state that functions more openly and bru-
tally to corral the domestic population for the purposes decreed
by the global market. But the change in the nature of the international imperial order in the last decade, the birth of the new
imperialism, the succession of military conflicts in which the
British state has played a role second only to the Untied States,
have also accelerated this transformation in the state's inner
constitution.

The growth of international corporations and their close association with national states are both aspects of an imperial system, as the Russian Marxist Nicolai Bukharin realised in the early years of the 20th century. Both aspects of imperialism tend to hollow out the parliamentary system as power is drawn upwards into the executive and non-elected parts of the state. The modern ruling class is less a hybrid of different elements and more concentrated in its largest economic powerhouses even before its will is collectively expressed by the state. As Bukharin put it:

> 'With the growth of the importance of state power, its inner structure also changes. The state becomes more than ever before an "executive committee of the ruling classes" ... It is true that state power always reflected the interests of the "upper strata", but inasmuch as the top layer itself was a more or less amorphous mass, the organised state apparatus faced as unorganised class (or classes) whose interests it embodied. Matters are totally different now. The state apparatus not only embodies the interests of the ruling class in general, but also their collectively expressed will. It faces no more atomised members of the ruling classes, but their organisations ... This is one of the main causes of the so-called crisis of parliamentarianism ... Parliament at present serves more as a decorative institution; it passes on decisions prepared beforehand in the businessmen's organisations and gives only formal sanction to the collective will of the consolidated bourgeoisie as a whole. A "strong power" has become the ideal of the modern bourgeoisie.'[9]

Bukharin may have underestimated the degree to which competition, even between very large multinational capitalist firms, still produces divisions among them when they confront the state but he is nevertheless pointing to an important shift in the power relations between the modern state and multinational corporations.[10]

One important political consequence of these changes in the relationship between the state and multinational capital has been to heighten the sense of popular alienation from the huge bureaucratic structures that dominate the lives of ordinary people. This political alienation, always a feature of modern capitalism, is now magnified by the sheer scale of the institutions, state and private, that confront working people.

The proportion of people having 'a great deal' or 'quite a lot' of trust in parliament fell from 54 in 1983 to 10 percent in 1996, the last full year of the Tory reign. It has only recovered to 14 percent under New Labour. Trust in the civil service shows a similar pattern. It fell from 46 percent to 14 percent in 1996 and has recovered to 17 percent under New Labour. Only 22 percent of the public tend to trust big business while 65 percent do not.[11]

There seems, for most of us, no way to 'get at' these bodies. No way in which complaint or protest, never mind real influence, can reach them. Pollution occurs, fatal rail accidents take place, in hospitals lives are lost and injury caused, savings disappear, working conditions are unilaterally altered and the path of individual redress begins and often ends with automated answering services of the great bureaucracies. The 'best' that most complainants get is to eventually talk to another human being on whom they can vent their frustration. This person is, without exception, another worker and not the manager, let alone the senior executive, whose decisions are ultimately at the root of the matter. This frustration has reached such epidemic proportions that in those services where the staff have to confront the public they either have to be physically protected by screens, as now happens in social security offices, or notices have to be posted warning the public of the dire consequences of assaulting staff, as now happens on London buses and tubes.

All this is further aggravated by the ridiculous market-inspired jargon that seems to promise exactly the opposite of this frustration. Trains now carry customers not passengers. Nurses tend clients not patients. Bewildering consumer choice is offered by the same few large corporations. Customer charters offer unredeemable rights. The near universal mechanisms supposedly designed to provide accountability – regulation, inspection, target-setting and audit – are in fact making things worse. 'Changes supposed to make them more accountable to the public in practice only make them more subject to central control. Far from increasing public trust, they often had the opposite effect.'[12]

This alienation, fused with the larger alienation caused by growing inequality, the intensifying demands of the work process and the erosion of welfare provision, has now begun to find a political expression.

Inequality at the core

There is one index that demonstrates this general situation more clearly than any other – the growth in inequality. In the US the ratio of the median worker's income to salaries of chief executives was one to 30 in 1970. It was one to 500 by the year 2000. The top 0.1 percent of income earners had increased their share of national income from 2 percent in 1978 to 6 percent in 1999. Over the same period the share of the top 1 percent had risen to nearly 15 percent of national income, close to its share in the 1930s.[13]

The same picture presents itself wherever we look. The United Nations Human Development Report for 1999 recorded 'the countries of Eastern Europe and the CIS have registered some of the largest increases ever ... in social inequality. The OECD countries also registered big increases in inequality after the 1980s.'[14]

In Britain the original income of the top fifth of households is now 18 times greater than that of the bottom fifth, according to the government's own figures. Even after tax and benefits the top fifth of households are still four times better off than the bottom fifth. Yet despite being 18 times better off, the top fifth of households only pay twice as much of their gross income in tax as the bottom fifth (24 percent as against 12 percent).

Moreover inequality has grown significantly in Britain in the last 20 years. Government figures for disposable income show a

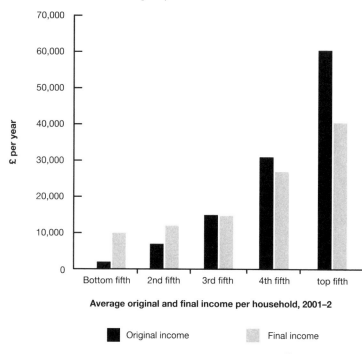

Figure 4.1 United Kingdom household income £ per year[15]

sharp rise in inequality in the second half of the 1980s, a slight decrease in the mid-1990s, and a rise under New Labour to the previous high of the Thatcher years. This is in 'complete contrast to the position in the earlier part of the post-war period. From the 1940s, average income had been rising, and until the late 1970s it has been rising fastest for those in the bottom income groups'.[16]

Inequality is as important in assessing the stability of society as levels of absolute poverty. If it were only absolute poverty that resulted in high levels of social resistance there would never have been any general strikes or revolutions after the first years of industrialisation. Few people in modern Britain wake in the morning to face a new day and content themselves with the thought that at least they are not living like 19th century weavers. They ask themselves different questions. Is my child's life

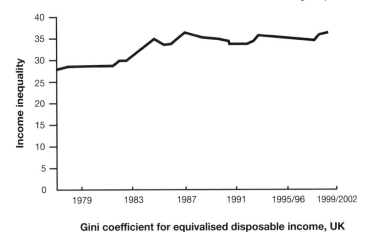

Gini coefficient for equivalised disposable income, UK

Figure 4.2 Income inequality (higher percentage = greater inequality)[17]

going to be harder than mine? Are we, the people who do the work, getting a fair share of all the wealth that we see around us in this society? It is therefore, as Marx pointed out, not the absolute poverty level but the socially relative poverty level that counts.

In a peculiarly Marxist moment the government's Office of National Statistics has given us a snapshot of relative poverty at the start of the 21st century. In interviews with panellists selected from the General Household Survey it drew up a list of items regarded as 'necessities': a bed, heating, a damp-free house, the ability to visit family and friends in hospital, two meals a day and medical prescriptions.[18]

The study found that four million people do not eat either two meals a day or fresh fruit and vegetables. Nearly 10 million cannot keep their homes warm, damp-free or in a decent state of decoration. Another 10 million cannot afford regular savings of £10 a month. Some 8 million cannot afford one or more essential household goods like a fridge or carpets for their main living area. And 6.5 million are too poor to afford essential clothing. Children are especially vulnerable –17 percent go without two essential items and 34 percent go without at least one.

We should not imagine that these conditions merely exist for a small 'underclass'. As the 21st century dawned the Organisation for Economic Co-operation and Development estimated that at some point over a six year period 55 percent of people in Britain had experienced poverty. Even when benefit payments were taken into account the figure remained 40 percent.[19] These figures are percentages of the whole population and so include the middle and upper classes. If we were to recalculate the percentages so that they showed the proportion of the working class that experience poverty (the only class that, in a general sense, is affected by poverty) we would have to conclude that a substantial majority of workers are, at some point over a six year period, poor.

There is, however, more to it than how much the working poor get to spend at the end of a shift. The intensification of work and the insecurity of working life are now part of the combustible material accumulating at the base of society. The end of the welfare state consensus, the decline of the public service ethos and the rise of the market-led consumerism of the Reagan-Thatcher era have had a profound effect on the regime within many workplaces. The defeat of the trade unions in the 1980s reduced the degree of day to day control that many workers had enjoyed over their working environment.

Short term contracts, part-time work, flexible shift patterns, mushrooming ranks of middle managers and supervisory staff, constant testing and assessment, punitive disciplinary codes, long working hours, short holidays and relentless 'downsizing' have materially and dramatically worsened the experience of going to work for many people.

What does all this mean? Just this: that for more than a generation the lives of working people have become harder, coarser, more difficult. It is a simple thing to say. But its political consequences are profound; especially when at the other end of society something very different is happening.

The ruling class and the upper ranks of the middle class have had a very different 25 years. They have become considerably wealthier. Just as we entered the 21st century, government figures revealed that Britain's biggest earners were enjoying their largest share of national income since the Thatcher years. The wealthiest fifth of the population controlled 45 percent of all disposable wealth. Senior executives in Britain's largest companies have seen their salaries rise by 92 percent in the last 10 years, more than double the increase in average wages.[20] Not only are the rich richer, but they are getting richer faster under New Labour. In the last two years of the Tory government the rich saw their incomes rise by 4.3 percent. But in the first two years of the New Labour government they rose by 7.1 percent.[21]

An important cultural change has flowed from this situation. Its most obvious face is the end of the public service ethos that was espoused, at least publicly, by the governing classes in the welfare consensus era. The now dominant free market ethic has given rise to an undisguised worship of wealth. One report notes, 'the redistribution of national wealth to the benefit of a narrow privileged elite has led to a "Roaring Twenties" mentality among this layer. Ostentatious consumption is *de rigueur*; the men's magazine *Arena* reports sales of champagne, cocaine and luxury sports cars have never been higher in the UK.'[22]

But more important than the conspicuous consumption of the middle and upper classes is the isolation from the rest of society that they now cultivate. This is an inevitable consequence of growing inequality. From the houses burglar alarmed and watched over by the unblinking eye of CCTV, out from the gated communities, drive the BMWs, Saabs, Audis and 4x4s, dropping the kids in schools increasingly segregated on class lines even when they are not fee paying. Or they board trains at 'peak times' for which even the second (sorry, 'standard') class fare is beyond the means of any person on the average wage. They holiday two or three times more regularly than working class people, dreaming of early retirement and a second home abroad. While the real welfare state declines the welfare state for the rich – the share options, pensions schemes, golden parachutes, travel allowances, private health plans, subsidised travel and accommodation – goes from strength to strength.

This way of life is validated for the rich in a thousand ways – in films and TV shows, in the Sunday newspaper supplements and the lifestyle magazines now divided into subsets for their houses (interior and exterior), gardens, holidays, cars, physical exercise routines, clothes, restaurants and cookery. And to help them in these arduous tasks there has reappeared, long after the decline of domestic servants, a new breed of casual domestic labour – cleaners, nannies, child-minders, au pairs, tutors, home helps, cooks, gardeners, personal fitness trainers, drivers and secretaries. Indeed spending on domestic service almost quadrupled to £4 billion annually between 1981 and 1998 and 'much of this was concentrated in households at the top of the income ladder and in London'.[23]

Many of those above the level of the upper middle classes now seldom meet a working class person in any other capacity than as a subordinate in the workplace, a sales assistant or as someone employed to work for them in their home. They move from one air-conditioned and socially controlled environment to another. Their knowledge of working class life is scant and they increasingly see the rest of society as a potentially threatening mob. The problems of workers – poverty, unemployment, bad housing, poor health, educational under-achievement – are of their own making. Social policy is no longer about treating the conditions that give rise to these problems but about coercing and containing the people who suffer from them.

New Labour inherited this mental world from the yuppie boom of the Tory years. It has accepted it with only minor rhetorical amendment. This gulf between the governing classes and the rest of society produces among them an extreme 'social Darwinism'. They think themselves better than others simply by virtue of being at the top of the pile. It is their own intelligence, savvy, flair, good taste, eye for a bargain and an opportunity that has got them where they are. The rest, those that suffer from 'social exclusion', must be helped to help themselves. No handouts mind you. Tough love. Encouragement for those that will help themselves. Scroungers with a 'dependency culture', 'bogus asylum seekers', those who refuse to 'modernise', the enemies of 'reform' must be swept aside. In other words, Victorian paternalism has returned as the dominant ideology of the governing classes. But, since the world doesn't work like this, the inevitable counterpart of Victorian paternalism has also returned – Victorian hypocrisy.

This ideology is fairly universal in the ruling class but it is not universal among the middle classes. The less well off sections of the middle class cannot rely wholly or mainly on private provision for such essentials as health care, pensions, education, care of the environment and transport. They too depend on the welfare state. Some heads of department and heads in schools, lecturers, middle ranking civil servants, managers in local councils, regret the passing of the public service ethos even as they preside over its destruction. Their work has become subject to the some of same modern day Taylorism that blights the jobs of workers. This is one reason why scepticism about neo-liberal economic and social policy has reached so deeply into the general population.

Global inequality

Capitalism has always increased the gulf between the rich and the poor. Even that relentless booster of globalisation, *The Economist*, noted 'over the past two centuries of rapid global growth, the gap between the rich and the poor countries has widened dramatically'.[24] A study by World Bank economists shows that the ratio between the richest and poorest country was nearly eight to one in 1870, 38 to one in 1960 and stood at 45 to one in 1990.[25] The wealthiest 20 percent of nations dispose of over 84 percent of global GNP, account for 84 percent of world trade and possess 85 percent of domestic savings. They use 85 percent of the world's timber, 75 percent of processed metals and 70 percent of the world's energy.[26]

The spread of neo-liberal doctrines and the deregulation that they promote has led to further disastrous economic consequences for much of the globe. The World Bank's figures on poverty give us one important indicator:

'These figures, rapidly becoming the most quoted economic figures in the world, show that about one-quarter of the world's population is below the lower poverty line

($1 a day) and about half below the upper poverty line
($2). The percentages have declined very slowly in the two
poorest regions, South Asia and sub-Saharan Africa, and
quite sharply in China and other parts of East Asia; but
they have risen sharply in the countries of the former
Soviet Union. Over the ten years covered by these estimates the total number of poor people in the world . . .
has either stayed about the same or risen.'[27]

In the last 50 years the gap between the rich and poor nations
has widened. It is no different in the era of globalisation.
Between 1960 and 1995 the growth rate of the developing
countries (including China, South Korea and Indonesia) was 1.3
percent per year. In the rich countries it was 2.4 percent.[28]

The United Nations Food and Agriculture Organisation
reports that the number of undernourished people in the world
actually rose by 18 million between 1995–97 and 1999–2001.
'Figures for the developing countries as a whole indicate that
the number of undernourished people has actually increased by
4.5 million per year' during this period. Among the 842 million
of the global total of the undernourished, 10 million were in
the richest countries in the world. Many of the 'new hungry' are
in India, where undernourishment is rising, and in the former
Soviet Union.[29]

Even these figures do not tell us about the growing inequality
between rich and poor in those societies, like China, where
industrialisation is lifting the general standard of living. Even
here there are 'extraordinary surges in income inequality and
wealth in China as it has adopted free market oriented practices.'[30] The cumulative effect of this process is to create economic turmoil, social dislocation, and political conflict. And in
this soil the seeds of war are sown.

Globalisation and 'rogue states'

The US and its allies are very clear about the link between globalisation and rogue states. For them it is the failure of such

states to jump on the globalisation bandwagon, rather than the failure of globalisation itself, which dooms certain states to failure. This view is expressed with great clarity by Dennis Sherman, former vice president for global business development at ExxonMobil, and Banning Garret, director of Asia Programs at the Atlantic Council, in their article 'Why Non-Globalized States Pose a Threat'.

Sherman and Garret argue that 'The most immediate threats to the interests and security of the United States and other globalizing nations in the 21st Century come not from each other or from rising powers but from declining states – weak, failing, and rogue nations that have become havens for terrorists and drug lords, seekers of weapons of mass destruction (WMD), incubators of disease, nurturers of religious extremists, and demographic time bombs of growing numbers of unemployed youth.'

The existence of such states is said to be a direct result of these societies' lack of participation in the globalised world economy: 'While globalization has created greater prosperity for states that have successfully integrated into the process, most states that have failed to effectively participate in globalization or have intentionally sought to isolate their countries from the process, have fallen farther behind. Weak and failing states are generally characterized by incomplete control over their national territories, an inability to provide basic services, a lack of legitimacy in the eyes of their populations, and widespread corruption and criminal violence. These states also usually have deteriorating infrastructures and weak, tenuous links to globalization.'

Sherman and Garret go on to distinguish between 'failed' states and 'rogue' states: 'The threats posed by the weak and failing states to the international community and their own populations emanate from the weaknesses of their governments. By contrast, the threats posed by rogue states, which also may have failing economies and impoverished populations and may be disconnected from globalization, emanate from the strengths of their governments. Rogue states threaten the international community through the acquisition of weapons of mass destruction (WMD) and pursuit of aggressive military actions against their neighbors and even sub-national groups within their own territories. Moreover, for rogue nations, WMD may be the balance of power equalizer of choice as they fall farther and farther behind economically and feel threatened by their neighbors or by the United States. . . . '

And with all the frankness that only close association with big oil can bestow they conclude that the most important global division is between the haves and the have-nots: 'All of these trends have led to a new fuzzy bipolarity between the world of order, prosperity, relative stability and increasing inter-dependence and the world of growing disorder, economic decline, and instability. The latter consist of weak, failing and rogue nations that are far less connected with and benefiting far less – if at all – from the globalization process . . . '[31]

Both the facts of the case and the line of causality have been horribly mangled in this analysis. Globalisation has not decreased the gap between rich and poor nations but widened it, as we have seen above. It is precisely the 'gale of creative destruction' caused by globalisation which has undermined the ability of weaker states to control their own destiny, develop their own welfare systems and, therefore, undermined their legitimacy in the eyes of their populations.

Part of the problem, as we have seen in earlier chapters, is that the US no longer has the absolute weight in the world economy to underpin economic stability in the way that it did after the Second World War. But the neo-liberal ideology, the view that the market can do no wrong, actually prevents a more stable international economic order even when resources could be mobilised to prevent states from 'failing'.

The entire value of the IMF 'rescue package' for Indonesia in 1998, for instance, is reckoned to be equal to the personal wealth of the deposed Suharto family. And on the estimate of one Indonesian economist 95 percent of the foreign debt of $80 billion is owed by 50 individuals – not the 200 million Indonesians who suffer from 'structural readjustment' pro-grammes.[32]

The general picture is the same: the debt of the 41 most highly indebted nations is of the same order as the bailout of the US Savings and Loans institutions in the 1990s. Or as another study points out, the defaults on foreign bonds by US railroads in the 1890s were on the same scale as the current developing countries' debt problems.[33]

The inability of the system and its defenders to contemplate the political alternative of cancelling debt or forcing the rich to carry the burden of their failure is closing off the long cherished belief in development even among the elites in developing countries. As Egyptian writer Mohammed Sid Ahmed concludes: 'It's all over. The North-South dialogue is as dead as the East-West conflict. The idea of development is dead. There is no longer a common language, not even a vocabulary for the problems. South, North, Third World, liberation, progress – all these terms no longer have any meaning.'[34]

The inevitable conclusion is that weak states do not fail as a result of their elites' wilful refusal to worship at the altar of the one true market. Rather their failure results from the functioning of the global capitalist system and of political and economic choices made by imperial powers. This is not to glorify the regimes in such states. Their weakness is often visited in the most brutal manner on their own populations. The ruling elites often respond to economic blackmail with military threats, which in turn are then met with further economic sanctions and military responses by the major powers.

But if both state-led developmental models in the third world and welfare-state models in industrialised countries are being progressively dismantled by the neo-liberal economic offensive there is, nevertheless, an alternative to globalisation.

The rise of anti-capitalism

There is one response to the process of globalisation and the internationalisation of state power which has the potential to express a real alternative to the global ruling elite – the revolt from below. This revolt stretches from the strikes and protests against privatisation, like the struggle against water privatisation in Bolivia, through the general strikes in Africa, to the near insurrectionary movements that overthrew Milosevic in Serbia and Suharto in Indonesia. It is a revolt that is far from homogeneous in methods or aims. Its subjects would not necessarily recognise each other as allies nor agree on strategy or tactics. But for all its variegation this revolt has gradually taken on an increasingly widespread and self-conscious form in the last ten years.

The emergence of a global anti-capitalist movement since the great Seattle demonstration of 1999 has provided a common language and identified a common enemy in a way that has not been true of any international movement of revolt since the defeat of the last great upturn in struggle in the mid-1970s.

In a report which could have been written about any of the anti-capitalist demonstrations of the recent years but was actually written about the protests at President Bush's inauguration in January 2001, *The Washington Post* said,

> 'The activists sometimes confound onlookers with the diversity of their concerns, from the environment and civil rights to Third World debt and corporate power. It's all the same struggle, they say … "We are all united behind a fear and loathing of corporate control in our country", says David Levy, 43, a think tank policy researcher … "The government is for sale, and big business bought it."'

It is specifically the global capitalist system that these demonstrators have in their sights. *The Washington Post* report continues:

> 'The international finance and trade bodies seek to make the world profitable for the same corporations that are running the show in US politics, the demonstrators say … Framing the issues in this way has allowed disparate causes to unite against common enemies. Save-the-rain-forest and anti-sweatshop activists, for example, stand against the same trade and development policies that might boost

corporate investment in a poor country engaged in selling off its natural resources. Global capitalism is unjust and ineffective in these situations, the activists say.'[35]

Where did these mobilisations come from? The long erosion of the pro-market consensus that reached its peak in the Reagan-Thatcher years was their period of gestation. This pro-market consensus was never absolute. A substantial section of the working class, often a majority, always rejected it. But a section of the working class, plus a majority of the middle class and the ruling class made it hegemonic during the boom of the mid and late 1980s. On the international level the economic disaster which accompanied the introduction of western style capitalism into Eastern Europe and Russia began to undermine this hegemony throughout the 1990s. The South-East Asian crash of 1997 and the subsequent crisis in Russia reinforced the growing ideological rejection of the market. The 1992 recession also eroded popular support for pro-market policies in the European and American heartland of the system paving the way for social democratic and Democrat election victories – despite the fact that the social democrats and Democrats continued to pursue neo-liberal economic policies.

As powerful a dissolvent of neo-liberal ideology has been the domestic experience of privatisation. In hundreds of ways the individual lives of millions of people began to get worse because of the practical effects of neo-liberal economic policies. Work became harder and longer and less secure. The provision of healthcare and education became visibly worse and, at the same time, equally visibly tied to market-style organisational structures. Transport deteriorated in the hands of private companies. Public housing declined, private house prices soared and then collapsed leaving many homeless or in negative equity. Then house prices soared again. Superstores so dominated the landscape, especially in medium size towns, that critical observers could be forgiven for thinking that the truck-stop system had found its contemporary form. Certainly credit card debt became the modern form of pawn-broking.

The 'public culture' of the post-war boom, of Beveridge and the welfare state, however far short of its idealised form the reality may have been, was replaced with something much worse. The old reformist consensus of 'Butskellism'[36] did at least admit that if there was something wrong with the society it might be the system itself that was at fault. If there was poverty or unemployment or poorly educated children for instance, then it might be necessary to regulate the market or reform the law in order to address the problem. But the neo-liberal doctrine assumes that the market is a more or less perfect method of distributing goods and services. Any attempt to 'interfere' with the market must end in a less efficient system. Any 'reform' must be aimed at allowing the market greater freedom of operation. This is the rock on which the modern social democratic critique both of Stalinism and of 'old Labour' ideology stands, just as it was the rock on which Thatcher's critique of the 'wet' one-nation Tories in her own party stood.

Consequently, for New Labour as much as for Margaret Thatcher, if there is poverty, unemployment or educational failure it cannot be the fault of the market. Indeed, failures like these can only have two sources. The first source is that the market is not yet free enough. If privatisation does not work, then more privatisation, more competition, must be the answer. The second source of failure is the individual. If someone is unemployed, and if the fault cannot lie with the market, then it must lie with the individual unemployed person. They must not have trained themselves 'to fit the needs of the market', or they must have become 'welfare dependent', or they must, more crudely and more commonly, be 'a scrounger'. Equally, if our 'reformed' schools are failing it must be the fault of the teachers, or the parents, or the children for not making the system work. They should be 'Ofsteded', or closed down, or have more market-derived structures imposed on them, or simply have their schools handed over to private companies.[37]

Whatever the issue, this logic is one that systematically blames the victim for the crime. It promotes a culture of scapegoating. At its extreme this logic ends in demonising beggars, or the homeless, asylum seekers or black people in general. But its effects are just as disgusting, if less obvious, among working people as a whole. This neo-liberal 'market morality' attempts to convince working people that they should blame one another for the failures of the system. The social service worker is encouraged to blame the unemployed worker, the parent to blame the teacher. It attempts to convince us that as long as we can buy a little better education, health care or transport provision than our neighbour then we are 'doing alright' and they are 'the problem'.

The great virtue of the anti-capitalist movement is that it expresses the pent-up anger at this world that has consumed many working people for the last two decades. It says to them that they and their kind are not to blame. It says, as many had long suspected, that it is not they who are failing the system but the system that is failing them. Moreover, it tells them that here, right in the heart of the system, hundreds of thousands reject the priorities of the system.

Anti-capitalism and modern Labourism

The modern social democratic parties are almost universally proponents of the neo-liberal economic orthodoxy. Their leaders are 'pro-market' and 'business friendly' to a degree that surprises even the most hardened right wing social democrats of the Cold War era. Consequently, there currently exists an enormous gap between the consciousness of most Labour voting workers and the policies of the social democratic leaders.

The Reagan-Thatcher 'revolution' pushed the entire establishment political spectrum to the right. Neo-liberal free market ideology became dominant, socialist ideas became marginalised. The collapse of the Stalinist states, because they were widely associated with socialism, confirmed the prejudices of ruling class and social democratic commentators. It also demoralised the Stalinist oriented left, which included many on the Labour left. Once the boom of the mid to late 1980s collapsed this right wing tide receded among those sections of the working class where it had taken hold. As it did so it revealed that the old Labour welfare consensus was largely intact, even if the unions and the Labour Party were now much less willing to defend it. At just the same time revulsion at the 'excesses' of the 1980s was spilling over into a wholesale popular rejection of privatisation, and attacks on the welfare state in general and the NHS in particular.

The 1990s marked a general move to the left in popular consciousness and therefore exposed the gap between the New Labour type of social democratic leader and the mass of their traditional supporters. This chasm exists over a number of central issues. The neo-liberal social democrats see the central role of the state as facilitating private capitalist corporations to compete more effectively in the market. Most Labour supporters see the role of the state as limiting the damage done to society by the unbridled pursuit of profit. The new social democrat leaders defend the pursuit of profit, the payment of huge salaries and bonuses, the appointment of corporate executives to positions in the state and the welfare state. Most workers oppose such moves. The New Labour ideologues are privatisers down to their bones. Most of the people who vote for them oppose it with increasing bitterness. The New Labour politicians think the welfare state is wasteful and needs cutting back. Most workers think it is underfunded. The neo-liberals are anti-union but most workers are not.

The passage of time since Labour's 1997 election landslide has done nothing to diminish this gap between the government and its supporters. The government's own Social Attitudes survey, in a chapter titled 'The working class and New Labour: a parting of the ways?', has examined this divide. It shows that 83 percent of working class people think that 'the gap between high and low incomes is too large'. Some 57 percent of workers think the 'government should spend more on health, education and social benefits'. Some 40 percent of workers agree, with only 29 percent disagreeing – 'even if it leads to higher taxes'.[38] Indeed the main development noted is that the opinions of many middle class people now shadow the attitudes of workers on these issues. Years of privatisation and cuts are now driving sections of the middle class to draw the same conclusions that many working class people reached long ago.

There have also been contrary indications that this disillusionment with the establishment political system could produce threatening right wing reactions. The election of British National Party councillors is one such indication, recent attacks on asylum seekers by the Labour government another. In Europe the threat has been more substantial: the rise of Le Pen in France, the Vlaams Blok in Belgium, the neo-Nazis in Germany and Haider in Austria underline the dangers. But in Britain, and to an even greater extent in France, it has been the left wing trajectory of popular consciousness that has been the dominant feature. This can change, of course. And part of maintaining this left trajectory is to vigorously meet and defeat such right wing threats as soon as they emerge. So far this has been the pattern.

A related fact is that on some social issues – 'family' issues, immigration, race, law and order – Labour leaders stand closer to the consciousness of many workers. The British Social Attitudes survey argues that 'There are in fact two types of class-related issues, and thus two potential sources of divergence between the working class and New Labour: traditional economic issues to do with redistribution, on which the working class are on "the left", and social issues to do with tolerance, morality, traditionalism, prejudice and nationalism, on which the working class are on "the right".'[39] And at times various politicians, both Tory and Labour, have attempted to mobilise popular opinion on these issues to re-establish a basis of support. Sometimes they have been at least partially successful. The initial phase of the Child Support Agency or Section 28, or the first phase of the recent scare over asylum seekers are examples. But resistance from the left, plus the obvious injustice of the measures themselves as they are put into practice, has often turned the ideological tables on the government and its supporters.

More fundamentally the working class consensus over issues which are essential to the success of any social democratic government – the welfare state most obviously – has remained resolutely opposed to the neo-liberal agenda. And this is what has prevented any further closing of the gap between the policies of the social democrats and the consciousness of most workers.

This does not mean that most workers have a socialist consciousness. Nor does it mean they will desert Labour at the ballot box, especially when the Tories are the only viable national alternative capable of forming a government. In many ways working class reformist consciousness has remained remarkably consistent since the 1970s. But mainstream reformism can no longer realize these aspirations. As a result 'reformist' consciousness now finds itself confronted with a crisis of political representation. No establishment politician will put forward a programme that represents these traditional working class needs. In a way this was always true. Labour always only partially represented these aspirations and was even more partial in realising them once in office. But there was some congruence. Now that area of congruity has been reduced to a bare minimum. Support for Labour now devolves more fully than ever to fear of the Tory alternative and less than ever on positive affirmation of Labour policies. Workers vote against the Tories, not for Labour. Or they simply don't vote at all.

The by-elections and council elections during the New Labour governments have seen the lowest turnouts since universal suffrage was introduced in Britain. Labour voters are less likely to turn out than Tories and the lowest turnout of all is in the Labour heartland seats.[40]

So many workers vote Labour with a heavy heart and many don't vote at all. In both groups there are great numbers who also begin to question how democratic the system really is. In one survey 58 percent thought that 'government ministers putting interests of business before people' was 'a major problem'. Another 29 percent thought it 'a minor problem' but only 6 percent thought it 'not a problem'. Financial sleaze in government is a major problem for 49 percent and a minor problem for another 39 percent. Again, only 6 percent think it is not a problem. But perhaps the most damning findings are the ones that show the lack of faith in the parliamentary system as a whole. In 1999 only 41 percent of people though the system of government was working well. That proportion has fallen to 31 percent by 2001.[41] Further evidence of this mood is contained in Figure 4.3.

The Iraq war dramatically accelerated the disillusionment both with New Labour and with the disengagement from the parliamentary system. Especially to those of us who stood with the two million on Stop the War demonstration of 15 February 2003 there could be no greater contrast between the political commitment of those around us and the fact that the previous election had seen the lowest turnout in Britain's modern democratic history. Clearly this was not political 'apathy'. There was plenty of appetite for extra-parliamentary politics. But there was little faith that any establishment political party would register the views of those who marched or the millions more who agreed with them.

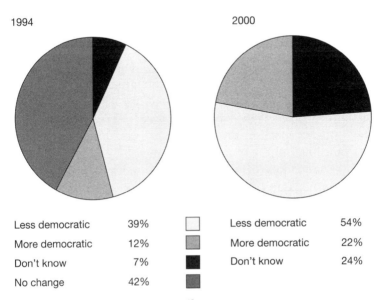

1994		2000	
Less democratic	39%	Less democratic	54%
More democratic	12%	More democratic	22%
Don't know	7%	Don't know	24%
No change	42%		

Figure 4.3 Losing faith in democracy[42]

This process is also reflected in the erosion of Labour's core organisation. Labour's membership has fallen during the course of its time in government. Even in Labour's Scottish stronghold membership 'has dropped to its lowest in modern times, with just 18,800 members in Scotland. In the run-up to the 1997 election, Scottish Labour membership peaked at 30,000 as large numbers joined amid the wave of enthusiasm to oust the Tories from office'.[43] Fewer now attend ward or constituency meetings. Fewer canvass at election times. Councillors regularly defect not to the Liberals or the Tories but to become Labour independents. A minority have begun to search for a new political home. As they do so, even though they start out from traditional reformist consciousness, the fact that the traditional organisational receptacle for this consciousness is no longer adequate forces them to begin to draw more left wing conclusions.

The crisis of Labourism

The Labour Party will not crumble simply as a result of its current crisis. To understand why, we have to look at the fundamental reasons why workers hold Labourist ideas in the first place. This, in turn, requires us to pay some attention to the social position that workers occupy in capitalist society. This position is a contradictory one. On the one hand the collective labour of workers is the basis of production in society. Just as at the birth of capitalism the steam engine could neither be built nor function, nor the spinning jenny move, nor ships put to sea without the labour of workers, so today power stations do not function, nor cars and planes get built, nor supermarkets operate without the labour of workers. This invests workers with a tremendous potential power to determine the fate of society.

On the other hand, workers cannot gain access to the means of production without selling their wage labour to the capitalist, the owner of the means of production. Just as at the birth of capitalism, so it is today. No power station today, just as no factory in the past, no car plant today, just as no textile firm in the past, no supermarket today, just as no department store in the past, will allow a worker access to the means of production unless he or she agrees to work for a wage. And this means that the hours of work, the type of work, the conditions of work, and the rate of pay are largely determined by the employers. Having to sell their ability to work to employers encourages workers to believe that they are powerless in the face of the vagaries of the 'labour market', depriving them of the sense that they can shape their own destiny.

This is the root of contradictory consciousness among the working class. They are the wealth creators, the potentially most powerful class in capitalist society, the class on whose action, both economic and political, the fate of the society turns. They are at the same time reminded on an hourly basis that they only work when the forces of the market permit, that their fate rests with this impersonal power, that they are subordinated by the very wealth they create.

The initial form in which this situation is reflected in the minds of workers is a consciousness that tries to bind together these contradictory impulses. On the one hand the impulse to transform capitalist society, on the other the feeling that such transformation must not exceed the limits stipulated by the ruling class. Reformism is one of the most characteristic forms that this consciousness takes. Reformism codifies and crystallises the notion that, although the society requires alteration, such transformation can only take place within the economic and political institutions provided by the system itself. Trade union-ism, the desire to better the terms on which workers are exploited, is one expression of this process. But trade unionism, operating primarily at an economic level, leaves unresolved the question of what sort of political organisation workers should build. Reformist political parities are only one possible, but to many workers the initially plausible, alternative.

It is for this reason that reformist consciousness, sometimes of a more left wing variety and sometimes of a more right wing variety, dominates the thinking of the majority of the working class for long periods of time. Consequently, both revolutionary ideas and outright reactionary or conservative ideas are for long periods minority currents within the working class.

There is, however, a problem with this account of reformist consciousness as it has so far been developed. This analysis would drive us to the conclusion that reformism is the 'natural' home of the majority of workers. Yet we know that this is certainly not the historical experience.

In decisive moments of historical change the majority of workers come to embrace the belief that they can transform the existing society by the direct use of their own power institutionalised in bodies of their own creation. Such was the situation in Russia in 1917, in Germany in 1918–23, in Spain in 1936, in Hungary in 1956 and in Poland in 1980–81, for instance. Such occasions, and also many more minor crises that have disrupted the existence of a reformist compromise in workers' ideology, are rooted in the fundamental economic instability of the system. The assumption that we can get some of what we need by working inside the system is challenged by periods where capitalism fails to meet the economic, social and political aspirations of working class people.

The system can at times become so economically, socially and politically unstable that it undermines the class compromise that is working class reformist consciousness. The Labour Party is currently caught in the coils of one such crisis. The capitalist system has been increasingly trying to shift the burden of the crisis on to the shoulders of working people for more than a quarter of a century. Economic growth is not only much slower than during the post-war boom, but lower in the 1990s than in the 1980s. As the *Financial Times* reports: 'Remember that economic growth between successive cyclical peaks was 3.3 percent a year in the 1980s, against about 3.1 percent in the 1990s'.[44]

Labour is grappling with the effects of this long cycle of attacks on workers. Its quick fixes fail and the system does not have the resources for a work of more substantial reconstruction in key areas such as public transport, health and education. This leaves many Labour supporters in as dire straits as they were under Tory rule. Indeed, some are worse off. Between 1995–96 and 1997–98 the number of people on very low incomes (less than two-fifths of the national average) grew by more than a million to a total of 8 million. In 1998 14 million people were below the government's poverty line. This included some 4.4 million children compared with an estimated 1.7 million in 1979. The number of children in poverty declined in Labour's third term but was still far short of the government's own target. The level of unemployment significantly affects poverty. And although Labour boasts that the official figure for unemployment is at a 25-year low, calculated by those claiming benefits, the real number of those who would like paid work but have none now stands at 4 million.[45]

Even the great good fortune of Labour's term in office coinciding with the upswing of the business cycle and buoyant government finances has not allowed Labour ministers to effectively deal with these structural issues. As Peter Kenway, co-director of the New Policy Institute, argues:

'Time will tell if the measures announced in recent budgets can succeed in turning the tide of poverty and social exclusion. But these figures show that an improving economy and falling unemployment are not enough on their own. As the government's policies for tackling these problems begin to bite, poverty is at levels close to the high-water mark reached in the early 1990s.'[46]

The high-water mark for the indices of poverty was reached in the early 1990s not only because of the effects of long years of Tory government but also because the early 1990s were a time of serious recession. Labour has so far avoided having to govern through such a period, mainly because of the reflationary measures taken in the US to avoid the 1997 crash in South-East Asia and Russia spreading to the Western industrialised countries. But Labour will not be able to avoid this conjuncture forever. Any recession will not only worsen the material conditions in which Labour voters live, it will also do great damage to some of the most cherished myths in the New Labour ideological lexicon.

One such myth was that the boom was the result of a 'new economy'. New Labour bought the 'new economy' theory wholesale from American economic pundits and Clinton spin-doctors. The theory was that the business cycle was at an end and that new flexible markets and new technology firms would ensure it never returned. Gordon Brown seemed at times to be repeating word for word the speeches of Nigel Lawson in the late 1980s – just ahead of one of the severest recessions of the post-war period. Now, once again, previous cheerleaders for the new economy theory are voicing their doubts. The *Financial Times* argues:

> 'The business cycle is decidedly alive. That should not surprise anybody … cycles can occur – and frequently have occurred – in flexible economies with credible monetary anchors. All that is needed is a big investment expansion fuelled by expanding credit and a strong stock market. Indeed, the firmer the belief that the business cycle is dead, the greater the confidence and the likelihood of business cycles.'[47]

Neither has the *Financial Times* now got much time for that other economic icon of New Labour, the reviving powers of the dot.com revolution:

> '… Internet mania looks like an only slightly less irrational version of the South Sea Bubble. The notion that information technology represents the greatest transformation since the industrial revolution is historically illiterate. The technological changes between 1880 and 1940 exceed, in both scope and intensity, all that has happened since.
>
>   Those changes included new sources of energy (electricity and petroleum), new industries (motor vehicles and pharmaceuticals) and new products (cars, washing machines, telephones, radio, television, penicillin). They profoundly altered what was produced and how. They also transformed the way people lived. Against all that, what are the personal computer and even the internet?'[48]

The end of the post-war boom in the 1970s and the decades of slow economic growth that followed have restricted the ability to grant meaningful reforms. The welfare state consensus and the toleration of some trade union influence on government are things of the past. Active participation in Labour Party organisation is at a historic low. The links between trade union activists and local campaigners and Labourism are weaker than at any point in the post-war period. As a consequence popular scepticism about the political system as a whole is at historically high levels.

But for all this Labourism is far from dead. The 7 million workers in the unions can still be addressed and influenced by union leaders deeply committed to the reformist project. The repellent power of the Tories is still a powerful call on the loyalty of class conscious workers. What is necessary to turn the crisis of Labourism into a step forward in the working class is to actively replace reformist organisation with an alternative. Social democracy never simply disappears. It always has to be actively replaced by a superior set of ideas embodied in an alternative organisation. Reformist workers have to be sure that the things that they thought could be fought for by joining the Labour Party can be better achieved by other methods before they will desert the Labour Party, even a Labour Party whose leaders have turned their backs on these workers' most cherished aspirations.

Conclusion

The period of slow economic growth and of the neo-liberal offensive, both beginning in the mid-1970s, has increased inequality both in the Third World and the developed world. This economic weakness at the heart of the system is the root cause of greater global conflict and greater social division in the advanced countries. The recomposition of the state so that it has progressively lost some of its social welfare functions has exacerbated these tensions

The revolt against neo-liberalism has also been on a global scale. In the heartlands of the system it is eroding the purchase of traditional social democratic organisation on the loyalties of masses of working people. It is also now combining with a popular rejection of the new imperialism which is accelerating this process. In other parts of the globe these same developments have produced revolutionary challenges to the existing order. These revolts have from 1989 onwards often taken the form of democratic revolutions, hailed by sections of both the political left and the political right. The next chapter looks at the experience of these revolutionary developments and measures them against past revolutions and the potential future of revolutionary change in the modern world.

5　Their democracy and ours

In the early 21st century both sides of the ideological divide define themselves as adherents of democracy. For the ideological defenders of capitalism the social and economic content of democracy is a 'free' market and social inequality. For their opponents it means, perhaps more vaguely, social and economic justice and, therefore, the restriction of untrammelled corporate rule. This latter is in the broadest sense socialist, although the exhaustion of the state capitalist and reformist models of socialism means that only a minority of activists claim this label for themselves.

Democracy has acquired a new meaning since the end of the Cold War. For democracy movements fighting authoritarian regimes the end of the Cold War means that their struggles are no longer automatically equated with 'communism' by Western governments. Democratic and anti-imperialist struggles may still pose a threat to Western interests but they can no longer be seen as a simple product of 'Soviet bloc' manipulation. This does not mean that the democratic aspiration among ordinary people has run its course.

In fact democracy as the aim of working people has forced ruling elites to reformulate their own notion of democracy as the 'best form of government for capitalism'. Ever since Francis Fukuyama wrote in the immediate aftermath of the fall of the Berlin Wall that a capitalist economy and a parliamentary government were the best and only viable society, Western politicians have increasingly insisted that 'democratic values' are the natural counterpart of globalised markets.

US and British governments have been at the forefront of developing a 'democratic imperialist' ideology to justify military interventions in Yugoslavia, the Gulf, Afghanistan and Africa. It has become the declared aim of the US administration to try and re-shape the Middle East according to a 'democratic' model. The 'velvet revolutions' which broke open the Eastern bloc serve as the starting point. The cases to which this model has been applied vary widely: from Lebanon to Uzbekistan. Even old US allies, like President Mubarak of Egypt, find themselves under pressure to make the 'democratic transition'. Of course pressure is applied to friends and enemies in very different degree – from a gentle diplomatic word to full scale invasion.

Yet today's new ideological definitions cannot disguise the 'social question' that arises in all democratic movements. The 'property question' as Marx put it comes to the fore in the course of every movement's development. Since at least the English Revolution of the 17th century there has always been a battle within the democratic camp between those who want to limit democratic rights to the political sphere (compatible with capitalist social relations) and those who want to extend democracy to the social and economic sphere (ultimately incompatible with capitalist rule). Marx identified the same dynamic in the 1848 revolutions and noted that it was given greater force by the emergence of the modern working class. In the early 20th century Russian socialists grappled with a similar question, the relationship between the democratic revolution and the social revolution.

In recent years revolutionary movements have repeatedly challenged the existing order. In 1989 the states of Eastern Europe were demolished, in part by mass movements from below. At about the same time South African apartheid was destroyed by a mass movement led by the African National Congress at the core of which stood the organised working class. At the end of the 1990s the 32 year old dictatorship of General Suharto was over thrown in Indonesia. In the first years of the new century in Serbia and a string of Central Asian states in new 'velvet revolutions' threw out their governments.

Democracy has been the aim of these revolutionary upheavals. Often enough no strong parliamentary democracy has emerged but none has led to a transformation of capitalist social relations. Is this because, as Francis Fukuyama first claimed and George W Bush later echoed, liberal democracy and capitalist economic relations are the natural boundaries of historical change? Or is it that subjective factors, the strength and ideology of the left, are the principal reasons why these movements failed to reach their potential?

To answer these questions we must first look at the period when the revolutionary challenge of the bourgeois revolution did indeed find its limit in the achievement of capitalist economic relations and a parliamentary republic. This is the era which runs from the English Revolution of 1640s, through the American Revolution of 1776 to the French Revolution of 1789. Secondly we will look at the period when the organised working class made its appearance, raising the spectre of revolutionary change that could run beyond these boundaries and establish a socialist society. I will also examine the occasions when defeat has robbed workers of this possibility and the role of political leadership in shaping these outcomes.

Under all these circumstances the dynamic of capital accumulation still produces great social crises which result in profound social transformations. The unification of Italy and Germany in the second half of the 19th century and the wave of anti-colonial revolutions in the second half of the 20th century are examples. The role of a key layer of the middle classes in these latter transformations is examined in order to shed light on the conflict between the competing strategies of the socialist revolution and the democratic revolution, as well as their differing relationships to wider class formations and conditions of capital accumulation, in the more recent revolutions. This examination sheds light on the relationship between the Western rulers' 'push for democracy' and the fate of revolutionary movements from below.

The classical bourgeois revolutions: England, America and France

The history of the great bourgeois revolutions can illuminate the radicalising dynamic which works at the heart of all revolutions. In these revolutions those who made the revolution had little notion of forcibly overthrowing the existing order when they entered the conflict. Only repeated internal crises in the revolutionary process eventually brought them face to face with this necessity. This polarisation is as marked in the great modern revolutions as it is in the bourgeois revolutions.

However, there is a second comparison in which the differences between the two sorts of revolution are most obvious. This concerns the differences between the socio-economic conditions under which the revolutions take place: the bourgeois revolutions against a pre-capitalist social structure, the modern against a developed industrial capitalism. This framework ultimately limits the revolutionary process, providing the practical barrier against which the furthest and most radical programmes of the revolutionary movements are tested.

Alexis de Tocqueville once said 'the most dangerous moment for a bad government is generally that in which it sets about reform'.[1] But the fate of Charles I shows that resistance to reform can be just as dangerous. It was Charles' determination to retain, indeed to strengthen, the absolutist cast of his regime in the face of social and economic change which was the immediate cause of the revolution. Marx, referring to John Hampden's refusal to pay the Ship Money tax with which Charles attempted to overcome the financial crisis of the state, put the point like this:

'It was not John Hampden ... who brought Charles I to the scaffold, but only the latter's own obstinacy, his dependence on the feudal estates, and his presumptuous attempt to use force to suppress the urgent demands of the emerging society. The refusal to pay taxes is merely a sign of the dissidence that exists between the Crown and the people, merely evidence that the conflict between the government and the people has reached a menacing degree of intensity.'[2]

In the American Revolution of 1776 the colonial relationship with Britain gives the forces and phases of revolutionary development a significantly different character. In 1763 the British emerged victorious from their war with the French for control of the North American colonies. But war debts concentrated the minds of the British ruling class on regaining full control of their colonial possessions. Again, new taxes provided the flashpoint.

In 1764 the Currency Act and the Revenue (or Sugar) Act aimed to make colonial merchants pay in sterling rather than their own coin and to slap duty on imported sugar even when, as had not previously been the case, it came from other parts of the British Empire. In 1765 the Stamp Act ruled that any transaction specified by the act was illegal unless the appropriate stamp was purchased. Legal, church, political and commercial documents, passports, dice and playing cards, books, newspapers and advertisements were all subject to taxation under the act. Furthermore, there was a directly political side to the act. Money raised under the act would be directly under the control of the British-appointed governors, not, as before, the colonial assemblies. Here was the origin of taxation without representation.

One reason for the unique depth and breadth of the French Revolution of 1789 is that the bourgeoisie's cumulative experience of challenging the old order fed into French events.[3] The French, like the Americans a decade or so before, drew on the political theory of John Locke and the Enlightenment tradition which owed so much to the impulse of the English Revolution. But these ideological influences are not the main reason for the great reach of the French Revolution. The fundamental causes lie in the social and economic conditions under which the revolution took place. France was a much more economically advanced society at the time of her revolution than either England in the 1640s or America in the 1770s.

In 1789 in France the proportion of national product coming from industry and commerce (18 percent and 12 percent respectively) is similar to England and Wales in the 1780s. Even the proportion of national income coming from agriculture, at 49 percent, is only 9 percent higher than the figure for England and Wales.[4]

Yet this is only half the story, because France's social and political development, unlike Britain's, stood diametrically opposed to her economic progress. France's class structure remained caught in the long shadow of feudalism. The monarch's absolutist pretensions overawed most of the bourgeoisie (and even some of the aristocracy). But the most important dividing line ran between the aristocracy as a whole and the rest of society, whose leading non-noble element was the bourgeoisie. Abbé Sieyes' famous pamphlet *What Is the Third Estate?*, the initial manifesto and rallying call of the bourgeoisie, complained:

> 'all the branches of the executive have been taken over by a caste that monopolises the Church, the judiciary and the army. A spirit of fellowship leads the nobles to favour one another in everything over the rest of the nation. Their usurpation is complete; they truly reign.'[5]

In the English, American and French revolutions it was mass mobilization from below which repeatedly sharpened the conflict between the revolutionary camp and the old order and caused crises within the revolutionary leadership itself.

In England, from the summoning of the Long Parliament by Charles I in 1640 to the outbreak of civil war in 1642, the broad parliamentary opposition polarised into those willing to take their opposition to the king to the point of armed conflict and those who would rather side with the king than countenance the threat to the existing order which civil war represented. It was the London crowd, composed of the lowest levels of the 'middling sort' of small craftsmen and traders bolstered by servants and labourers, which drove the parliamentary opposition forward. And, by repulsion, they also obliged the King and his supporters to define themselves clearly as a reactionary political force.[6] This tripartite division is characteristic of bourgeois revolutions.[7]

In America, even before the Stamp Act, a coalition of merchants, professionals and slave-owners together with artisans, labourers, farmers, servants and sailors had emerged to oppose the British. At first their pamphlets and speeches were cautious, but they grew bolder with each imperial crisis, graduating from resistance to revolution and from protest to a war for independence. Resistance to the Stamp Act was the first phase of radicalisation. A Stamp Act Congress brought nine colonial delegates to New York City to pass strongly worded resolutions and addresses to the King. But in the towns from which the delegates came tax collectors were being tarred and feathered by angry Sons of Liberty groups that sprang into being. The first of the various Sons of Liberty organisations were the Loyal Nine of Boston and among their members were a printer, a brazier, a painter and a jeweller. These artisans were joined by men like Sam Adams and, later, Tom Paine, intellectuals whose lives were closely intertwined with those of the artisans, but able to command both the respect and fear of the merchants and slave-owners of the revolutionary coalition.

Popular mobilisation defeated the Stamp Act which was repealed the year after it was introduced. But the British were not by any means done with the American colonies. Just as the Stamp Act was repealed the Declaratory Act was passed, insisting that Britain could 'make laws ... to bind the colonies and people of America ... in all cases whatsoever'.[8] In 1767 the Chancellor of the Exchequer, Charles Townshend, passed acts taxing paint, paper, lead, glass and tea. Colonial America responded with a tax strike which ran until 1770. Throughout this period the popular mobilisations typified by the Sons of Liberty response to the Stamp Act continued. They culminated in the event which precipitated the repeal of the Townshend duties, the Boston massacre of 5 March 1770. British redcoats opened fire on an angry crowd of protesters, killing five of them. The dead give an accurate social cross-section of the movement: an African-Indian sailor, a ship's mate, a leather-maker, a rope-maker and an ivory-turner's apprentice. Their deaths helped to cement the lower levels of the revolutionary alliance to their leaders.

The movement in America deepened and radicalized again after the Boston Tea Party in December 1773 when protesters disguised as Mohawk Indians dumped tea, the one remaining commodity subject to Townshend duties, from ships into Boston harbour. Even before the Continental Congress met in 1774, Committees of Correspondence staffed by the same sort of people who had formed the Sons of Liberty, indeed often by the very same individuals, to resist the Stamp Act a decade earlier carried the newly revolutionary message throughout the colonies.

The French was the greatest and most complete of all the bourgeois revolutions but in 1789 no leader of the French bourgeoisie realised how great a struggle would be needed to vanquish the old order.[9] At first it even seemed as if sections of aristocracy might be willing to participate in the work of reforming the old order. But by the time the King was forced to call the Estates General on 5 May 1789 the challenge of this 'aristocratic revolution' had run its course.

In this first internal crisis the Third Estate nominally represented the whole of the non-noble, non-clerical nation. In fact they represented the bourgeoisie. Of the 610 delegates of the Third Estate, the biggest single element (25 percent), as in so many capitalist parliaments since, were those professionally engaged in advocacy for the wealthy: lawyers. Some 13 percent were actually manufacturers; another 5 percent were from the professions; only 7 to 9 percent were agriculturalists.[10]

The Third Estate declared itself the leadership of what, at this stage, remained an attempt to force the king into reform without destroying the entire ruling institutions of society. The first radicalisation of the revolution took place when sections of the Third Estate left the revolutionary camp to join the majority of the clergy and the aristocracy to work for compromise, despite the fall of the Bastille and the first eruption of the peasant struggle.

Each of these revolutions was to radicalize a second time as the pressure from below, and the intransigence of the old regimes, resulted in a renewal of the revolutionary leadership.

In the English Revolution when civil war became a reality between 1642 and 1645 a further polarisation in the parliamentary ranks took place; this time it was between those who were willing to prosecute the war to the point of destroying the King and possibly the monarchy. These were the Independents grouped around Cromwell and Ireton. On the other side were Presbyterians who would, even now, only fight in order to weaken the King to the point where compromise once again became possible. Indeed the Presbyterians claimed they were fighting for 'King and parliament'. To these moderates Cromwell replied that: 'I will not cozen you with perplexed expressions in my commission about fighting for King and parliament. If the King happened to be in the body of the enemy, I would as soon discharge my pistol upon him as upon any private man.'[11] In this phase of the revolution the decisive act was Cromwell's creation of the New Model Army, made possible by mobilising the lower orders of society.

In the American Revolution the second phase of radicalization was witnessed by the fact that by 1775 popular committees had replaced the ruins of royal government as the effective power in the colonies transacting 'all such matters as they shall conceive may tend to the welfare of the American cause'. Committees raised militias, organised supplies, tried and jailed the revolutions' enemies and began to control goods and prices. They called mass meetings to 'take the sense of citizens'. They frustrated British plans to regain control by calling an election for a provincial assembly and ensuring that radicals won. In January 1776 Tom Paine published a revolutionary manifesto, *Common Sense*, which used the plain language of ordinary artisans and farmers to urge the movement on to a final break with Britain. It sold 150,000 copies and its arguments were repeated wherever revolutionaries met to convince others that resistance must lead to independence.

This decade long radicalisation could not help but alarm the elite figures who strove to stay at the head of resistance to the British, even as they realised that the British could not be beaten without such popular agitation. The War of Independence helped them to keep this movement within bounds. Unlike the conflict of 1642–45 in England, this was not a civil war but a colonial war for independence from Britain. Consequently, the effect of the war was not to further polarise the revolutionary camp, as war had done with the creation of the New Model Army or was to do during the French Revolution. Once war broke out, the Colonial Army under Washington increasingly replaced the guerrilla methods of the first battle at Lexington with regular army discipline enforced by the rich and powerful who dominated the officer corps. By contrast, the creation of the New Model Army required the 'internal coup' of the self-denying ordinance against the aristocrats who had stayed with parliament.

In France the second phase of the revolution began when the long and fruitless search for compromise was cut short by the King's flight to Varennes on 21 June 1791. This made it clear to even the most ardent compromiser that no agreement was possible. The nobility now fomented open counter-revolution both at home and by conspiring with the crowned heads of Europe to wage war from abroad, hoping that the experience of war would unite the nation behind the traditional ruling class. 'Instead of civil war, we shall have war abroad, and things will be much better', wrote Louis XVI.[12]

The popular response to this threat took not only the aristocracy but also the existing leadership of the revolution by surprise. In 1792 the popular mobilisation against the threat of counter-revolution within and without sealed the fate of the monarchy and marked a further radicalisation of the revolution. The Girondins, named after the area of France from which they came, insisted that the 'passive citizens', the lower orders of ordinary people, now be called upon to defend the nation and the revolution. But the mobilisation of the popular masses under the banner of the *sans culottes* and the enragés brought with it demands which the Girondins could not countenance. In Paris in May 1792 the 'red priest' Jacques Roux demanded the death penalty for hoarders of grain; a year later he was insisting that 'Equality is no more than an empty shadow so long as monopolies give the rich the power of life and death over their fellow human beings'.[13] This message was carried through Paris by means of direct democracy: the assemblies and meetings of administrative 'sections' of the city, the associated political clubs and left wing newspapers.

At first the newly aroused popular classes, the small bourgeoisie and the journeymen and labourers below them, in addition to the continued peasant risings in the countryside, forced divisions between the Girondins, only yesterday the most radical leaders of the revolution with Danton as their leader, and the Mountain (or Montagnards, the left deputies so called because they occupied the upper tiers in the National Assembly, led by Robespierre and the Jacobins). The Girondins stood aside from the revolutionary movement of 10 August 1792 which overthrew the monarchy and the restrictive electoral system of the previous year's Constitution. It was a critical abstention and the Girondins shared the fate of the King.

The Jacobins were the recipients of the laurels of 10 August. But the Jacobins themselves relied on the support of two different class fractions, the small bourgeoisie and the artisans, and the day labourers and journeymen whom they employed. This alliance and the popular mobilisation which underlay it reached its high point in 1793–94. By 1793 the Jacobin revolutionary government finally constructed itself in such a way that it was capable of effectively and definitively dealing with its aristocratic enemy, in part by granting the popular demand for a law setting maximum prices for essentials (and also for wages). But at the very moment of victory the alliance between the Jacobins and the *sans culottes*, which made victory possible, fell apart.

Even the Jacobins could not allow either an economic programme which limited the bourgeoisie in this way, or a redefinition of 'the people' to mean the *sans culottes* alone, thereby excluding the section of the bourgeoisie on which the Jacobins predominantly relied. 'It is hardly surprising' notes George

Rudé, 'that the political ideas and social aspirations of such men should differ in important respects from those of proprietors, lawyers, doctors, teachers and businessmen who sat in the Convention or even from those of the smaller lawyers, trades-men, and civil servants who predominated in the provincial Jacobin clubs and societies'.[14]

In all these revolutions the final division among the leaders of the revolution reveals the underlying class contradictions and the economic limits of what was possible. In England the radical democracy of the Levellers and the Agitators elected by regi-ments of the New Model Army is defeated by the stable centre of the 'middling sort', led by Cromwell and Ireton. In America the slave-owners and business class win through. In France the *sans culottes* and the Jacobins are defeated by counter-revolution.

Shortly before Charles' execution, Leveller leader John Lilburne was summoned before Cromwell and his Council of State to account for the Levellers' continued agitation in favour of their radical democratic programme *The Agreement of the People*. Lilburne was, as ever, unyielding. He was told to retire, but from the next room he heard Cromwell say: 'I tell you, sir, you have no other way of dealing with these men but to break them, or they will break you ... and so render you to all rational men in the world as the most contemptible generation of silly, low-spirited men in the earth, to be broken and routed by such a despicable, contemptible generation of men as they are, and therefore, sir, I tell you again, you are necessitated to break them'.[15] Cromwell proceeded to do just as he promised and a few months later the Leveller mutiny in the army ended in the shooting of three of the radicals at Burford churchyard.

Nevertheless, these same developments and the remaining challenge from the left also forced the Cromwell to abandon compromise with the King and to embark on the road which led through regicide to the establishment of a republic. At this time there was one last attempt to radicalise the revolution fur-ther: the Diggers' dozen or so attempts, most famously at St George's Hill in Surrey, to found 'communist' communities. As expounded by their best known spokesman, Gerrard Winstanley, the Diggers' programme ran well beyond the democracy expounded by John Lilburne and the Levellers and raised the issue of social and economic equality. But even at the height of popular radicalisation there was no social class, because there was no underlying economic development, which was capable of implementing the Diggers' radical dream. Their bequest to radicals who came after them, down to our own times, is the dream of political, social and economic freedom even though they lacked the means to realise it in their own time.

In America popular disaffection with the war was, if anything, greater than in England, although in both cases some felt, wrongly but understandably, that it was a 'rich man's war' which would change little regardless of who won. Daniel Shays, a poor farm hand and former soldier, led a rebellion in 1786 which briefly raised the spectre of renewed popular radicalism. The rebels used the same tactics that had proved so effective against the British, gathering in arms to close the local court house. But now their allies of 1774, the Boston radicals, were divided. Some, allied with conservative merchants, ran the state government and sent loyal militiamen to scatter the Shaysites. Sam Adams was one such, helping to draw up a Riot Act and to suspend habeas corpus and so allow the authorities to keep prisoners in jail without bringing them to trial. One defeated Shays supporter pleaded, 'Tis true I have been a committeeman', but, 'I am sincerely sorry ... and hope it will be overlooked and pardoned'.[16] Unmoved by such sentiments, Adams argued: 'In a monarchy the crime of treason may admit of being pardoned or lightly punished, but the man who dares rebel against the laws of a republic ought to suffer death.'[17] The Shays Rebellion never developed either the programmatic clarity of *The Agreement of the People* or the political weight of Lilburne's organisation; nevertheless the parallel with the defeat of the Levellers at Burford is obvious.

The triumphant ruling class, led by the Federalists Alexander Hamilton and James Madison, like Cromwell before them, moved to create a stronger unitary state. And in both England and America the bourgeoisie asserted itself within this more conducive framework in the longer run. In England in 1689 the ruling class frustrated renewed Stuart attempts at establishing monarchical power and by 1832 the industrial bourgeoisie established complete hegemony over its old land-owning partner. In America the epilogue was more dramatic than the prologue. The second American Revolution, fought as the American Civil War, utterly crushed the power of the Southern landowning slavocracy.

The differences in class base and political programme among those in the revolutionary camp are clearest of all in the French Revolution. The *sans culottes* united petty bourgeois and craft workers in one organisation at a time when these layers found themselves pitted against a more developed layer of bigger capitalists. The *sans culottes* could not form a working class organisation, because this class did not yet have the capacity to frame its own demands and form its own movements. But they were an organisation that channelled the economic desperation of the common people, the wage labourers, journeymen and artisans who did not own the capital. The *sans culottes* wanted restrictions on capitalist wealth and a republic of small proprietors; but they were small capitalists themselves (or under the influence of small capitalists) and could hardly bridle the accumulation of capital with any consistency.[18]

The leadership of the Jacobins, who perhaps form a more accurate French counterpart to the Levellers, found in the *sans culottes* a force they needed to employ against the entrenched resistance of their aristocratic enemy. But as soon as its necessity was past they reacted against this pact with the devil even more furiously than Cromwell reacted against the Levellers. Cromwell had ten years, and the full term of his life, before counter-revolution repaid him for the suppression of the Levellers. Robespierre survived a matter of months before Thermidor (as the month was called in the new revolutionary calendar, 27 July 1794 in the old calendar) repaid him for the suppression of the *sans culottes*.

The radical left once again enjoyed a bright but brief Indian summer. In the footsteps of Winstanley and Shays came Babeuf.

But this 'revolution after the revolution' was, again, different to its forerunners. If the *sans culottes*' programme ultimately expressed a nostalgic reaction of a half-emerged artisan working class to the contradictions of capitalism, then Babeuf's Conspiracy of Equals came close to connecting a utopian vision of communism, which gave it some continuity with the Diggers, with a class of wage workers far more developed than that in 17th century England. Moreover, in the Conspirators' organisation, despite the misleading indications of their title, the first dim outlines of modern working class political organisation can be traced.[19]

History is full of such intimations of the future by social movements and individuals alike. Leonardo da Vinci's drawing of a 'helicopter' is one such magnificent presentiment of things to come, even of some of the technical principles which might make such a dream work. Hundreds of years of economic development were necessary before Leonardo's drawing could become a practical proposition. So it is with the Diggers and the Conspiracy of Equals. Nevertheless, we do not turn our back on the genius of Winstanley or Babeuf any more than we would on the genius of Leonardo. We look to combine their image of the future with what we now know to be the material means of making the image real.

What changed in 1848?

Even before the outbreak of the 1848 revolutions Marx and Engels were clear on two points. The first was that the coming revolution would be a bourgeois revolution; that is, it would issue in a capitalist state, hopefully democratic and republican in form. The second was that the bourgeoisie would have to be pushed to a decisive settling of accounts with the old order since the growing strength of the working class made them fearful that unleashing the full power of the revolution would sweep them aside along with the feudal state. For Marx and Engels the revolution in Germany would be 'carried out under far more advanced conditions of European civilisation, and with a much more developed proletariat, than that of England in the seventeenth, and of France in the eighteenth century' and would therefore be 'the prelude to an immediately following proletarian revolution'.[20]

Thus in the early stages of the revolution Marx and Engels fought as the furthest left wing of the democratic revolution. But even the *Communist Manifesto*, written before the outbreak of the revolution, urged that although the working class should 'fight with the bourgeoisie whenever it acts in a revolutionary way' socialists should also 'instil into the working class the clearest possible recognition of the hostile antagonism between the bourgeoisie and the proletariat'.[21] Marx and Engels' approach at the start of the revolution was 'to spur on the bourgeoisie from an independent base on the left, organising the plebeian classes separately from the bourgeoisie in order to strike together at the old regime, and to prepare this democratic bloc of proletariat, petty bourgeoisie and peasantry to step temporarily into the vanguard should the bourgeoisie shows signs of cold feet, by analogy with the Jacobin government in France of 1793–94'.[22]

But this position was significantly altered by Marx and Engels as the 1848 revolutions developed. For the first three months of the German revolution it looked as though the bourgeoisie, though irresolute, might be pushed into decisive action. But the longer the revolution continued the more timid and paralysed the bourgeoisie became. By the time of the 'June days' all the exploiting classes, including the bourgeoisie and most of their democratic spokesmen, were ranged on the side of reaction. Marx and Engels were increasingly driven to the conclusion that only the exploited classes, the workers and the peasants, could drive the revolution forward. As Marx wrote in his paper *Neue Rheinische Zeitung*, whose bourgeois backers were abandoning it because of its radical stance,

'The German bourgeoisie developed so sluggishly, so pusillanimously and so slowly, that it saw itself threateningly confronted by the proletariat, and all those sections of the urban population related to the proletariat ..., at the very moment of its own threatening confrontation with feudalism and absolutism ... The Prussian bourgeoisie was not, like the French bourgeoisie of 1789, the class which represented the whole of modern society ... It had sunk to the level of a type of estate ... inclined from the outset to treachery against the people ...' [23]

Faced with far greater treachery on the part of the bourgeoisie than they had at first expected Marx and Engels altered their strategic position. Marx and Engels now concluded that independent action on the part of the working class and a more critical stance, on tactical issues as well as theoretical ones, towards the bourgeois democrats was essential. Marx's explanation of the attitude of the workers to the democrats is of great relevance:

'The workers must drive the proposals of the democrats to their logical extreme (the democrats will in any case act in a reformist and not a revolutionary manner) and transform these proposals into direct attacks on private property. If, for instance, the petty bourgeoisie proposes the purchase of the railways and factories, the workers must demand that these railways and factories simply be confiscated without compensation as the property of reactionaries. If the democrats propose a proportional tax, then the workers must demand a progressive tax; if the democrats themselves propose a moderate progressive tax, then the workers must insist on a tax whose rates rise so steeply that big capital will be ruined by it; if the democrats themselves demand the regulation of state debt, then the workers must demand national bankruptcy. The demands of the workers thus have to be adjusted according to the measures and concessions of the democrats.' [24]

As the revolution develops, political divisions within the revolutionary camp based on underlying class differences begin to harden:

> 'It is the fate of all revolutions that this union of different clas-
> ses, which in some degree is always the necessary condi-
> tion of any revolution, cannot subsist long. No sooner is
> the victory gained against the common enemy, than the
> victors become divided amongst themselves into different
> camps and turn their weapons against each other. It is this
> rapid and passionate development of class antagonism which,
> in old and complicated social organisms, makes revolution
> such a powerful agent of social and political progress.'[25]

In response to this polarisation Marx urges revolutionaries to
concentrate on the independent political organisation of the
working class, confident that the more powerful this is the more
it will push the bourgeois democrats to the left whether they are
in government or not. Marx hopes the movement of workers
can become so strong that it can result in a revolution against the
liberal democrats. Marx now believes, as he did not clearly believe
before the 1848 revolutions, that this will be a socialist revolution.

It is this new perspective which leads him to conclude that,
since the state apparatus is not a neutral body that can simply be
passed from one class to another, the working class must concentrate on building up its own state apparatus alongside and in
opposition to that of the propertied classes. Such organisations
will emerge from the struggle against the old regime: strike
committees, local delegate bodies of workers and mass meetings,
and so forth. Where conditions of struggle allow, these will
involve the formation of workers' militias, armed with what
they are able to find or to take from the armed forces of the
state. These 'counter-state' organisations Marx describes as
'revolutionary local councils' or 'revolutionary workers' governments' and they cannot co-exist with the bourgeois state for
long without a decisive settling of accounts in which either the
workers will smash the state or the state will smash the organs
of workers' power:

> 'The German workers ... must contribute most to their
> final victory, by informing themselves of their own class

interests, by taking up their independent political position as soon as possible, by not allowing themselves to be misled by the hypocritical phrases of the democratic petty bourgeoisie into doubting for one minute the necessity of an independently organised party of the proletariat. Their battle-cry must be: the Permanent Revolution.'[26]

Thus we see that the perspective of permanent revolution originated with Marx in 1850. Here is the origin of the idea that there should be, from the beginning of the revolution and even while a workers' party is supporting 'democratic demands', a strategic perspective of independent working class socialist organisation, aiming first at the creation of dual power and then at a socialist revolution.

The bourgeois revolutions from above

The 1848 revolutions definitively brought to a close the epoch in which the bourgeoisie was willing and able to act as a revolutionary class. After this date there were no more attempts by the bourgeoisie to lead the mass of the people in open revolution against the old order. But this did not mean that the bourgeoisie were now the effective political power, even in all the economically most developed countries. Nor did it mean that the dynamic process of capital accumulation came to a halt. Far from it. The effect of the bourgeois revolutions was to increase the tempo of capital accumulation and forge a world market more completely than had previously been the case. Neither did the unwillingness of the bourgeoisie to provide political leadership for the mass of the population mean that popular revolts against the old order were a thing of the past.

Instead, there were two broad lines of determination which ran out from 1848 and on through the 19th century. One was the element of continuing popular revolt, increasingly involving self-conscious working class activity and organisation. The high tide of this current was reached in 1871 when the first successful workers' revolution flowered briefly in the Paris Commune. But even where such peaks were not scaled, popular and working class action could be seen, for instance, in the New Unionism of the 1880s in Britain, the growth of Marxist influenced unions and social democratic parties throughout Europe towards the end of the century.

The second process of change which followed 1848 was the bourgeoisie's continuing attempt to develop political and state forms adequate for the new conditions under which capital accumulation was now taking place. National unity and the attendant reshaping of the state machine to meet capitalist needs, a key prize won by the English, American and French revolutions, was now a pressing necessity for every capitalist class, especially since the competitive advantage which the forerunners gained from their revolutions was increasingly obvious to the laggards.

In the American Civil War Lincoln chanelled popular mobilisation in to the military struggle against the South, thus recasting American capitalism as a whole in the image of the Northern bourgeoisie. In so doing he forcibly unified the ruling class and enabled it to pursue its 'manifest destiny' of conquering the land to its west as far as the Pacific. In Italy national unification and the creation of a bourgeois state involved popular mobilisation around the figures of Garibaldi and Mazzini, but this was kept well within the limits of Cavour's constitutionalism. In Germany, Napoleon's armies had done much to clear the ground for Bismarck's state-building enterprise. The defeat of 1848 allowed this process to surge forward with little popular impediment until the rise of the Social Democratic Party and the organised working class at the end of the century.

The importance of briefly sign-posting this process is to demonstrate that the bourgeoisie did not cease to pursue its own political goals, including those which involved major social transformations, when it renounced revolutionary methods of action. Neither did it wholly dispense with the desire to utilise the energies of social classes beneath it. It simply refused to give such classes revolutionary leadership. The bourgeoisie feared their action and yet at the same time sought to profit from the upheavals which popular movements created.[27]

Lenin and Trotsky on the socialist revolution and the democratic revolution

Lenin's initial estimation of the forces involved in the Russian revolution is contained in his *Two Tactics of Social Democracy in the Democratic Revolution*. This work predates the experience of 1917; in fact it even predates his full absorption of the lessons of the 1905 Revolution. In some important respects it is a regression to a point less politically developed than that of Marx and Engels in 1850. In *Two Tactics* Lenin argued that the economic and social conditions in Russia were not sufficiently advanced for the coming revolution to be a socialist revolution. The revolution would be bourgeois democratic in content:

> 'The degree of Russia's economic development (an objective condition), and the degree of class consciousness and organisation of the broad masses of the proletariat (a subjective condition inseparably bound up with the objective condition) make the immediate and complete emancipation of the working class impossible. Only the most ignorant people can close their eyes to the bourgeois nature of the revolution which is now taking place.'[28]

Lenin thought the Russian bourgeoisie was too weak to lead the democratic revolution in the way that the English bourgeoisie had done in the 1640s, or the French bourgeoisie had done in the 1790s. The working class would therefore have to lead an insurrection which would overthrow Tsarism and establish a democratic republic. But for the working class to be able to perform this task it would have to be led by a revolutionary party which insisted on a political strategy free of compromises with the vacillating bourgeois democrats and their fellow travellers inside the organisations of the working class, the Mensheviks.

This position clearly had a number of strengths. The greatest of these was the assertion of the leading role of the working class in the democratic revolution and the insistence on the building of a revolutionary party carrying out socialist propaganda, even though socialism was not the immediate aim of the revolution. And such a strategy required sharp criticism of, and political independence from, both the bourgeois democrats, the emerging Cadet party, and the Mensheviks.

But, for all Lenin's insistence on these crucial elements, *Two Tactics* contains a weakness which allows for constant back-sliding, especially by those who claimed to be Lenin's supporters but who did not share his revolutionary intransigence. For, if the revolution is to result in a bourgeois democratic settlement, if a 'democratic dictatorship' is the furthest stage to which the revolution can advance, then the working class is reduced to being the furthest left wing, the most consistent element, in the democratic revolution. That is, its political representatives would play the role of the Levellers in the English revolution or the sans culottes in the French revolution. This situation contains the inherent danger that the revolutionary party will underestimate the consciousness and activity of the working class, tailoring its slogans to the democratic tasks of the day and forgoing independent socialist agitation. If such a situation arises the party can become a force retarding the development of the class by failing to formulate a strategy which crystallises the aspirations of the class. Instead it can channel their energies into fighting for goals far short of those which workers are capable of attaining.

The crucial advance made by Trotsky in his 1906 work *Results and Prospects* was to point out that if the working class was the leading element in the revolution it would not limit itself to merely democratic demands – it would demand the arming of the workers, the expropriation of the capitalists, and that power be given to the workers' councils. Capitalist industry had developed to the point where Tsarism was in a terminal crisis. Although industry had not developed on the scale of, say, Britain or Germany, where it did exist in Russia it existed in a very advanced form. So it was that St Petersburg's Putilov works (destined to become a 'citadel of Bolshevism' in 1917) was the largest and one of the most technologically advanced factories of its kind anywhere in the world. This is what Trotsky called 'combined and uneven development': the most advanced forms of capitalist development are transplanted, often by international investment, into the heart of underdeveloped countries.[29]

Trotsky went on to agree with Lenin that the Russian bourgeoisie was too timid to lead a democratic revolution, largely because the working class which had grown up around the new industries frightened the bourgeoisie with the spectre of a revolution which could sweep away both Tsarism and the bourgeoisie in a single blow. Consequently, the working class would not limit itself to bourgeois democratic demands. When the working class fought it could only do so using working class methods: strikes, general strikes, workers councils and so on. But these methods of struggle are as much directed against the bourgeoisie as they are against Tsarism. They raise the question: 'who will run the factory?' as well as the question 'who will run the state?' The revolution will therefore be a social revolution (i.e. an economic and political revolution) not simply a political (i.e. democratic) revolution.

Trotsky completed his analysis by showing that the socialist revolution will be able to sustain itself, despite Russia's backwardness, because Russia is part of the world economy, because the crisis of capitalism is international and, therefore, because the revolution can spread to the advanced capitalist societies of the West. In so doing it provides the material base to develop a socialist society, making the revolution permanent. In other words, the democratic revolution, by virtue of its dependence on the working class as its leading force and by virtue of its international dimension, would immediately grow over into the socialist revolution.

This is, of course, exactly what happened in 1917. But in 1917 the Bolshevik party was still operating the perspective of *Two Tactics*. This is why it tail-ended the Provisional government and the Mensheviks between February and April 1917. This is why the entire leadership of the Bolsheviks thought Lenin was mad when he returned to Russia and, at the Finland station, made a speech calling for a second, socialist revolution. This is why Lenin's *April Theses* at first found virtually no support among the Bolshevik leadership. Lenin had, in essence, accepted Trotsky's theory of permanent revolution.

The Russian Revolution

The main novelty which the 1917 Russian Revolution added to the pattern of the 1848 revolutions was that some socialists were, from the first, the willing assistants of the petty bourgeois democrats in their efforts to contain the revolution. The Mensheviks and the Social Revolutionaries (SRs) and, until Lenin's return to Russia in March 1917, a sizeable section of the Bolsheviks including Stalin and other leaders of the party, were willing supporters the provisional government. The Mensheviks and the SRs at first performed this service from their seats in the Petrograd Soviet, but in April they formally joined the government. The Bolsheviks, despite the misgivings of some party members, supported the government without joining it.

Only Lenin's *April Theses* rearmed the party by adopting Trotsky's (and Marx's) perspective of permanent revolution. From that point on the Bolsheviks were in opposition to the provisional government and solely concerned with strengthening the soviets, as these were the independent organisations of the working class. As Trotsky wrote:

'In all past revolutions those who fought on the barricades were workers, apprentices, in part students, and the soldiers came over to their side. But afterwards the solid bourgeoisie, having cautiously watched the barricades from their windows, gathered up the power. But the February revolution of 1917 was distinguished from former revolutions by incomparably higher social character and political level of the revolutionary class, by the hostile distrust of the insurrectionists towards the liberal bourgeoisie, and the consequent formation at the very moment of victory of a new organ of revolutionary power, the Soviet based on the armed strength of the masses.'[30]

It was by strengthening the power of the soviets that the Bolsheviks both managed to defeat the Kornilov coup against the provisional government and to lead a successful socialist revolution in October 1917. But victory did not go uncontested, and nor did the strategy of permanent revolution. The great division between revolutionary socialism and Stalinism was fought over precisely this issue. Internationalism was at the core of the October revolution, not as an abstract moral injunction but as the very means of the revolution's survival. Lenin repeated again and again, both before October and afterwards, that the Russian Revolution could only survive if the revolution spread to the West:

> 'It is not open to the slightest doubt that the final victory of our revolution, if it were to remain alone, if there were no revolutionary movement in other countries, would be hopeless ... Our salvation from all these difficulties, I repeat, is an all-European revolution.'[31]

Trotsky, repeating the prognosis he first made in *Results and Prospects* after the 1905 revolution, argued:

> 'If the peoples of Europe do not rise and crush imperialism, we shall be crushed – that is beyond doubt. Either the Russian revolution will raise the whirlwind of struggle in the West, or the capitalists of all countries will stifle our struggle.'[32]

Neither was this the isolated view of Lenin and Trotsky. It was 'the European revolution' on which 'the confident calculations, not merely of a few optimists but of every Bolshevik of any account, had been based'.[33] Most of all Lenin and Trotsky hoped the revolution would spread to Germany. Had it done so it would not only have altered the whole international balance of class forces, making it impossible for the imperialist powers to continue their wars of intervention and unnecessary for the revolutionary government to cede the huge territories it lost in the peace of Brest-Litovsk. It would also have transformed the domestic situation of the revolution. Industry, and with it the numbers and confidence of the working class, could have been restored. The crucial alliance with the peasantry, on which the revolution depended, could have been maintained as manufactured goods were sent to the country to be exchanged for grain to feed the starving cities.

But without such an international victory, the Russian Revolution remained isolated. The working class, decimated by the civil war, the wars of intervention and the starvation and famine which followed, recovered at a snail's pace if at all. Grain had to be requisitioned from the peasantry at the point of a gun. Eventually the regime introduced a partial restoration of the market – the New Economic Policy – which gave rise to a profiteering layer of bureaucrats and richer peasants. Indeed the bureaucracy remained the only stable element in a society whose revolutionary institutions had been undermined by the terrible price the working class had to pay in the fight to defend them.

These are the conditions under which the Stalinist trend in the bureaucracy began to assert itself. It came to represent a layer which set its face against the whole idea of internationalism: Stalin's slogan was 'Socialism in One Country'. Trotsky defended the principle on which the October Revolution had been, and could only have been, won: internationalism. As we have seen, Trotsky and Lenin had realised that if the revolution was to be a socialist revolution, rather than simply a democratic revolution which at best would issue in a capitalist economy and a parliamentary republic, it must spread to the advanced industrialised countries. This was the whole theoretical basis on which the Third International was formed.

Once Stalin broke the link between the possibility of socialist revolution at home and the fight to maintain it by spreading it internationally, the whole basis of the Bolsheviks' revolutionary policy in October collapsed. Stalin's 'Socialism in One Country' insisted that the Russian state could 'go it alone' and castigated Trotsky for 'underestimating the peasantry'. In the international arena this returned Bolshevik policy to the Menshevik position in 1917. The model of revolution which Stalin now propagated throughout the third world was the 'two stage' revolution. First the democratic revolution in which the working class should subordinate specifically socialist aspirations to a broad alliance aimed at achieving a democratic revolution. Only after this stage had been completed could socialist demands be raised.

Stalin's approach meant that the revolution did not need the international working class to ensure victory, since a 'democratic revolution' could be achieved by a cross-class alliance of progressive forces acting within a purely national arena. Thus, it became acceptable for socialists to argue that the working class should ally itself with the peasantry and 'progressive sections of the bourgeoisie' in future revolutions. In China in 1927 and in Spain in 1936 this led to disaster because it subordinated working class revolution to bourgeois nationalists (Chiang Kai Shek) or bourgeois parliamentarians (the republican parties in Spain). The result was counter-revolution and dictatorship in both cases.

The bourgeois revolution after the defeat of the Russian Revolution

The working class movement suffered a series of crushing defeats as fascism triumphed in the inter-war period. In Italy the two 'red years' of revolutionary struggle immediately following the Russian Revolution were ended by Mussolini's consolidation of fascism in the 1920s. The charge of the German revolution took longer to dissipate, but ultimately the failure of the Stalinist dominated German Communist Party to resolve the crisis of the Weimar republic in the working classes' favour paved the way for Hitler to take power in 1933. The following year a belated workers' rising in 'Red Vienna' was crushed as the fascists took power. In 1936 the Spanish Revolution and the struggles around the election of the Popular Front government in France briefly raised the hope of turning the Nazi tide, but again the conduct of the Comintern destroyed the opportunity. The scene was set for world war.

The destruction engendered by the war, and the further demobilisation by the Communist Parties of the post-war wave of popular left wing struggles, especially in Italy, meant that the widespread revolutionary mood which attended the end of the First World War was present only in a more muted form after the Second World War. Furthermore, sustained arms spending at a level quantitatively higher than during the inter-war period led to a 30 year period of economic expansion unparalleled in capitalism's past. In this respect the period after the Second World War was quite unlike the crisis ridden 1920s and 1930s. The international scene was also transformed during the long boom. The old European colonial powers, whether victors or vanquished, ended the war economically exhausted. Faced with twin pressures to open their markets to competition from newly dominant American corporations and from growing anti-colonial resistance, they were unable to sustain their empires. The second half of the 20th century became the great era of decolonisation, although economic power wielded by the imperial states proved to be as disabling for the mass of the population in the former colonies as the old set-up of direct rule had been.

These great anti-colonial transformations combined with the previous defeats suffered by the international working class movement and the economic growth which attended the long boom to throw the dynamics of the revolutionary process into a unique new pattern. The assumptions which lay behind Trotsky's theory of permanent revolution were called into question by these new developments. Trotsky's theory had been constructed between two poles. One was the fact that the bourgeoisie was incapable of recreating its revolutionary past under modern conditions and therefore of carrying through the construction of a unified, independent capitalist state in the face of concerted opposition from pre-capitalist or colonial ruling classes. The second was that the working class would fill the political vacuum thus created, simultaneously solving the problems of the democratic and the socialist revolution. But what would happen if the first of these conditions, the objective weakness of the bourgeoisie, remained true while the second, the subjective potential of the working class, remained unrealised?

The cadre of the middle class revolution

Trotsky could not foresee the unprecedented conditions which conspired to bring about just this situation after the Second World War. Nevertheless, such conditions required a fresh analysis. This was provided in Tony Cliff's pioneering essay 'Deflected Permanent Revolution'.[34] In analysing the Chinese revolution of 1949 and the Cuban revolution of 1959, Cliff demonstrated that in periods where the working class was unable to mount a challenge to the old order, and yet the old order was decomposing as a result of a wider social crisis, other social forces were able to play a significant political role. The peasantry often provided the forces for popular mobilisation in these circumstances but, since modern revolutions are overwhelmingly urban events, they could not provide indigenous or effective political leadership. This leadership could be provided, however, by sections of the middle class intelligentsia – lawyers, state bureaucrats, teachers, literary figures, owners of small businesses, academics.

This layer had, in an earlier incarnation, often been a crucial element of the practical leadership of the classical bourgeois revolutions. The greater bourgeoisie do not often directly provide their own political representatives. The middle classes are often professionally engaged in forming general ideological conceptions of society and live closer to the mass of the population whom they are trying to lead. They are, therefore, better political representatives of bourgeois political programmes than the oligarchs of the bourgeoisie themselves. This is a relationship which holds to this day: better for the ruling class that they be represented by a university educated grocers' daughter like Margaret Thatcher (and the lawyers who dominated the House of Commons), than that Rupert Murdoch and his fellow plutocrats attempt to directly represent themselves.

One of the great strengths of the analysis which Cliff provided was a political profile of this layer of people as they appear in

modern 'developing' societies. The intelligentsia in these societies is peculiarly open to playing a leadership role in popular
movements when the working class is quiescent. But the revolution made under these circumstances is a modernising,
nationalist, anti-colonial revolution, not a socialist revolution.

> 'The intelligentsia is ... sensitive to their countries' tech-
> nical lag. Participating as it does in the scientific and tech-
> nical world of the twentieth century, it is stifled by the
> backwardness of its own nation.'[35]

Thus the intelligentsia turns its face against the ruling class
whose 'mismanagement', 'corruption' and 'cowardice' in the
face of imperialism has brought the nation to this pass. Such
individuals are in search of a new God, which they find in the
abstract notion of 'the people', especially those sections of the
people who have the greatest difficulty in organising for themselves, the peasantry.

> 'The spiritual life of the intellectuals is also in crisis. In a
> crumbling order where the traditional pattern is disin-
> tegrating, they feel insecure, rootless, lacking in firm
> values. Dissolving cultures give rise to a powerful urge for
> a new integration that must be total and dynamic if it is to
> fill the social and political vacuum, that must combine
> religious fervour with militant nationalism.'[36]

But this desire to be part of 'the people' and to end the subordination of the nation is always combined with a sense of
superiority, the elite feeling that the masses are too backward or
apathetic to accomplish a revolution for themselves.

> 'They are great believers in efficiency, including efficiency
> in social engineering. They hope for reform from above
> and would dearly love to hand a new world over to a
> grateful people, rather than see the liberating struggle of a
> self-conscious and freely associated people result in a new

world for themselves. They care a lot for measures to drag
their nation out of stagnation, but very little for democracy. They embody the drive for industrialisation, for
capital accumulation, for national resurgence. Their power
is in direct relation to the feebleness of other classes, and
their political nullity.'[37]

This political profile made the whole strategy of autocratic,
state-led, capital accumulation very attractive for this social class
throughout the 30 years of the long boom. China was only the
purest expression of this trend. But, as Cliff noted, 'other colonial revolutions – Ghana, India, Egypt, Indonesia, Algeria etc –
more or less deviate from the norm. But ... they can best be
understood when approached from the standpoint of, and
compared with the norm.'[38]

In Egypt this social layer had been at the heart of the main
nationalist party, the Wafd, from its early days. As Beinin and
Lockman's classic *Workers on the Nile* explains, 'The Wafd can best
be characterised as a bourgeois nationalist party, representing
the most directly the interests of the urban and rural middle
classes: the owners of medium sized agricultural properties and
the urban *effendiyya* [westernized journalists, teachers, lawyers,
university students etc]. It was from this latter group that the
party's political activists were drawn, although wealthier elements continued to dominate the top leadership.' Yet the party's
radical rhetoric allowed the effendiyya political activists to 'play
an important role in the labour movement during the interwar
period.'[39]

Later in Egypt and Syria, Cliff argues, the social base of Nasserism and the Ba'ath regime was 'army officers, civil servants
and teachers, sons of merchants and prosperous artisans, better-
off peasants and small-scale landowners ... The characteristics
of "Arab socialism" spring from this equivocal position.' Consequently, both Nasser and the Ba'ath accepted 'criticism of
feudalism, imperialism and monopoly capitalism ... They
advocate the transfer of key parts of the economy to state
ownership ... '. But, since this perspective rejected working

class activity as the core of socialism, state ownership had nothing to do with socialism.[40]

This contradictory attitude stems from the position of the middle class. 'The attitude of the middle class to state enterprise and planning is very ambivalent indeed. As part of the state bureaucracy, they are interested in the rapid advance of state enterprise. However, as sons, brothers and cousins of small property owners they are quite willing to let the private sector milk the state sector. Hence the Egyptian economy suffers from both bureaucratic inertia of state capitalism and the speculative working of private capitalism.'[41]

As the post-war colonial revolutions ran their course, the long boom came to an end and the terminal crisis of the East European regimes set in, this model lost its attractiveness. But the class who saw modernisation as the key objective of popular movements did not disappear. And although they no longer held to Stalinist derived economic models, they continued to see the state as the crucial vehicle for their political strategy. In some cases, for instance in South Africa, they remained caught within the old Stalinist ideology until the very collapse of Stalinism itself. As the leadership of the liberation movement, and the working class struggle as it revived, they influenced it accordingly.

In Eastern Europe, where opposition necessarily defined itself against Stalinism, other ideologies were pressed into service and often had to contend with socialist and revolutionary alternatives for hegemony. In the Indonesian revolution very little of the old nationalist and Stalinist ideology survived the 1965 coup which brought Suharto to power, simultaneously overthrowing the nationalist founder of Indonesia, Sukarno, and crushing the Indonesian Communist Party. Some 32 years of dictatorship united aspirant members of the excluded middle class around pro-democratic sentiments. They sought to benefit from the overthrow of Suharto, principally by pacifying the movement which achieved it.

We can see the same social pattern developing in the Islamic revival that has followed the Iranian revolution of 1979. As

Oliver Roy has written of the supporters of the Islamic revival in the third world:

> 'they live with the values of the modern city – consumerism and upward social mobility; they left behind the old forms of conviviality, respect for elders and for consensus, when they left their villages ... they are fascinated by the values of consumerism imparted by shop windows of the large metropolises; they live in a world of movie theatres, cafes, jeans, videos and sports, but they live precariously from menial jobs or remain unemployed in immigrant ghettos, with the frustration inherent in an unattainable consumerist world ... Their militant actions exist in symbiosis with the urban environment ... '[42]

The new radical Islamists have a great deal in common with the radicals of the nationalist era:

> 'They are young people with school and even university education who cannot find positions of professions that correspond to their expectations or visions of themselves, either in the saturated state administrative sector or in industry because national capitalism is weak, or in the traditional network because of the devaluation of religious schools ... Thus the newly educated of the Muslim world find no social ratification, either real or symbolic, for what they perceive as their new status.'[43]

This social stratum is as combustible in the modern world as it was at the time of the bourgeois revolutions or in the more recent anti-colonial revolutions – but it now interacts with a wider imperialist and capitalist social structure very different to earlier periods.

Nevertheless, wherever other social forces, principally the working class movement, are weak or lacking in coherent, socialist leadership, this crucial layer of the middle classes have continued to play a role long after their state capitalist ideological incarnation has passed away.

The velvet revolutions of 1989

The causes of the East European revolutions of 1989 are three-fold: firstly, they are international, defined by economic and military competition between the West and the Eastern bloc; secondly, they are the internal economic and political decay of the national economies and the Russian empire; and thirdly, the class struggle determined how these forces expressed themselves as social struggles and political strategies.

The deepest and most lengthy processes culminating in the East European revolutions are found in the first register. The nature of these regimes was that the 'normal' political function of the state, the exclusive use of force in a given territory, is combined with the 'normal' function of a capitalist class, the exclusive right to hire and fire wage labour. It is therefore best captured in the designation 'state capitalist'. The Eastern European regimes resulted from the Russian occupation at the end of the Second World War. Although the Russian model and its East European copies saw the state capitalist method of industrial development at its most extreme, elements of this approach were clearly visible in many economies of the 1930s and 1940s. The international experience of the 1930s economic crisis, followed by the centralising imperative of total war, meant that a state capitalist element was present in Hitler's Germany as well as in Stalin's Russia, in New Deal America as well as in wartime and welfare state Britain. State-led economic development became an attractive model for post-colonial regimes as well.

The attraction was not illusory. In the immediate post-war period the state capitalist regimes' economic expansion was faster than that of the Western powers. Indeed, the correlation appeared to be that the more state capitalist the regime, the faster the economic expansion. The index of industrial production in East Germany rose by more than five times between 1950 and 1969. In the same period West Germany's index rose sevenfold – but Poland's rose by almost the same amount. Britain's rose less than twofold, while Hungary's rose nearly five-fold. France's increased by just over two times, yet in the same period Romania's index rose over 10 times.[44] These figures only measure the rise in industrial production, not the absolute size of the various economies. But they show that the picture of the state capitalist economies as stagnant is a myth.

In the same period of state capitalist growth the world economy expanded massively. And the dynamic of the world economy transformed as it expanded. Private monopoly and multinational firms came to dominate the Western economies. International trade grew as never before. These developments began to undermine the progress possible using state capitalist methods of accumulation.

For the autarkic state capitalisms of Eastern Europe, those states which had attempted the most complete isolation from the rest of the world market, state capitalism had been very good at developing an industrial base from weak beginnings in a post-war world where the international economy was itself weak. However, when the Western economies recovered and grew, and as international trade expanded, the isolation worked to their disadvantage: Western corporations, both private and state owned, were free to organise and trade on a global scale, searching the globe for the cheapest raw materials, plant and labour, and for new and lucrative markets. The Eastern state corporations traded in a bloc which had always been weaker than its Western rivals, even in the pre-war years. Non-convertible currencies, restricted resources and the imperial demands of the Russian state undermined their competitiveness on a world scale.

Domestically, it was obvious that the industrial progress of the post-war period was not being converted into a 'second revolution' in consumer durables. Internationally the inability to keep up economically eventually meant an inability to keep pace with the West militarily. The state capitalist ruling class were losing the Cold War. Détente was the result: an attempt to transfer resources from the military to the civilian economy, the better to be able to develop military capacity in the future. The stakes in this game had become very high by the 1980s when Ronald Reagan proposed the Star Wars defence system and

Mikhail Gorbachev, fearful of another huge hike in defence spending, countered with a series of disarmament proposals which he hoped the United States could not refuse. He was right, but it was too late.

Developments in the class struggle would close down this road to reform. This revolutionary narrative, however, begins much earlier. In the 1970s the leader of Poland, Edward Gierek, attempted a new strategy to deal with waves of strikes and factory occupations which had toppled his predecessor in December 1970. He attempted a 'second industrial revolution' by borrowing from the West. New plant would be built with Western loans and repaid by exporting Western quality goods back to the West. The plan was a catastrophic failure, in part because the world economy was no longer expanding as it had done in the post-war period but entering the current prolonged era of slump and slow growth. In 1976 Poland's hard currency debt stood at 10 billion dollars. Three years later it had reached 17 billion dollars.[45]

Other East European leaders had tried the same 'consumer socialism' experiment – Janos Kadar in Hungary, Erich Honecker in East Germany – and by the late 1970s per capita debt in these countries had reached the same level as in Poland. Economic failure led to political change: Honecker tried cautious rapprochement with the Protestant Church, Kadar implemented a slight easing of restrictions on intellectual freedom. But Poland had sustained the longest and deepest tradition of mass working class resistance to the state and it was this which was to be the decisive factor in the overthrow of the Eastern bloc regimes.

In 1976 workers were once again involved in a huge wave of strikes against price increases. The Baltic shipyards were occupied, as they had been six years earlier. Several thousand workers of the Ursus tractor factory in Warsaw marched to the rail lines, ripped them up and stopped the Paris-Moscow express. In Radom, south-west of Warsaw, workers burnt down the Communist Party headquarters. The price rises were withdrawn, but the workers paid for their victory in other ways: thousands were sacked, many jailed and, in Radom and Ursus, those who kept their jobs were beaten back to work between lines of truncheon wielding police.

To defend the workers in the aftermath of the 1976 strikes, activists and intellectuals formed the Workers' Defence Committee (KOR, by it Polish initials). In September 1977, a year after KOR was founded, it began to produce its own newspaper, *Robotnik* (*The Worker*). On May Day 1978 the Founding Committee of Trade Unions on the Coast was founded in Gdansk and it soon began producing its own paper, *Robotnik Wybrzeza* (*The Worker on the Coast*). 'KOR worked very much as Lenin recommended (in *What is to be Done?*) the conspiratorial communist party should work, raising the political consciousness of the proletariat in key industrial centres'.[46] The activists drawn together in these and other similar initiatives were to become the leadership of Solidarity in the wake of the largest of all Polish strike waves in 1980. Their political development was crucial to the whole process of revolution in Eastern Europe.

The workers' movement which gave birth to Solidarity was insurrectionary in its scope. In July 1980 the government announced another round of price rises and again these were met with a series of rolling strikes. Despite the regime's attempt to pacify the workers with a wage increase, the strikes spread. By August they had reached Gdansk and the Lenin shipyard was occupied in response to the sacking of *Worker on the Coast* activist Anna Walentynowicz. The yard management conceded the occupiers' demands, but the occupation continued in solidarity with the local strikes which the action at the Lenin yard had sparked. An Inter-Factory Committee (MKZ) was established for the whole of Gdansk. Strikes and occupations spread, and mines and steelworks in southern Poland struck for the first time. The MKZs also spread across the whole country. In September they united in one national organisation, Solidarity. The government was forced to negotiate an unprecedented agreement, the '21 points', granting a host of reforms, most importantly the right to 'independent, self-governing trade unions'.[47]

Such an unprecedented rupture in the authority of a Stalinist state created a situation of dual power. The state tried, but failed, to undermine Solidarity in the months after the initial strike wave. And Solidarity for its part came to take on more and more of the actual running of society. One KOR activist paid eloquent testimony to this fact, though he saw it as more of a problem than an opportunity:

> 'At this moment people expect more of us than we can possibly do ... In Poland nowadays, however, society gathers around the free trade unions. That's a bad thing ... It would be a good thing if the party took the lead and removed the people's expectations from our shoulders. But will it do so now? In the eyes of the people the new trade unions should do everything: they should fill the role of trade unions, participate in the administration of the country, be a political party and act as a militia ...' [48]

Solidarity leaders were unwilling to meet these expectations by overthrowing the government and this was bound to disappoint its supporters. Worse, they began to limit the actions of its rank and file in the name of not provoking the government. Worse still, such a policy divided and exhausted the movement, allowing the ruling class to regain the initiative and to organise the military coup headed by General Jaruzelski in August 1981.

What brought the Solidarity leadership to act in this way? Why did they not support the demands of the rank and file, and of the radicals within the Solidarity leadership, and use the power, which they acknowledged the union to have, to overthrow the government? Crucial to this decision was the political strategy developed by the KOR leadership in the period before Solidarity was created. Jacek Kuron is perhaps the pivotal, certainly the emblematic, figure in this story.

Kuron was a long-standing militant with an impressive record of opposition to the Polish regime. As early as 1965 he had written, with Karol Modzelewski, the path-breaking *Open Letter to the Party*. This document, which still has an impressive power when read today, was a Marxist critique of the Polish state. Similar in its social analysis to the theory of state capitalism, it insisted on revolutionary conclusions: it called for a return to genuine workers' councils, for the arming of the workers and for an 'anti-bureaucratic revolution'. Indeed, it went on to call for 'the organisation of workers' circles, nuclei of the future party'.[49] However, by the time he played a leadership role in KOR and then Solidarity Kuron would abandon this revolutionary perspective.

Paradoxically, the economic and social fate of the state capitalist regimes played an important part in Kuron's shift to the right. The economic success of Stalinism in the 1950s and 1960s allowed the opposition in Poland and throughout Eastern Europe to believe that a renewal of socialism, a return to the genuine Marxist tradition and to the democracy of the early Russian Revolution was necessary. Even those who broke completely with the notion of 'reform Communism', as Kuron did, were influenced by evidence that state ownership was a viable economic model.

The *Open Letter* had argued that the threat of armed Russian intervention would be met by the spread of the revolution to the rest of the Eastern bloc. It could therefore paralyse the Russian ruling classes' ability to intervene. By 1980, however, Kuron was defending the reformist perspective precisely by reference to the Russian military threat. Just as the Western left was abandoning the revolutionary perspectives of 1968 in favour of the reformist perspective of the 'long march through the institutions', so Kuron was coming to believe in a 'self-limiting revolution' in which the institutions of civil society would be built up within the old order, gradually forcing it to accommodate to liberal democratic norms.

Kuron's change of heart was equally marked on the question of party organisation. The *Open Letter* had been unambiguous on this issue:

> 'In order that the working class can have the chance to play the leading role, it must be conscious of its distinct, particular interests. It must express them in the form of a political programme and organise itself – as a class fighting for power – into its own political party or parties.'[50]

By the time KOR was founded Kuron and fellow activist Adam Michnik were writing a series of essays calling for a 'New Evolutionism'. KOR itself was renamed the Committee for Social Self-Defence. Although the central role of the working class was never abandoned, as it would have been difficult to do given the combativity of Polish workers, this force was now to be harnessed to a gradualist political strategy. New political allies were to be sought, especially among the intellectuals gathered around the Catholic Church. This new 'popular front' reformism had little need for the revolutionary organisation outlined in the *Open Letter*. When, in the midst of the crisis which engulfed Solidarity in 1981, radicals began to call for the formation of such a party Kuron spoke against them.[51] Such ideas were not peculiar to Kuron but became the common coin of oppositions throughout Eastern Europe in the 1980s.

The military coup of 1981 was a brutal refutation of this perspective. Yet the reformist vision continued to be held by the leaders of Solidarity even as they were imprisoned and chased into the underground by Jaruzelski's troops. But if the 1981 coup was a defeat for Solidarity, it was not a victory for the regime. The Polish ruling class were so burnt by the cost of imposing martial law that it could not be repeated. Marian Orzechowski joined the Central Committee of the Polish CP in 1981, its politbureau in 1983, and was effectively the Party's last foreign minister. He says,

'I personally feel that the 13 December 1981 had been a hugely negative experience for the army and the police. I had discussions with General Kiszczak and General Siwicki that martial law could only work once. The army and the riot police could not be mobilised against society. Most of the party leadership realised this … You couldn't rerun martial law.'[52]

The Russian ruling class had been unwilling to act, ironically given Kuron's fears, and seemed to have drawn the conclusion that it would henceforward not be possible to intervene against civil unrest in its Eastern empire. The 'Sinatra doctrine', 'I Did it My Way', as Gorbachev's spokesman Gennady Gerasimov would later call it, was sung to a Polish tune. General Jaruzelski himself recalls:

'Gorbachev on many occasions said that Polish changes were an impulse to perestroika … He often requested materials about what we had tried and tested … I was closely linked to Gorbachev. We spoke to one another without reserve, saying that old men like Zhivkov [of Bulgaria] and Honecker [of East Germany] did not understand a thing.'[53]

And as the crisis sharpened again with the 1988 strikes, Gorbachev had an immediate political motivation for continuing to support the Polish government's decision to attempt to hang on to power by compromising with, rather than cracking down on, Solidarity. Polish foreign minister Orzechowski again:

'When in February 1988 I told him [Gorbachev] that the position of Jaruzelski was under attack, he was very worried … Gorbachev realised that if economic reforms in Poland were to collapse, his hardliners could argue that deviation from the principles of socialism must lead to catastrophe. He came to Poland in June 1988 to provide moral support. At every meeting with Jaruzelski, Gorbachev approved of what was happening in Poland.'[54]

The ultimate cause for the change of political heart towards Solidarity was rooted in economics: Poland and other East European states were now connected to Western regimes by trade and debt. Poland's external debt totalled over 38 billion dollars in 1988, the highest in the Eastern bloc. Armed intervention would endanger both trade and loans, worsen an already dire economic crisis, and precipitate civil unrest – the very thing intervention was meant to suppress. Beyond these internal consequences the whole project of détente would have been destroyed by Russian police action in Eastern Europe.

Solidarity itself maintained an underground structure. Renewed strike action in 1988 left the Polish regime with no other option but to try and negotiate its way out of the impasse. Despite continuing strikes, which Lech Walesa tried to demobilise, student protests and protests from the radical wing of Solidarity, 'round table' negotiations with the government began in January 1989. Kuron's response to the radical critics of the 'round table' strategy reveals the degree to which he had now adopted a fully articulated reformist strategy:

> 'Many of our friends, members of the opposition in Poland, asked us: Why did you go to the roundtable discussions? Wouldn't it have been better to continue organising people and to increase the potential for social explosion – a social explosion which would wipe out the totalitarian system? Our answer was 'No'. We don't want to destroy the system by force … the road to democracy has to be a process of gradual evolution, of gradual building of democratic institutions.'[55]

The round table went ahead and resulted, in June 1989, in elections which the regime thought it might win, especially as they were rigged in its favour. In the event Solidarity swept the board with an electoral victory far greater than many in Solidarity had imagined possible. The path to the 'velvet revolutions' in Eastern Europe now lay open. But Jacek Kuron was right when, looking back from 1990, he wrote:

> 'The real breakthrough took place in 1980, when a massive wave of strikes led to the founding of Solidarity, an independent union that the government was forced to recognise. This was truly the moment when the totalitarianism system in Poland was broken.'[56]

At the same time as these events were unfolding in Poland, the Hungarian ruling class were feeling their way towards a similar reconstruction of the political regime. Indeed, six days after

Solidarity swept the board in the Polish elections the Hungarian government opened their own round table discussions about reform. A week later over 100,000 people gathered at the reburial of Imre Nagy, the murdered leader of the 1956 Hungarian revolution. But there was comparatively little popular mobilisation in Hungary in 1989 and certainly no re-creation of the workers' councils of 1956. Yet if the Hungarian events do not tell us very much about the role of the working class in the revolution, the very quietude of the transition in Hungary allows us to see the reconstruction of a ruling class in its purest form.

In the 1970s Hungary followed many of the same policies and confronted many of the same problems as Gierek's Poland. Opening the economy to the West meant accepting Western loans and increased indebtness. Hungary's external debt rose from 0.9 billion dollars in 1973 to 5.8 billion dollars in 1978.[57] Economic liberalisation was combined with a degree of intellectual liberalism. Elemer Hankiss, a Hungarian academic and, after 1989, head of Hungarian television writes,

'In the 1970s, in certain places a kind of social democratisation began. Already during the late sixties, in Hungary the Kadar regime introduced a more tolerant policy to the opposition and society in general. It allowed a 'second economy' to evolve; it allowed a process of cultural pluralisation to emerge, though of course it did not allow political pluralisation.'[58]

The formal economy continued to slide into deeper crisis during the 1970s and 1980s, but the 'second economy' grew. The number of independent craftsmen in Hungary was 50,000 in 1953. By 1989 it had risen to 160,000. In the 1970s there were reckoned to be two million Hungarian families involved in the 'second economy'. The numbers of entrepreneurs, shopkeepers and employees rose from 67,000 in 1982 to almost 600,000 in 1989. These figures were tiny compared to the formal economy and the economic activity these forces generated could not reverse economic decline, but they were of sociological and ideological importance. They were one indicator showing the Hungarian ruling class a way out of the crisis.[59] By the mid-1980s this growth was combined with limited but real political change: a popular ground-swell, unsuccessfully resisted by the state, got genuinely independent candidates elected in the 1985 general election. Independents won 10 percent of parliamentary seats.

The question of whether or not the whole Hungarian ruling class would attempt a transition to a more market oriented form of capitalism would be decided by the behaviour of the upper echelons of the state bureaucracy and the managers of the major industrial enterprises. In this respect Hankiss notes, 'Since the writing appeared on the wall in 1987, the Party and state bureaucracy have been trying to convert their bureaucratic power into a new type of power which will be an asset that can be preserved within the a new system, namely in a market economy or even a democracy.' The result 'may be called the rise of a kind of nineteenth century *"grande bourgeoisie"*.'[60] This class is an amalgam of different elements of the old ruling class.

Firstly, the state bureaucracy of the old order used its family ties to diversify its power.[61] Secondly, as the dam broke in 1989, party bureaucrats found they 'could convert power on an institutional level' and so they began to transform high value properties and real estate, including Party buildings, training centres and holiday complexes, into semi-private or joint stock companies. And besides the party bureaucrats proper there were managerial bureaucrats, the 'Red Barons', who relocated themselves as private capitalists. A third way for the regime to convert power was 'to transform the Hungarian economy into a market economy. This ... has been carried out in such a way that this new *grande bourgeoisie* profit most from the new laws.'[62] Indeed, this generalized consciousness among the ruling class predated the upheaval of 1989 and provides a part of the explanation of the peaceful nature of the transition in Eastern Europe. The political institutions of Eastern Europe were transformed in 1989 but the ruling class was not overthrown and no new mode of production was advanced by the revolutions. The ruling class transformed one method of capitalist accumulation, the autarkic state capitalist method, into another involving a combination of private monopoly, orientation on the world market and a continuing element of state ownership and regulation. They reproduced the really existing capitalism of the West, but not the fantasy 'free market' model of ideological fame.

> 'In the late 1980s a substantial part of the Hungarian party and state bureaucracy discovered ways of converting their bureaucratic power into lucrative economic positions and assets (and also indirectly into a new type of political power) in the new system based on market economics and political democracy ... When in the late 1980s they discovered the possibility of ... becoming part of an emerging new and legitimate ruling class or **grande bourgeoisie**, they lost interest in keeping the Communist Party as their instrument of power and protection. And, as a consequence, on the night of 7 October 1989 they watched indifferently, or assisted actively in, the self-liquidation of the Party.'[63]

This metamorphosis by the ruling class was more extreme in Hungary than elsewhere in Eastern Europe. It was inconceivable without the actions of the Polish working class in 1980–81 and again in 1988. The Polish workers' struggle demonstrated to the ruling classes of Eastern Europe the penalty to be paid if they persisted in trying to rule in the old way. Furthermore, it was the experience of Solidarity combined with Russia's own economic problems and the consequent need to break into the world economy which created the Sinatra doctrine of non-intervention. This created the space in which the Hungarian and other ruling classes could recompose themselves.

The Hungarian events did however contribute one vital link to the chain of the East European revolutions. Early in 1989 the still ruling Hungarian Communist Party decided to open its border with Austria. It was a dramatic move which broke apart the still intact Eastern bloc. The then Minister of Justice, Kalaman Kulcsar, recalls:

> 'we wanted to show that we meant what we were doing and saying. Poland and Hungary were then the only two countries on the road to reform and it was by no means excluded that others in the Warsaw Pact would try something against us. We were pretty sure that if hundreds of thousands of East Germans went to the West, the East German regime would fall, and in that case Czechoslovakia was also out. We were not too concerned about Romania, the only danger to us came from the DDR [East Germany]. We took the step for our own sakes.'[64]

Although the Hungarian government correctly foresaw the international implications of opening the border, they did not see the domestic consequences. 'Our internal situation changed completely. Suddenly conscious of the strength of its position, the opposition was able to advance the date of the elections, and that was the end of the party'.[65] Even so, it was still not clear in all cases that a peaceful transition was inevitable, as the case of East Germany shows.

The East German ruling class instantly grasped the implications of Hungary's open borders. Erich Mielke, the head of the Stasi secret police, 'called it treason'.[66] The East German leader Erich Honecker described it as 'nothing short of treachery'.[67] Some 24,000 East Germans left the country via Hungary between 10 September and 30 September.

East Germany was the western watchtower of the Russian empire. Its fate was always closely tied to the fate of the empire which created it. Two-thirds of East Germany's trade was with Russia. Honecker himself remembers being told by Russian leader Brezhnev in 1970: 'Never forget that the DDR cannot exist without us; without the Soviet Union, its power and strength, without us there is no DDR'.[68] East Germany could not simply be 'hollowed-out' by its own ruling class in the way that the Hungarian regime had been. Neither had there been the long tradition of combativity by which the Polish working class had worn down the resistance of its ruling class.

Consequently, the East German regime fell as a result of the decay of the empire which sustained it and the simultaneous pressure, both through mass demonstrations and mass emigration, of its ordinary people. The fact that the regime did not attempt a violent counter-revolution was not a result of lack of will on the part of its leaders, but the result of an imperial implosion running just ahead of popular mobilisation, eroding the regime's capacity for repression.

The East German state marked its 40th anniversary on 6 October 1989. Gorbachev arrived to attend the celebrations. *Neues Forum*, the dissident civil rights organisation, had already been banned shortly after its formation the previous month. Some 1,000 people were arrested the day Gorbachev arrived, and another 3,456 during the few days of his visit. To mark the anniversary a triumphal torchlight procession marched past a saluting stand in Berlin on the night of 6 October. But, though they marched to order, the crowds could not be made to chant to order. Instead they chanted 'Gorbi, Gorbi'. The following morning Gorbachev and Honecker held their final private meeting. In the corridor afterward Gorbachev deliberately let slip a phrase which, although it was not his intention, damned the East German state: 'Whoever acts too late is punished by life'. He then delivered a speech to the SED (communist party) central committee which was an oblique attack on the speed of reform in East Germany, beginning the process of upheaval in the SED leadership which would see Honecker replaced by Egon Krenz on 18 October.

But as the succession was being decided in the old way, very different things were happening in the streets. On 7 October violent arrests accompanied a 6,000 strong march in East Berlin; the next day 30,000 marched in Dresden. On the same day, 8 October, special security forces were put on alert. For the following day's demonstration in Leipzig huge numbers of police, plus ambulance and hospital services, were mobilised. Honecker is reported to have ordered the use of live ammunition. On 9 October 50,000 marched in Leipzig. There was no shooting.

Honecker's order to shoot had been lost by one vote at the central committee.[69] Local district party bosses also refused to carry out Honecker's orders any longer.[70]

The governing class as a whole were no longer willing to follow Honecker. He had been publicly deserted by Gorbachev and his rivals were already beginning to campaign for his removal. Honecker had lost the trust of Moscow and with it the confidence of his fellow rulers. Consequently, the East German government stayed its hand.

The effect of such governmental paralysis was dramatic. A week later, on 16 October, 100,000 marched in Leipzig. By 23 October the marchers were 150,000 strong; by 30 October 300,000 marched. On 4 November 500,000 attended a rally in East Berlin as tens of thousands left the country through the now open border. In an attempt to stem the tide the regime announced, on 9 November, that border crossings to West Germany were open. The unexpected consequence was that crowds gathered on both sides of the Berlin Wall and began to dismantle it with picks, hammers and chisels.

A round table on the Polish model followed, but its only real achievement was to set the date for elections: 18 March 1990. Helmut Kohl and the Christian Democrat machine filled the void left by the collapse of Stalinism, winning the election and setting its own stamp on the process of German unification.

For events to have taken a left wing direction during the East German revolution would have required a left wing organisation and ideology of rare consistency. In the polarised ideological atmosphere of a partitioned country only an alternative as clear and consistent as either the old Stalinist certainties of Honecker or the Western imperial realpolitik of Helmut Kohl, and equally opposed to both, could have sustained support. The East German opposition had few of these qualities. One of the founders of *Neues Forum*, Jens Reich, recalls the atmosphere of the opposition in the early 1980s:

> 'The new opposition was individualistic and bohemian, and composed of a kaleidoscope of 'counter-culture' social

groups: hippies, Maoists, anarchists, human rights groups, greens, gays, lesbians, the protesting "church from below" – a very colourful mixture ... in fact, to professional people, frankly somewhat alien! My wife Eva and I felt like fish out of water ...'[71]

Of course it is perfectly possible that out of such a milieu a core of people could emerge who clarify their ideas, formulate a strategy and start to build links with workers. This, for all their ultimate weaknesses, was the path taken by KOR in Poland. But this was not the path taken by the people who founded *Neues Forum*. Jens Reich argued,

'We had to reach out to a more "respectable" middle-aged generation, to give them the courage to come out of their snail-shells ... We wished to ensure that we were properly representative; to ensure that *Neues Forum* incorporated not only clergymen, not only Berliners, not only intellectuals, not only young dropouts from the social ghetto. This criterion brought us together ... a cross-section of normal people with normal professions and different political leanings.'[72]

Such a strategy was initially successful, but as the revolution radicalised, and as global political issues quickly came into play with the fall of the Berlin Wall, *Neues Forum* was thrust aside by more robust political forces. On one side it was undermined by Helmut Kohl's pro-market capitalist ideology and the huge CDU and state machine. Despite this many East Germans rejected this model, and many more came to reject it as they experienced life under 'really existing capitalism'. But *Neues Forum* could not even present itself as an adequate vehicle for discontent. So, from the other side, it was undermined by the reconstituted social democratic SED, now called the Party of Democratic Socialism.

This is not the inevitable fate of the kind of petty bourgeois groups who formed the core of *Neues Forum*. They can often play a very effective political role. But the East German opposition could not align themselves with the ruling class, did not align themselves with the working class and were a dispensable commodity for the West German ruling class. They bloomed briefly in the revolution of the flowers, but wilted quickly in the heat generated when real class forces came to dominate the scene.

The fall of the Berlin Wall signalled that the end of state capitalism throughout Eastern Europe was only a matter of time. Jan Urban, a leading figure in Czechoslovakia's Civic Forum, recalls,

> 'Poland, Hungary and now East Germany were moving. What about us? On the 9 November 1989 the Berlin Wall was breached. Now it was completely clear that Czechoslovakia would be next on the list.'[73]

The difference between the Prague Spring of 1968 and the revolution of 1989, as far as Urban is concerned, is that 'twenty years ago it was predominantly a matter of a crisis of legitimacy within the governing Communist elite in one country of the Communist bloc, in 1989 ... it was the Czechoslovak variant of the crisis of legitimacy of whole Communist system'. Although the Czechoslovak regime did not accumulate debt on the Polish scale it did, consequently, create a 'painful internal debt ... so the structure and equipment of industry became unmaintainable. The transportation system was old, services undeveloped and natural environment devastated.'[74] In common with other ruling classes in Eastern Europe, the Czechoslovaks were losing faith in the state capitalist method of accumulation. The onset of perestroika in Russia from the mid-1980s deepened this mood.

There had long been dissident groups in Czechoslovakia. The most famous of them was Charter 77, patterned on KOR in Poland but more oriented on achieving 'civic rights' and less on working class activity. But the real mobilisation of the mass of the population only really took hold after the fall of the Berlin Wall. Throughout 1988 and 1989 many thousands signed petitions of protest against the Czechoslovak regime, the largest of these were organised by the Church. Demonstrations did not attract more than 10,000. Indeed, as late as 28 October this was the number in Prague's Wenceslas Square when at the same time Leipzig was seeing demonstrations of 150,000 to 300,000. These demonstrations, and the ones that followed, were met with beatings and mass arrests by the police.

Sections of the regime clearly hoped they could stage-manage a transition which would maintain nearly all their power. But events ran beyond their control, although not so far beyond as to endanger the whole process of transition to capitalist parliamentary democracy. On 17 November riot police made a violent attack on a Prague demonstration, and a carefully planned security operation was mounted to make it seem as if a student, Martin Smid, had been killed. The incident was meant to be reported by the dissident press. The security forces then planned to produce the unhurt student, discredit the opposition and pave the way for 'reform communist' Zdenek Mlynar to replace Husak as president. At the same time a StB security service briefing was arguing:

'Use influential agents to intensively infiltrate opposition parties. Aim to disinform the opponent. Compromise the most radical members of the opposition and exacerbate divisions within the opposition. At the same time, create conditions for StB officers to obtain civil service promotions and posts at selected companies. . . .'

The narrower part of this plan, to replace Husak, failed for two reasons. Firstly, Mlynar refused to play his allotted part, even though Gorbachev sought to persuade him. Secondly, and more importantly, after the fall of the Berlin Wall the mass movement took on a momentum which swept aside such plans for an orderly succession.[75]

A week after the Berlin Wall came down the numbers in Prague rose to 50,000. Two days later, on 19 November, they doubled to 100,000. The next day the numbers doubled again to 200,000. Four days later, 24 November, 500,000 demonstrated in Wenceslas Square and listened to Alexander Dubcek, the disgraced leader of the Prague Spring in 1968. The same day the entire politbureau of the CP resigned.

On 25 November, another crowd of 500,000 gathered to hear Civic Forum leader Vaclav Havel and Dubcek speak. Two days later three million workers took part in a two-hour general strike, and 200,000 demonstrated in Wenceslas Square. The result of this massive spasm of popular activity was that Civic Forum announced the suspension of the demonstrations and the government conceded free elections. Within a week the leaders of the CP resigned from government and a majority reformist administration took over.

The Civic Forum leaders were thrown to the head of the movement, but they did not create it. Indeed, it was not until 19 November 1989 that 400 activists founded Civic Forum. But the long history of dissent by the leaders of Civic Forum, many of whom were Charter 77 activists, made them natural figure-heads, symbols of the revolt. But it could not be said that they *actively and organisationally prepared* the revolt in the way that the KOR activists prepared for, and then built and led, Solidarity. The deficiencies of organisation and ideology were made good by the cumulative weight of the revolutions in Eastern Europe, which led directly to massive mobilisations, and the internal decay of the regime. Jan Urban's recollections make explicit both the rapidity of the regime's collapse and the limited aims of the opposition:

> 'The entire political power structure collapsed in front of our eyes. We didn't want to allow the state to collapse with it, so we had to act. There was no one else to do so. There were even moments when we had to support some Communist Party officials against whom we had just fought.'[76]

Martin Palous, a philosopher at the university in Prague and a founder of Civic Forum, underlines this view:

> 'Civic Forum leaders were constantly shocked that their proposals, dreamlike, turned into reality. It gave everyone a

false impression that they were really marvellous politicians ... The party structure of communications and power disintegrated.'[77]

The crucial weakness lay in the 'popular front' style political strategy which the Civic Forum leadership had long espoused: Urban again:

'In a few hours we had created, from the far Left to the far Right, a coalition with only one goal: to get rid of Husak ... We did it ourselves, and having done so, we found out it was not enough. Now we had to change the whole system! We decided that the best way to achieve this was through free elections.'[78]

Here the forces which determined the fate of the Czechoslovak revolution stand out in high relief. An exhausted empire was in collapse. The national regime fell apart under the impact of popular mass mobilisations. The working class was willing to take part in general strike action under the leadership thrown to the fore by the revolution itself. But these leaders had previously committed themselves to a perspective which limits the revolution to achieving the kind of political structure which dominates the Western powers. They chose to pursue this aim by a cross-class alliance stretching from the political left to the far right. At the crucial juncture they found that this ideology, and the consequent lack of real roots among the mass of the working class, led them to suspend further mass mobilisations and strikes. What followed was an accommodation between the Civic Forum leaders and members of the ruling class which allowed that class as a whole, barring only a few symbolic political figures, to maintain their power.

The Christmas revolution in Romania was significantly different from the revolutions in the rest of Eastern Europe. Here the violent overthrow of the Ceausescu regime requires careful analysis. Certainly, the Romanian regime was engulfed by the rising tide which had already swept away nearly all the East

European dictators by the time it overcame Ceausescu. Demonstrators in Romania chanted 'We are the people', copying those in East Germany. But if the mass movement was inspired by and had much in common with the other revolutions of 1989, the state against which it was pitted was significantly different.

Romanian state capitalism was an unreconstructed and unreformed model. External debt had peaked in the early 1980s and been reduced by means of impoverishing the working class. By 1988 food and fuel rationing was in operation. In Bucharest electricity was reduced to one kilowatt per day per household. The Romanian regime had been less undermined by growing economic links with the West. There was some of the gradual demoralisation obvious elsewhere in Eastern Europe, but it found an impenetrable barrier at the core of the state machine in the tightly knit clique of the Ceausescu family circle. Ceausescu had a long history of distancing himself from Russian foreign policy and defence strategy, and had no sympathy with 'reform communism' of any description. This independence from Moscow earned Ceausescu the admiration of Western rulers and resulted in the granting to Romania of 'most favoured nation' trade agreements with the United States. Consequently, when faced with unrest the Romanian regime was far more inclined to take the traditional stance of East European rulers: military repression, the response of Jaruzelski in 1981 not the response of Jaruzelski in 1989.

The first open signs of unrest came late in the East European revolutionary calendar when, on 15 December 1989, pastor Laszlo Tokes of the town of Timisoara was served with a deportation order. Tokes was an ethnic Hungarian, a fact that was significant for two reasons. Firstly, Ceausescu had announced the previous year a 'systemisation' plan for agriculture which involved the demolition of 7,000 of Romania's 12,000 villages, many of them in areas heavily populated with ethnic Hungarians. Secondly, a diplomatic war between Hungary and Romania had been raging ever since Hungary began its reform programme and Ceausescu responded with a series of public hard-line criticisms. A few months before the deportation order was served on Tokes Hungarian TV had broadcast an interview with the pastor.

The day after the deportation order was served, 16 December, several hundred blockaded Tokes' house to stop it being enforced. The following day Ceausescu ranted to his Political Executive Committee about the necessity of opening fire with live ammunition: 'I did not think you would use blanks; that is like a rain shower ... They have got to kill hooligans not just beat them'.[79] The same day the Securitate police opened fire, killing 71 protesters. In the following days the protests grew both in Timisoara and around the country. Troops withdrew from Timisoara on 20 December after workers threatened to blow up the petrochemical plant and 50,000 demonstrated and sacked the CP headquarters. The next day Ceausescu's power collapsed after a staged rally turned into protest demonstrations. The scale of resistance required more than the Securitate to repress it, but the conscript army refused to intervene. The Securitate did fight back, firing on demonstrators. Fighting spread and during the course of the revolution 700 lost their lives. Ceausescu tried, on 22 December, to address a crowd outside the CP central committee building. The crowd broke into the building and Ceausescu had to flee by helicopter from the roof. The army joined the battle against the Securitate as crowds captured the TV and radio stations. Ceausescu and his wife were captured and shot three days later, on Christmas Day 1989.

The newly formed National Salvation Front dominated the provisional government which also included some 'dissidents' and religious leaders. Romania was one of the most repressive states in Eastern Europe. Its dissidents were hardly numerous or well organised enough to be called a movement. There existed no widely recognised programme of reform even among the intelligentsia. There was no KOR, no Charter 77, no *Neues Forum*. The National Salvation Front was therefore not a dissident organisation, but one of the groups competing for power which emerged from the old governing class. Given the vacuum of political leadership such a group was always most likely to be composed of former Stalinists who knew the system and were able to take it over more or less intact. The National Salvation Front's President, Ion Iliescu, was a former leader of Ceausescu's youth organisation from the 1960s; the NSF's second in command was a former Securitate officer and diplomat; another senior NSF figure, Silviu Brucan, was a former editor of the party daily paper and an ambassador. Their 'opposition' to the regime was limited to the fact that they had all quarrelled with Ceausescu in the past.

The background of some of the leading figures of the revolution, and their relationship to the apparatchiks of the NSF, is revealing. Ion Caramitru took part in the invasion of the TV studios. He was a well known actor and head of Romania's National Theatre. Octavian Andronic was a cartoonist and news editor of the party paper *Informatia* before he launched the free paper *Libertatea* during the revolution. Nicolae Dide made film sets before he helped storm the central committee building. Later he became a parliamentary deputy. Petre Roman was a professor at the polytechnic when he pushed into the central committee building with the first wave, making his way to the balcony to famously declare that the people had taken power.

The relationship between these middle class activists and the core of the old regime that survived in the NSF is described by geologist Gelu Voican-Voiculescu. He was involved in fighting around the Intercontinental hotel. He remembers coming to the TV centre the following day: 'I entered the television centre, just like that, someone off the street. By five o'clock I was one of Iliescu's team, and five days later I was deputy Prime Minister. It's almost unimaginable!'[80] Petre Roman found that his brief moment of revolutionary heroism gained him a similarly swift induction to the elite. At a meeting in the central committee building he remembers: 'The former top bureaucrats of the communist system were gathered and I remember how everyone was of the opinion that Iliescu should assume responsibility ... Among the old guard, Brucan, General Militaru and so on, I was the only one to come from the street'.[81] Nicolae Dide also remembers the scene inside the central committee building:

'In the afternoon Iliescu arrived and that was the point where we lost the revolution. We gave it to him not because we wanted to but because we were not good at revolution. For about two hours we had been an alternative government, the first government of the revolution. When Iliescu and company entered the building they spread out ... General Gheorge Voinea appeared. He said, I want to talk to the revolutionary political structure. All of us remained rooted on the spot. None of us had any conception of political structure. At that moment Petre Roman stepped up from behind us, to say, We are here. And he took general Voinea off to meet up with Iliescu and his friends to form the National Salvation Front and then they went off to television. General Voinea was part of it. And that's the way they did it.'[82]

Thus a paradox was created: the most complete revolutionary experience of 1989 resulted in the least fundamental social change of 1989.

The velvet restoration

The experience of revolution in Eastern Europe in 1989 was a mixture of achievement and disappointment. The real achievement of the 1989 revolutions is that they overthrew a dictatorial political system and replaced it with a form of government in which working people have the right to join trade unions which are not state controlled, to express themselves and to organise politically with a freedom they did not have under the Stalinist regimes. The disappointment is that such a powerful international revolutionary movement ended with the installation of a new economic and political order which preserved the wider power of the ruling class, enabling it to renew the process capital accumulation by further exploiting the working population. This disappointment manifested itself, firstly, in the disillusionment of many of the leading figures of the 1989 revolutions and, secondly, in the economic exploitation and political exclusion of the most workers throughout Eastern Europe.

Many of the leading opposition figures now look on the results of the 1989 revolutions with a profound sense of dis-illusionment. Most still regard the limits which they imposed on the revolutionary development as necessary, but they regret the effects of what Adam Michnik calls 'the velvet restoration'. Comparing the mood in Poland in the 1990s with previous periods of restoration Michnik writes,

> 'The mark of restoration is sterility. Sterility of government, lack of ideas, lack of courage, intellectual ossification, cynicism, and opportunism. Revolution had grandeur, hope, and danger. It was an epoch of liberation, risk, great dreams, and lowly passions. The restoration is the calm of a dead pond, a mar-ketplace of petty intrigues, and the ugliness of the bribe.'[83]

It is the conduct of Solidarity itself which Michnik holds mainly responsible for this state of affairs:

> 'One does not have to like the Solidarity revolution anymore ... With that revolution the time of Solidarity and Walesa had passed. The great myth turned into caricature. The movement towards freedom degenerated into noisy arrogance and greed. Soon after its victory it lost its instinct for self-preservation. That is why the post-Solidarity formations lost the last elections ... Let us emphasise this: it is not so much that the postcommunist parties won as the post-Solidarity parties lost.'[84]

But Solidarity lost its imagination and its ability to preserve itself because the aims to which it was limited by its leaders had been achieved − a capitalist economy and a fragile and corrupt par-liamentary system. Only a deeper revolutionary policy could have maintained Solidarity's engagement with its base, but this was precisely the policy that Michnik was instrumental in jettisoning from Solidarity in the 1980s.

Michnik is not alone in his disillusionment. Jens Reich of *Neues Forum* says, 'Strange to say, I am not happy and neither are others around me. Now that the state is decaying, people begin to yearn for some of its more sympathetic traits. In a peculiar way, many of us feel homesick for that inefficient and lazy society which is so remote from the tough and competitive society into which we have been thrust.'[85]

Jan Urban of Czechoslovakia, predicts 'real problems before us' and that 'economic difficulties await us', including 'nationalist frictions' and 'clashes with dissatisfied workers'. But for Urban this is simply the price which has to be endured in order to secure the 'beginnings of parliamentary democracy'.[86]

These are not the disappointments of a few revolutionary dreamers but those of the leaders of the 1989 revolutions. The programme with which they entered those events incorporated an idealised view of parliamentary democracy and a misapprehension that the kind of economic performance demonstrated by America in the 1950s was the norm for any capitalist economy. What they got was the crisis ridden, monopoly dominated, anti-welfare capitalism of the 1990s wedded to barely reformed state machines, glossed by a thin varnish of parliamentary representation.

The extent of the failure of capitalist democracy in Eastern Europe is captured in the economic statistics. In all the major economies of the area, except Poland, real GDP was lower in 1997 than in 1989. In Hungary it was 10 percent lower; in the Czech Republic 11.4 percent lower; in Romania 17.8 percent; and in Russia there was a drop of over 40 percent. Real wages in the same economies dropped by between 8 and 54 percent between 1989 and 1995. Full employment gave way to unemployment of over 10 percent in most of the economies, excepting Russia (3.4 percent), Romania (6.3 percent) and the Czech Republic (3.1 percent). Those suffering low income have risen to between 20 and 60 percent of the population across the region.[87] As the *Financial Times*' Philip Stephens conceded,

'The common assumption was, and still is, that the defeat of communism marked the triumph of democracy. In fact, the victor was capitalism ... the EU's contribution to the creation of a democratic Russia has amounted to a few billion euros and the despatch of a handful of economists from the Chicago school. And to Moscow's former satellite states, the Union has offered plentiful promises and precious little else.'[88]

The mass unemployment, the destruction of welfare rights, the speed-up and intensification of the work process is what lies beneath the disappointment of the revolutionaries. Two major social forces have emerged to fill the vacuum, reformism and nationalism. National rivalry made two countries of Czechoslovakia and ignited internal conflict across the former Eastern bloc, but by far the most catastrophic effect of the 1989 nationalist revival has been the break up of Yugoslavia.

The destruction of Yugoslavia was a child of the revolutions of 1989. Like Romania, there was an enormous upsurge of class struggle inspired by the other East European revolutions. And the former Communist ruling class met this challenge by playing the nationalist card, notably in Kosovo. This process was enormously accelerated by the acts of the western powers who were keen to dismember the country. Germany led the way, flushed by its unexpectedly easy victory in shaping the unification of the country, it encouraged the independence of wealthy Slovenia. But at every step of the way in the 1990s all the major powers have concentrated their efforts in the continued dismemberment of the Balkans, finally provoking in 1999 the first war involving the main imperial powers on European soil since 1945.

Thus the disillusionment of the revolutionaries of 1989 was qualitatively different from that which afflicted their forebears. The Levellers, the Sons of Liberty and Babeuf were disappointed because their programmes could not be realised. The Bolsheviks' programme was simply defeated by counter-revolution. But the democratic revolutionaries of 1989 were disappointed because their programmes *were* realised. The fault lay in the programme, not in the limits of the objective situation or the power of the forces opposing them.

The pattern of revolution after 1989

The decade that followed the velvet revolutions saw two other great transformations in long-standing tyrannies. South Africa and Indonesia were both different from the East European societies and different from one another. Yet both the economic structure of these societies and the course of the revolutionary movements also had important similarities with the East European experience. Here I give a brief outline of the similarities although I have examined these revolutions in detail elsewhere.[89]

South Africa, like the Eastern Bloc, industrialised by a process of strong state direction and in relative isolation from the world economy. South African apartheid, like the Eastern bloc, faced its terminal crisis because it was unable to transform this method of capital accumulation when new realities faced it in the 1970s and 1980s. And the South African ruling class, like their East European counter-parts, tried to meet the opposition movement with a strategy of partial reform and negotiation.

Indonesian society in the 1950s and 1960s, the two decades after independence from the Dutch, was dominated by a state bureaucracy which became the leading force in investment and corporate ownership. No great landed families existed as they had done in Europe and Latin America. Consequently the state bureaucracy which led the industrialisation process was not subordinated to the same degree to a pre-existing conservative oligarchy. The middle classes, the other crucial contending class force in earlier transitions to capitalism, were also weak. This small layer of professionals and intellectuals were allied to a wider group which depended almost entirely on the state bureaucracy for their employment. This state machine and its huge military industrial complex increasingly dominated Indonesian society from independence under Sukarno, through Suharto's bloody coup in 1965, until the 1980s.

Over this period the international economic climate changed dramatically and so did the economic role of the state. As the world economy grew in the post-war period the Indonesian state adopted the autarkic, isolationist model of development common to the Stalinist states and many post-colonial third world regimes in the 1950s and 1960s. As late as the early 1980s the economy was more highly regulated and controlled than at any time since the 1930s.

In both South Africa and Indonesia the exhaustion of the state-led model of economic development in the face of an expanding world market led to a social crisis. Both regimes faced the rise of mass opposition, although the movement in South Africa was altogether more long-lasting and profound than the student-led opposition that confronted the Indonesian state.

The South African opposition was led by the African National Congress, born in 1912 as a predominantly middle class led organisation focused on constitutional change. 'The ANC ... drew its leadership largely from the small urban elite – teachers, priests, lawyers and doctors. Its policy was termed "moderate" – removal of discrimination, constitutional means of change, the gradual extension of a qualified franchise'.[90] The relationship with the South African Communist Party and the ascension to the ANC leadership of Nelson Mandela, Oliver Tambo and Walter Sisulu radicalised the organisation in the late 1940s. In 1955 the ANC adopted the Freedom Charter, the document demanding a number of democratic and civil rights' reforms. It remained the foundation of ANC politics until the victory over apartheid in the early 1990s.

The guiding principle of the Freedom Charter, the ANC's general strategy, and the politics of the Communist Party which informed both, was the stages theory of revolution. The principle argument of this approach was that South African society is a 'colonialism of a special type' in which the colonial ruling class resided within the borders of the colony. The first stage of the revolution would a democratic anti-colonial struggle and only after this struggle was complete would it be possible fight for socialism. In the course of defending the Freedom Charter in 1956 Nelson Mandela put it like this:

> 'The Charter does not contemplate economic and political changes. Its declaration 'The People shall govern' visualises the transfer of power not to any single social class but to all the people of the country, be they workers, peasants, professionals, or petty bourgeoisie.'[91]

As Mandela makes clear, the adoption of the stages theory not only precluded a struggle for socialism, but also effectively submerged specifically working class activity in an all-class 'popular front'. Furthermore, the aim such an 'anti-colonial' movement was to rid the country of apartheid, but not to smash the capitalist state. As Ronnie Kasrils, leader of the ANC's armed wing, explained in 1990:

> 'There are revolutionary movements which, at their foundation, addressed the question of seizing state power. These immediately recognised and analysed the use of state power and the need to develop a force to seize state power. With us that was not the ethos.'[92]

The leaders of the Indonesian revolution arrived at a similarly self-limiting perspective by a different route. The Communist component of the movement was much weaker because Suharto's rise to power had rested on the annihilation of the CP. So the rise of a newly confident middle class still tied to the state in many ways but chaffing against the limits of the old Suharto power structure became critical in Indonesia.

This layer of the middle class and their allies in the ruling class were certainly not the moving force behind the overthrow of Suharto. But once that had been achieved by other forces their political representatives, whether in the elite already or figures who had been excluded from it during previous dynastic quarrels, moved to ensure that their own agenda dominated the movement. They, like a previous generation of middle class activists in the deflected permanent revolutions discussed earlier, could only act because of the space created by the actions of other classes. And, unlike their forbears, the Communist Party had not been their political organisation nor revolutionary nationalism their ideology. For this generation the NGO's and academic forums provided much of the organisation and the 'western values' of democratic civil society and free market economics provided the ideology.

In South Africa, as in Eastern Europe, the political strategy of the leaders of the movement was crucial in shaping the outcome. The ANC's stages theory of revolution allowed it to negotiate a settlement with capital. In 1987 the ANC's national executive unequivocally stated:

> 'Once more we would like to affirm that the ANC and the masses of our people as a whole are ready and willing to enter into genuine negotiations provided they are aimed at the transformation of our country into a united and non-racial democracy. **This, and only this, should be the objective of any negotiating process**.'[93]

The path to the eventual majority rule settlement was still the subject of great conflict between the mass movement and the regime. But this conflict was no longer over whether or not there would be a social revolution in which capitalist relations would be challenged. Now the conflict was reduced to one in which the contending parties fought to decide who would have how much power inside a new parliamentary capitalist system. The regime was quite willing to use the violence of the security forces, and to stir up reactionary forces like Inkatha, to force the ANC into accepting a more disadvantageous settlement than it wanted. The ANC for its part realised that it could not operate effectively without mass mobilisation as a counter-weight to the violence of the state. But on both sides it was now understood that these forces were now adjuncts to the negotiations.

Just 12 weeks after the fall of the Berlin Wall, the government ban on ANC and the SACP was lifted. This, and the freeing of

Nelson Mandela nine weeks later, was a watershed. The regime could not go back to full-blooded apartheid and the ANC would not go forward to a struggle against capitalism. Even those who were critical of the slow pace and inadequate gains made in the negotiations, like Ronnie Kasrils, saw the mass movement as a tool which could create a 'Leipzig option' in which the government 'is propelled out the exit gate'. That is, the democratic revolution was attained by faster, 'bottom-up' methods.

The Indonesian revolution provides a weaker version of these developments. In May 1998 the Suharto dictatorship was broken by a mass student movement which coincided with, and gave political direction to, an uprising of the urban poor. The student demonstrations, the occupation of the parliament building and the urban riots made it plain that if Suharto did not go then the entire economic system, as well as the existing political system, stood under threat. The elite reacted to the economic crisis under pressure from below – and so began a process of governmental transformation.

The political leadership of the movement became critical when, after the overthrow of Suharto, demonstrations revived on an even grander scale at the November 1998 meeting of the People's Consultative Assembly (MPR). The November demonstrations failed to unseat the government and replace it with a 'proper' provisional government as many of the organisers hoped it would. But the regime's attempt to break the opposition movement in a 'Tiananmen-style' crackdown also failed. The killing of demonstrators outraged students, workers and the urban poor but did not break the movement. The armed forces were weakened by internal divisions as some army units either sided with the demonstrators or remained neutral, including elements of the elite marine units.

All these factors meant that the Habibie, Suharto's successor, already unstable, was propelled down the road of reform. Elections, which there had been plans to delay, were called. Early in 1999 a pledge was given that a referendum would be granted on autonomy for East Timor. East Timorese and other political dissidents began to be released from jail.

The People's Democratic Party (PRD), the furthest left on the Indonesian political spectrum was legalised and allowed to stand in elections, although its leading figures remained behind bars. All these reforms were urged on by the US, backed-up by Australia. As in South Africa, a variety of NGOs, often with links to the opposition, had been urging on the rapid transition to capitalist democracy.

But the regime did not just trust the outcome of the elections to pro-democratic sentiment. It reshaped the armed forces, giving the police a separate structure it did not have before. And it continued to feed religious and ethnic conflict. The aim was not to totally suppress the movement in the Suharto manner, but to keep it within the bounds of the election process and so destroy the possibility of a revolutionary alternative arising among the mass of the population, a fear rife in the ruling circles at the start of 1999.

The Indonesian bourgeoisie, including its liberal wing, was in an analogous position to the bourgeoisie that Marx described in 1848. It was 'grumbling at those above, trembling at those below'. The liberal leaders, like Sukarno's daughter Megawati and Islamic leader Amien Rais were, like their German precursors, 'revolutionary in relation to the conservatives and conservative in relation to the revolutionaries, mistrustful of their own slogans, which were phrases instead of ideas, intimidated by the ... revolution yet exploiting it; with no energy in any respect, plagiaristic in every respect'.[94]

Megawati ultimately emerged victorious because the Indonesian student movement and the left were caught off-guard by these developments. The central theoretical weakness of the Indonesian left was its view that conditions were not right for socialist transformation of society and, therefore, that the left should limit itself to the demand for a democratic republic.

The South African and Indonesian examples are by no means the only cases where this pattern of revolutionary development has occurred. In a precursor to these events, in Latin America the IMF and World Bank imposed austerity programmes of the 1980s 'led to economic contraction, de-industrialization, savage reduction in wages and declining living standards, and popular revolt *everywhere*.'[95] Moreover, 'in a cruel twist of history ... the debt crisis and the structural adjustment coincide with Latin America's return to (more or less) democratic rule ... '[96]

The transition to democracy in Latin America also had, in some cases, the backing of the US and the other imperial powers. This confronted the left with difficult strategic choices. 'It is certainly interesting that intellectuals from the traditional Marxist-Leninist left joined the grassroots movements in a struggle for electoral democracy, in what appears to be a lasting reversal of traditional priorities'.[97] These developments have meant that the left has had to rethink its ideas on the relationship between democracy and revolution. But so far much of what has resulted is 'confusion and disarray'.

Nowhere has this been more evident than in Brazil where the rise of the Workers Party and the election of Luiz Inacio Lula da Silva as President raised the hopes of the left in Latin America and across the globe. But the eventual outcome of this experiment shows all the dangers that arise for the left in the 'transition to democracy'. Lula's rule is a neo-liberal fist in a social democratic glove.

Quite how secure international capital feels with the Brazilian government was apparent in when *The Economist* interviewed Lula. Lula boasts that few 'countries have achieved what we have: fiscal responsibility and a strong social policy ... Never in the economic history of Brazil have we had the solid fundamentals we have now.' With his stress on 'strong investment in education and training' and 'tax relief to encourage new investment' Lula's rhetoric is interchangeable with that of neo-liberal social democracy the world over. Even *The Economist* cannot resist a sardonic smirk – 'solid fundamentals are nor what the world expected from Lula' – as it praises his abandonment of the Zero Poverty scheme. Moreover the same pragmatic adaptation to prevailing orthodoxy seems to be influencing foreign policy. Lula says of the threats against the Chavez government in Venezuela: 'Chavez is convinced that the coup attempt against him was organized to benefit American interests. President Bush doesn't accept that. This will be resolved only if they talk.'[98]

Similar disarray can be seen in the left's response to the second wave of velvet revolutions in the former Eastern bloc beginning with the overthrow of Slobodan Milosevic in Serbia in 2000 and following on through the fall of Edward Shevardnadze in Georgia in 2003, the Orange revolution in Ukraine in 2004 and Askar Akayev's demise in Kyrgyzstan in 2005. These revolutions run across a very wide-spectrum of experience – from genuine examples of people power to virtually unalloyed elite transition aided by the US, as Dragan Plavsic's analysis clearly shows.[99]

The Serbian revolution was 'caught between two epochs'. It both contained a genuine element of mass mobilization and also a 'concerted attempt by the Clinton administration to trigger Milosevic's removal by means of a "velvet revolution".'[100] The Serbian revolution could only succeed because of the depth and intensity of the popular mobilization, most importantly by the striking miners. But the ultimate outcome was seen as a success for Washington's strategy of 'electoral interventionism', exploiting rigged elections in order to precipitate regime change.

In Georgia the incumbent President was familiar to the US from perestroika days, Mikhail Gorbachev's foreign secretary, Edward Shavardnadze. But the level of popular mobilization against Shevardnadze obliged the US to switch horses in midstream. As Boris Kagarlitsky explains,

> 'As soon as Washington realises that popular dissent is rising in a country and that regime change is imminent, it immediately begins to seek out new partners among the opposition ... The money invested in the opposition by various (non-governmental organizations) is a sort of insurance policy, ensuring that regime change will not result in a change of course, and that if change is inevitable, it will not be radical.'[101]

The Ukraine's Orange revolution certainly drew enthusiastic crowds into Kiev's Independence Square, but those crowds were carefully controlled by Viktor Yushchenko, once out-going president Kuchma's prime minister. The US anticipated electoral fraud by Yushchenko's rival and channelled funds and other assistance to him for two years before the election. Consequently, Ukraine marks 'the low-point of the "democratic" wave ... because it also marks the high-point of ruling class and imperialist manipulation of people power.'[102]

Krygyzstan's revolution escaped the controlled environment of Ukraine. Despite intense interest by both Moscow and Washington in the fate of the country, events in Krygyzstan ran beyond the imperial writ. In Osh and Jalalabad a mass uprising and people's congresses demand the end of the old government. The revolt spread to the capital and drove Akayev from power. And even after the revolution subsided and many of the old guard returned to governmental office, landless squatters were still insisting that 'it was their revolution and ... they have a right to take land after years of requests went unanswered.'

The outstanding fact from this entire range of international experience is that the pre-existing theoretical understanding and organizational capacity of the left are critical to the outcome of modern revolutionary crises.

Results and prospects

The pattern of revolution described here is not an historical absolute. It is not the case that the transition from authoritarian rule to capitalist democracy is in some way the inevitable outcome of modern economic trends. China, to name only the most populous country on earth, is set on a course of 'totalitarian market capitalism'. The Tiananmen Square massacre reminds us all that the price paid for adopting a 'democratic revolution' strategy can be a great deal higher than a velvet restoration.

The pattern of revolution in the last ten years is also distinct from developments in the parliamentary democracies of the West. Most of the revolutions examined above took place in collapsing dictatorships. In these cases the reformist and centrist currents necessarily emerge as interior to the revolutionary camp. This was true of the Mensheviks, the ANC, KOR and the PRD.

In the West reformism is already organisationally and politically distinct and feels no need to adopt a revolutionary stance in the face of an authoritarian regime. Here, consequently, the undermining of reformism involves a longer process utilising united front tactics to win layers of workers away from established labour party type politics.

But, after all the qualifications have been duly noted, the patterns described in this chapter are now common enough to justify close examination. And these experiences become doubly important when the major imperialist powers adopt the model of the velvet revolution as one of their chosen tools for intervention around the globe. If these international elites batten on to the indigenous pro-capitalist 'democratic' forces in order to better reshape politics in their favour then there is an even greater need for the left to clearly understand the process of change the better to shape it to the needs of working people.

In the English, American and French revolutions the level of industrial development and the restricted size, organisation and consciousness of the working class prevented any socialist solution emerging within the revolutionary camp. But for the revolutions in Eastern Europe, South Africa, Indonesia and Latin America this is not the case. These are all industrialised societies in which the ruling class is a capitalist class and the working class is not only a substantial proportion of the population but also possess a considerable history of self-organisation and a developed class consciousness.

The revolutionary crises which have occurred in these societies have been crises of capital accumulation. A particular form of state-led capital accumulation which was laid down in the post-war period has proven an inadequate vessel for the renewed conditions of world-wide capital accumulation which have emerged in the period since the end of the long boom in the late 1970s. In each case, authoritarian regimes previously thought impervious to revolt from below were brought to the ground.

Once the rebellion was underway a process of polarisation within the revolutionary camp took place, much as it had done in all the revolutionary situations analysed in this account – 1649, 1776, 1789, 1848 and 1917. What determined the eventual outcome in all these cases was the way in which the revolutionary leadership interacted with the wider class forces of which they were a part. What separates the early bourgeois revolutions from the later revolutions is that the organisation of the revolutionaries in the first case largely emerged only in the course of events. With KOR in Poland, the SACP in South Africa and the PRD in Indonesia the fact that such organisations existed and influenced even quite small numbers *before* the outbreak of large scale struggles allowed them to varying degrees to become the political beneficiaries of those struggles.

Yet even those organisations with an orientation on rank and file workers were unable to overcome the problems with which they were confronted by the development of the revolution. In these cases there was a political failure to correctly apprehend the importance of the debate over the socialist revolution and the democratic revolution. KOR had an orientation on the working class and so did the activists who built the independent unions in South Africa in the early 1980s. And many of the best activists in the PRD and the student movement in Indonesia also acknowledged the importance of organising workers. But the key activists in KOR came to see Solidarity as the engine of a democratic revolution and did not maintain their earlier commitment either to the goal of a socialist revolution or to building a revolutionary party. In South Africa a syndicalist orientation on rank and file workers could provide no adequate alternative to the political strategy offered by the SACP – and so eventually became absorbed by it.

This points to the high premium to be placed on theoretical clarity and the determination to give this adequate organizational form. In 1848 Marx insisted that workers stay one step ahead of the liberal opposition and that their demands, while 'democratic', should have a specific class content which would set the workers at odds with the liberal democrats. For Marx this approach to the tactics and slogans of the day was part of a wider strategic understanding that a socialist revolution was the goal to which the movement was headed. Marx and Engels understood that class polarisation would divide the democratic camp. Engels noted that all revolutions begin with a cross-class 'democratic unity' against the old order. But, as the revolution develops, the initial phase, the 'revolution of the flowers', gives way to political divisions within the revolutionary camp based on underlying class differences. This has been the case in all previous revolutions, including the very first bourgeois revolutions. But in all the revolutions after 1848 there was the potential for this class differentiation to develop to the point where workers created their own distinctive organs of power: workers' councils.

Conclusion

The democratic revolution is one of the predominant forms of social change in the modern world. Revolutions always take place at the intersection of the economic and the political, the imperial and national lines of determination. Today the outcome of revolutions is decided by a huge contest between, on one side, the imperial powers and the national ruling classes and, on the other, the working class, urban poor, agricultural labourers and peasants. Who wins, and how much they win, is decided to a significant degree by the organizational and political capacities of the left.

Where the left is weak the imperial powers and their local accomplices are able to impose their own solution on an emerging social crisis. There are occasions when these 'managed revolutions' would be farcical if they were not tragic. The low point so far is the borrowed iconography of the East European revolutions that the US army deployed on the day in 2003 when Saddam's statue was pulled down in Baghdad. But in other cases revolution seems to be now reduced to a Washington scripted formula: find big central square, set up a public address system, get popular rock combo, draw a crowd and, hey presto, a seamless elite transition is accomplished.

All this simply underlines the fact that the outcome of revolutions depends on how clearly the left see the nature of the system they are opposing and how effectively they organize the forces on their own side to confront their opponents. It is to these issues that we turn in the final two chapters of the book.

6 War and ideology

The new imperialism is a product of the 'neo-liberal' period of capital accumulation beginning in the late 1970s fused with the reordering of the state system that began with the end of the Cold War in 1989. This fusion has produced a particular form of popular resistance which combines protest at the effects of globalisation with a movement against war. This is the modern form taken by the struggle between nation-states, corporate competition and the resistance of working class and poor – our three titans discussed first in the introduction.

The precursors of such struggles can be seen in earlier incarnations: from the inter-imperialist rivalry of the hey-day of the European empires, through the First World War and the revolutions in Russia and Germany which ultimately brought that conflict to a close, to the great wave of anti-colonial struggles during the Cold War. But just as it is important to see the continuities between each of these forms of imperialism, it is also important to see what differentiates them. It is in this debate that the real nature of the new imperialism can be further delineated.

On the political right the new era has given rise to a series of justifications for imperialism rarely heard since the days of European colonialism. The defining ideological counter-position of the Cold War was 'democracy' versus 'communism'. With the demise of 'communism' the argument from the right has reverted to an older polarity – 'democracy' versus 'barbarism'.

The civilising mission of the major powers is to bring democracy where the indigenous people are too benighted or religiously blind to achieve it for themselves. In this chapter these arguments are examined.

On the political left there have also been some who have argued that the new form of empire is so different from what went before that both the old methods of analysis and resistance are of little use. These approaches commonly underestimate the contradictions inherent in the relationship between competing units of capital and nation-states, thus attributing greater strengths to the system than it actually possesses. Or they tend to underestimate the potential power of those who oppose the modern imperial system.

In what follows, and in the next chapter, I examine some of the most commonly heard arguments from both the right and the left about the nature of the new imperial system and the resistance to it.

A war for democracy?

The Cold War staple of 'democracy versus communism' was too good to be relinquished just because communism had been defeated. No sooner had the Berlin Wall fallen than right wing commentators were insisting that parliamentary democracy on the western model was now the only viable form of political organisation. The favoured polarity now became 'democracy versus dictatorship'. 'New Hitlers', variously Slobodan Milosevic, Saddam Hussein, or Syria's Bashar Assad, would have to embrace democracy or face the consequences.

This argument has been most persistently and volubly advanced by the political right but on each occasion some previously left wing figures have also accepted that the nature of the regime in question was so dastardly, the capacities of its people so limited, that recourse to armed intervention by the major powers in order to impose democracy was justified. Academic Fred Halliday and journalists Christopher Hitchens, Nick Cohen, David Aaronvitch and Johann Hari have all taken this path in response to the first Gulf War, the Balkan and Afghan wars or the invasion of Iraq.

The democracy argument can only be sustained if one believes (i) that the major powers are genuinely in the business of pursuing a global democratic agenda, (ii) that democracy can be imposed at the point of a gun and (iii) that the people of the country concerned are not capable of achieving democracy themselves.

Assessing the major powers' commitment to democracy requires an examination both of democracy in the imperial countries themselves and of their record of supporting democracy abroad. It is a remarkable fact that the democratic rhetoric of the leaders of the major powers has reached a new pitch just at the time when the health of democracy in their own countries is probably worse than it has been at any point since the inter-war years. Voter turn-out in the US has always been low but even in countries where it has historically been much higher it is now in decline. In Britain the turn-out at the last two general elections has been the lowest since universal suffrage was introduced. Tony Blair's third successive term in government was achieved with the support of just 36 percent of those that voted and a mere 22 percent of those eligible to vote. Indeed Tony Blair won the 2005 election with less support than Neil Kinnock lost elections in the 1980s. Noam Chomsky's description of US politics as 'a totalitarian system with two factions' famously underlines the limited choices facing voters in the America. And it is of course a truism that it is impossible to become US President without being a millionaire, or having the support of millionaires.

The tightly drawn limits of democracy in the US are now increasingly being reproduced in other countries as all the establishment parties crowd into a 'middle ground' defined by neo-liberal economics and neo-conservative foreign policies. The growth of corporate power, and especially the wave of privatisation that has swept the industrialised countries in the last 25 years, is itself a major blow to democracy since it takes control over very large parts of social life out of the hands of elected politicians and places it in the hands of unelected corporation executives. To take but one example: 'freedom of speech' is the watchword of every western politician out to buttress pro-war sentiment, but what can this mean in their own societies when a single media mogul like Rupert Murdoch controls a third of the press? What can it mean when a media mogul of such power is also the prime minister, as was Italy's Silvio Berlusconi?

Moreover, it is commonly acknowledged that the 'security state' that has grown up since 9/11 has meant a significant erosion of civil liberties. The Patriot Act in the US and similar anti-terror laws in Britain have diminished the very freedoms which our governments insist make us superior to other nations.

None of this is meant to diminish the real difference between the degree of political freedom in parliamentary democracies and that in authoritarian regimes. The point being made here is a different one: those governments most insistent on propagating the idea that they are fighting for other people's freedom are precisely the same governments that are presiding over the erosion of freedom in their own countries. Conversely, those forces in the anti-war movement and on the left that have most resisted the 'wars for democracy' have been in the forefront of defending democracy and civil liberties in their own countries. So this argument speaks to the intention and motivation of the 'pro-war democrats'. It questions whether those who move so quickly to limit freedom at home can really be as enthusiastic as they claim about freedom abroad.

But even if we were to grant that the motivation is pure, can the chosen means deliver the declared goal? Is it possible to deliver democracy at gun-point? The balance of historical experience suggests that it is not. Modern democracy is, if anything, the product of revolution, revolutionary war, or anti-colonial uprising. It is rarely the product of military intervention by the major powers. The foundations of the modern democratic states of Europe and North America were laid by the English revolution of the 17th century and the American and

French revolutions of the 18th century, a process more fully examined in the chapter on 'Their democracy and ours'. This model was established as the aspiration of the European continent in the 1848 revolutions. In our times great swathes of humanity have achieved parliamentary regimes in Portugal, Iran, the Philippines, South Africa, Eastern Europe and Indonesia by the exercise of 'people power'. Even where the transition from authoritarianism to parliamentary democracy has not involved great popular mobilisation, as in the post-fascist Spain, the process has certainly had nothing to do with military intervention by the major powers.

Some neo-conservative commentators point to the Second World War as a counter-example. Germany and Japan, it is argued, had democracy imposed by invasion. But a little thought raises some difficulties with these examples. Germany was actually partitioned by the allies at the end of the war. Democracy was certainly not restored in East Germany. Its population continued to languish under an authoritarian regime until they took matters into their own hands in 1989. And in West Germany US backed unions and a kind of 'siege democracy' was installed with the express aim, as in post-war Italy, of excluding the left from power. In Japan the aim of war was certainly not to impose democracy. The US was perfectly happy to allow the Japanese Emperor to continue ruling undisturbed until the attack of Pearl Harbor. A war and two nuclear bombs later the aim was to impose a docile regime under US economic and military tutelage. The Japanese Emperor still sits on his throne. Just as in post-war Iraq today, the aim was to construct a pro-western social structure open to western economic penetration with only such democratic rights as are compatible with this fundamental goal. More frequently the historical record shows that democratic rights, at least outside the core of the system, have not been compatible with this goal.

Indeed the intervention of the major powers has been most frequently used to try and stifle democracy and anti-colonial movements. One only has to think of the British in India, the British, French and Israeli aborted Suez invasion, the CIA coup that installed the Shah of Iran, the Vietnam War, British support for the white settler regime in Zimbabwe, US support for South African apartheid, General Pinochet's coup against the democratically elected government of Salvador Allende in Chile, and the long US semi-covert war against the Sandinistas in Nicaragua, to make only a small selection from a long list. And today US and British support for dictators and authoritarian regimes continues unabated. President Mubarak enjoys lavish US military and economic support despite the rigged elections and torture routinely practised in Egypt. Oil ensures that the brutal House of Saud is still assiduously courted by the US and other western powers. The greatest dictatorship in the world in China is mildly rebuked and enthusiastically embraced as a trading partner because introducing the market is more important to the West than introducing freedom. General Musharaff's dictatorship in Pakistan was instantly transformed from 'rogue state' to 'ally in the war against terror' because of its mercenary role in the Afghan war. North Korea is respectfully negotiated with, not because it lacks weapons of mass destruction but precisely because it possesses them, a lesson not lost on other states threatened by the US.

Above all, the catastrophic failure of the invasion of Iraq proves that democracy cannot be delivered by cruise missile. The speed with which armed resistance to US and British occupation grew, its intensity and longevity are all testimony to the malevolent naiveté with which the planners of post-war Iraq approached their task. The impasse into which the occupation descended has led the occupiers into a 'democratic' strategy which is dividing Iraq on communalist lines and risks fragmenting it geographically. Moreover the group which has most benefited from this divide and rule strategy is the Shia sympathetic to Iran. So the fruit of the occupation has turned out to be political and economic chaos in Iraq and, internationally, the possibility of Iran emerging as the most influential power in the region.

The record in Afghanistan is hardly more encouraging. Five years after the invasion more troops are being committed in order to suppress areas of the country where, we are now told, 'the Taliban were never defeated'. Opium production increased exponentially after the invasion and special military operations are now mounted to destroy the crop. The democratic institutions of the new Afghanistan are stuffed with warlords and the head of state, Ahmed Karzai, while welcome at table in Downing Street and in the White House, is little more than the 'King of Kabul' in his own country, unable to move outside the capital without US protection.

More generally, the US government are now becoming more cautious about 'democratising' the Middle East since elections in Iraq, Iran and for the Palestinian Authority have not produced the results for which they wished. As a leader in the *Financial Times* noted,

> 'The Bush administration has dropped its Panglossian habit of banking each and every vote or protest in the region as a triumph for its strategy and started noticing that these are mostly won or led by Islamists inimical to its world-view: the Hamas victory; the Islamist landslide in Iraq; the stunning wins of the Muslim Brotherhood in Egypt; Hizbollah's entry into the Lebanese cabinet.'[1]

So if the motivations and the experience of the democratic warriors speak against occupation as an effective method of spreading democracy, what of the third argument: we have to act because the people of the country have no capacity to end dictatorship by their own efforts?

This is a particularly mendacious argument in at least two of the cases of post-Cold War conflict. In Iraq, in the wake of Saddam Hussein's expulsion from Kuwait, there was a popular rising against the regime. Its failure is entirely due to the US decision to stick with the devil they knew, Saddam, and allow him to crush the rebellion. So any later incapacity on the part of the Iraqi people is a product of US policy not the innate weakness of the Iraqi people. And even if Pentagon planners believed their own arguments about the lack of capacity that Iraqis might have to challenge an unpopular regime before they invaded Iraq they can surely not still sustain such beliefs now they have experienced the resistance to their own occupation. And in Serbia, of course, it was not the NATO war over Kosovo that toppled Slobodan Milosevic but an insurrection which crucially involved mass action by miners. More generally this theory has less to recommend it than in practically any other era since the 19th century. When, in living memory, half the European continent, South Africa and Indonesia have defeated dictatorship by means of popular mass mobilisation and revolution it would seem positively perverse to advance a theory resting on the incapacity of ordinary people to change the world around them.

The timescale of internal revolt may not suit foreign powers but it is the only sure way of achieving real and sustainable democratic change. This is not the same as saying that all such revolts are successful. But it is to say that only their success can bring such change. War can sometimes be a catalyst for such revolutions and such revolutions can sometimes encompass wars of liberation, as did the American Revolution. Invasion by the major powers is no substitute for this method. The reason, ultimately, is straightforward: those who do the liberating tend to do the ruling afterwards. Being liberated by the 82nd Airborne tends to leave you in their hands at the end of the day. When a people liberate themselves it is at least up to the further course of events in that revolution to decide which part of the people get to decide the fate of the society.

A clash of civilisations?

The West's battle with Islam is now a standard justification for the advocates of military intervention in the Middle East and beyond. Samuel Huntington's *The Clash of Civilisations* argues that since the end of the Cold War,

> 'The overwhelming majority of faultline conflicts ... have taken place along the boundary looping across Eurasia and Africa that separates Muslims from non-Muslims. While at

the macro or global level of world politics the primary
clash of civilisations is between the West and the rest, at
the micro or local level it is between Islam and the
others . . .

Wherever one looks along the perimeter of Islam,
Muslims have problems living peaceably with their neighbours. The question naturally arises whether this pattern of
late-twentieth-century conflict between Muslim and non-
Muslim groups is equally true of relations between groups
from other civilisations. In fact, it is not. . . .

In the 1990s Muslims were engaged in more intragroup
violence than were non-Muslims, and two-thirds to three-
quarters of intercivilisational wars were between Muslims
and non-Muslims. Islam's borders **are** bloody, and so are
its innards.'[2]

This, like the 'democratic' justification for war, is not a view
confined to the neo-conservative right. Plenty on the left see
Islam as a threat globally and domestically. They dislike religious
thought in general and conservative, as they see it, religious
doctrine in particular. They reject, for good reason, terrorist
methods and associate these with Islam. They point out, accurately, that in the Indian sub-continent and in the Middle East,
some Islamic currents have been or are the declared and bitter
enemies of the left. But they draw from these observations the
conclusion that Islam is in general an enemy of the left either
worse than or equal to the local and international ruling classes.
It follows, of course, that the left cannot ally itself with any
Islamic current.[3]

The first problem with this approach is that it ignores the
redefinition of Islam that the imperial powers have accomplished since the attack on the World Trade Center. Since that
time opposition to Islam has become one of the main justifying
ideologies of war. This is not to say, of course, that opposition
to Islam is the *explanation* for war. That lies in the economic and
geopolitical interests of the major powers. But opposition to
Islam has become the mobilising chauvinism of the new

imperialism. The racism inherent in the new colonial era expresses itself most forcibly as Islamophobia. Globally, Islam is overwhelmingly the religion of the poor in the industrialised world and of poor countries in the rest of the world. Muslims are overwhelmingly on the receiving end of the new imperialism, the victims of an ideological offensive unleashed by the 'war on terror'. This at least should give many on the left pause for thought before joining in with the establishment demonisation of Muslims.

Of course not all Muslims are poor and not all Muslims are victims of imperialism let alone opponents of imperialism. But in order to make such vital political distinctions much of the left will have to stop assuming that all Islamic political currents are the same. Islam is politically heterogeneous. It includes everything from the Wahabbism of the Saudi Royal Family, through Hamas and Hezbollah, to the poor backstreet mosque in a working class suburb of a north European city.

Let's examine this issue in more detail by first looking at the situation of Muslims in the industrialised countries. Even in the West there are certainly some rich and some white Muslims. But in their vast majority Muslims in the West are poor and Asian or African. As immigrants or the sons and daughters of immigrants they were already discriminated against long before the ideological offensive that followed 9/11 redefined their religion as a racial category. Since that time 'anti-terror laws' have systematically targeted these communities, physical attacks have increased, mosques have been attacked and the far right, once obsessed with Afro-Caribbean communities, have specifically focussed their propaganda on Muslims. The international reaction both to the French government's ban on the wearing of political and religious symbols in schools, the 'hijab ban', and to the reprinting throughout the press in mainland Europe of the anti-Islamic Danish cartoons in early 2006, shows how differently the 'enlightenment left' treat this form of discrimination. One only has to imagine, for instance, that the Danish cartoons had been of the Reverend Jesse Jackson as a golliwog or of a hook-nosed Jew counting money to realise that far from being reprinted by the liberal press the length and breadth of continental Europe they would have been, rightly, met with outrage at their racist content.

The 'enlightenment left' conducts its argument under the banner of secular opposition to religion. Islam is, they say, a religious belief and not a racial category. Yet it is obvious that in the West this religious definition is applied only to people who are not white. The 'enlightenment left' proudly displays the very weakness of enlightenment thought that Marxists have long pointed out: its rationalism is incapable of seeing beyond the conflict of ideas to examine the social context in which they are used and therefore to understand their real meaning.

The same inability to see the material forces behind religious abstractions is present in the 'enlightenment left' view of international politics. Just ask yourself this simple question: are any of the top ten economically and militarily most powerful states in the world run by 'Islamic' governments or do they contain large Muslim populations? In general it is true to say that Islam is the religion of poorer, weaker states subject to the bullying of richer, more powerful states. This simple fact makes a mockery of Samuel Huntington's assertion that

> 'Muslim states have a higher propensity to resort to violence in international crises ... While Muslim states resorted to violence in 53.5 percent of their crises, violence was used by the United Kingdom in only 11.5 percent, by the US in 17.9 percent, and by the Soviet Union in 28.5 percent of the crises in which they were involved.'[4]

Even if these statistics were accurate, might they not reflect the fact that superpowers and their allies use their overwhelming economic strength and the threat of their overwhelming military might to get their own way without recourse to the actual use of force? Perhaps the *Financial Times* was closer to the truth when it reported that 'in the current phase of globalisation, it hurts to be distant, it hurts to be poor and it hurts to be Islamic.'[5]

But within this over-arching reality Islamic governments and ruling classes differ greatly in their attitude to the imperial powers. This varies from being the willing accomplices of imperialism – for the most part the stance of the House of Saud – to being inconsistent opponents of imperialism – the stance of Iran. In both cases such Islamic ruling classes, like ruling classes everywhere, are the enemies of the left and the working class movement. But both in their inconsistent opposition to imperialism, as much forced on them by the imperialists as embraced as a matter of principle, and in their hostility to the left these Islamic ruling classes are little different from their nationalist precursors or contemporaries. The hostility, for instance, of Arab nationalist governments to the left is simply a matter of record from Gamal Abdul Nasser to Saddam Hussein and Bashir Assad.

In these societies some Islamic movements are more consistent opponents of imperialism than Islamic states – for example Hamas in Palestine and Hezbollah in Lebanon. In other cases the left currents are more consistent than Islamic or nationalist governments. The attitude of the socialist left should be that 'political Islam' has arisen because of the failure of the nationalist left. It fills very much the same political space as the nationalist current. It has a very similar relationship with the left in that it can, at certain times and under certain conditions, be an ally of the left and, at other times and in other conditions, turn on the left and the working class movement as an enemy. Accordingly the left should treat Islamic movements much as it should have, but often did not, treat the nationalist movement, including the Communist Party influenced nationalist left. That is to say certain Islamic currents are opponents of imperialism and advocates of democratic revolutionary change in their own countries. In so far as they are in opposition to imperialism and the domestic ruling classes the left should work with them. But the left should always maintain its own organisational and political independence. It should seek to strengthen the independence of the specifically working class resistance to imperialism and capitalism. In this way it should be the furthest left wing of the democratic and anti-imperialist movement. But it should also be preparing to fight for a transformation not only of the political system but of the economic system as well.

One empire?

Are we now facing a global empire in which the old imperial pattern of rivalry between major powers has been subsumed? This, ironically perhaps, is not a theory widely held among neo-conservatives but on the political left. It is most famously advanced by Antonio Negri and Michael Hardt in *Empire*. Hardt and Negri's 'basic hypothesis is that sovereignty has taken a new form, composed of a series of national and supranational organisms united under a single logic of rule. The new global form of sovereignty is what we call Empire.' This is a result of the 'declining sovereignty of nation-states and their inability to regulate economic and cultural exchanges.'[6]

Similar, if less abstract, notions of post-Cold War empire are widespread. Leo Panitch and Sam Gindin, for instance, argue that the economic interpenetration of nation-states by the foreign direct investment of multinationals has created a single US led system. This rules out a return to inter-imperialist rivalry between states.

' . . . what is at play in the current conjuncture is not the contradictions between national bourgeoisies, but the contradictions of "the whole of imperialism", implicating all the bourgeoisies that function under the American imperial umbrella.'[7]

The argument goes that 'With American capital a social force within each European country, domestic capital tended to be "dis-articulated" and no longer represented by a coherent and independent national bourgeoisie'.[8] Thus 'We cannot understand imperialism today in terms of . . . competition giving rise again to inter-imperial rivalry'.[9]

The Hardt-Negri and Panitch-Gindin analyses share one further similarity: both accounts of this 'simplified' imperial structure conclude with the seemingly radical point that if contradictions between imperial states have been sublimated in a global empire then the remaining major contradiction is between the system as a whole and, in Hardt and Negri's case, a declassed 'multitude' and, in Panitch and Gindin's case, the working class. In Panitch and Gindin's critique of *Empire*, while they disagree with Hardt and Negri on what constitutes the agent of change in the new empire, they have no disagreement with the idea that inter-imperialist rivalry has given way to a single, if articulated, empire.[10]

Thus in both *Empire* and the analysis offered by Panitch and Gindin interstate rivalry has been suppressed but struggle between the masses, however constituted, and the system goes on. This is not a minor theoretical innovation and its consequences are much more far reaching than their authors seem to acknowledge.

There might plausibly be two reasons for the believing in the attenuation of inter-state rivalry. It might be argued that globalisation, the rise of multinationals and the management of the world market by the IMF and similar bodies has so undermined economic competition that there is no longer any reflection of economic competition in the rivalry between states. But if we really are now living in the 'managed economy' only dreamt of by liberal economists in the 1960s then the absence of economic competition must affect the class struggle and undermine the very possibility of resistance to the system. Why? Because it is the competition between units of capital which produces within each individual unit the pressure for employers to lower wages, lengthen hours, intensify work, discipline the workforce and break unions. In other words, without competition between units of capital the motor of the class struggle is removed. So too is the competitive drive of the system towards self-expansion. An empire without economic competition will be a stagnant empire. Or as Marx summarised the case 'Capital can only exist as many capitals.' To deny this is to see the system as a clock without a spring.

The point about globalisation is that it intensifies this competition between units of capital on a global scale, not that it has in some way abolished it. But perhaps it is not the intention of these theorists to deny the continued prevalence of economic competition. Certainly this would seem to be Panitch and Gindin's stance since they have not travelled the post-Marxist, postmodernist path of Hardt and Negri. But if economic competition roars on unabated then we are being asked to believe that this competition between the giants of the economic world will never express itself in rivalry between states. That is, we are being asked to believe that there is an effective disassociation between politics and economics.

In the first case we have an Orwellian model of society in which a global empire confronts an atomised mass of plebs; or, in the second case, we have an Althusserian model of society in which the state is radically divorced from the economic competition raging beneath it. If the first case is true we may wish for new and creative acts of resistance by the oppressed but there is no inherent reason why the society should generate such opposition. If the second case is true such resistance may be generated for economistic reasons but it will confront a single, monolithic ruling class which has no effective contradictions between its constituent parts. In both cases the apparent radicalism turns into a utopian dream of resistance.

The theoretical incoherence of these views derives from the fact that they do not accurately describe the world. They radically underestimate the importance of the nation-state. As we have seen in chapter two, multinational capital remains closely tied to nation-states and there is no alternative institution that can perform their domestic police and social functions or their foreign military function on behalf of capital. Globalisation may have required less nationalisation but it has not required less state intervention in a more general sense. As Ellen Meiksins Wood notes,

> 'The critical point about the "internationalisation" of the state is that the nation-state is useful to global capital not to the extent that it is unable to "regulate economic and cultural exchanges". On the contrary, it is useful precisely

because it **can** intervene in the global economy and, indeed, remains the single most effective means of intervention.'[11]

And because states have this capacity, and because they are geographically bounded entities that are acted on both by their most proximate capitalists as well as by the local exploited classes, they exercise it in ways which contradict other states. The result is that 'the political form of globalisation ... is not a global state or global sovereignty but a global system of multiple states and local sovereignties, structured in a complex relation of domination and subordination'.[12]

In such a system imperial rivalry is central. It is no doubt useful to discuss between which states rivalry takes place, the degree of rivalry, the timescale over which such rivalry unfolds, or whether earlier periods of rivalry like that before the First World War are useful analogies. But it is not useful to declare that such rivalry is not a feature of the current era since this is patently not the case. Indeed, the one point that the analysis presented in this book has been at pains to demonstrate is that interstate rivalry is now both more volatile and is actually resulting in more wars when compared to the relative stasis of Cold War imperialism.[13]

That this situation has not yet resulted in a clash between two major powers should not surprise us. Such conflicts are many years in the making and the new imperialism is still only emerging from its Cold War chrysalis. To date the US has conducted the business of disciplining other major powers by the 'demonstration effect' of humbling minor powers in the Balkans, Afghanistan and the Middle East – whether China, Russia, France, Germany or anyone else like it or not. That this is what the US intends has been stated and restated a thousand times in official and unofficial documents, statements and speeches. The belief that this will always be accepted peaceably by the other imperialist states as in the 'greater interest' of the global system could only be sustained if some 'global committee for the management of the common affairs of the capitalist class' had replaced a system of competing nation-states. Capital would then no longer exist as many capitals. It would, therefore, no longer be capitalism but some new form of oppressive society.

This, the rhetoric of *Empire* notwithstanding, does not correspond with reality. A much more realistic projection has been made by Larry Elliott, the *Guardian*'s economics editor. Reporting a PricewaterhouseCoopers study, he suggests that the combined size of the Chinese, Russian, Indian, Indonesian, Mexican and Turkish economies will be at least 25 percent larger, and possibly 75 percent larger, than the G7 economies by 2050. Using purchasing power parity calculations which allow for the fact that a dollar buys more in China than in the US, China's economy is already 75 percent of the size of the US economy and could be one and a half times the size of the US economy by the middle of the century. Even without using purchasing power parity calculations China's economy is already 18 percent of the size of the US economy and will be virtually the same size in 2050, according to PricewaterhouseCoopers.

These shifts in economic power rarely happen without engaging the military capacity of states. 'History suggests that shifts in the balance of power causes geo-political upheaval – witness the period between 1890 and 1945 – as the new kids on the block flex their muscles and the old guard seeks to maintain the status quo. The US is already wary about the growing economic strength of China ... The scene is set for a period of tension between the current top dog and its east Asian rival.'[14]

The point here is not to deny the 'internationalisation of the state' or the degree to which the neo-liberal state sees itself as the servant of multinationals. Both issues have been explored earlier in this book. The point is that if this observation is carried too far it obliterates either the continued independent existence of the state or the continued competition between capitals. In doing this it prevents us from understanding that the instability of the system resides precisely in the dialectical relationship between the internationally competitive nature of the economic system and the indispensable but necessarily nationally limited nature of the capitalist state. Both Hardt and Negri and Panitch and Gindin have lost sight of the fact that it is the renewed ferocity of international competition between multi-nationals which is driving the military extensions of the nation-states into the vacuum created by the end of the Cold War.

Who resists?

For almost as long as there has been a working class there have been social theorists proclaiming its disappearance or its inability to change society. So far these claims have been unfounded but that does not seem to deter more writers from entering the lists. Hardt and Negri are the best known exponents of this view. In *Multitude*, the sequel to *Empire*, they insist that the working class is of no special importance as an agent of social change and that its place has been taken by 'the multitude' of those excluded from the empire.

Hardt and Negri insist that the multitude be distinguished from the narrow definition of the working class as simply the industrial proletariat. Since this is a position more regularly advanced in crude anti-Marxist caricatures of the left than by the left itself we need not disagree with Hardt and Negri on this issue. For nearly all socialists, Marxists or otherwise, the working class includes service workers, workers in the arts, 'brain' workers and so on. Indeed for Marxists the working class includes all those who must earn a wage because they have no way to subsist other than to sell their labour power. But Hardt and Negri go on to distinguish the multitude from even this broader definition of the working class on the grounds that it does not include 'the poor, unpaid domestic laborers, and all others who do not receive a wage. The multitude, in contrast, is an open, inclusive concept.'[15] This is a strange claim since there is a great deal of Marxist literature, beginning with Engels' *The Family, Private Property and the State*, that demonstrates that those dependent on the wages of workers, like those doing household labour, even if they do not earn a wage themselves, are part of the working class.

It is not clear quite what the point is of replacing a concrete and specific class designation with an abstract and ambiguous generality – except that it serves Hardt and Negri with a socio-logical justification for introducing an entirely subjective notion of the agent of social change. For them the multitude has to define itself since it has no objective economic definition: 'the multitude must discover *the common* that allows them to com-municate and act together. The common we share, in fact, is not so much discovered as it is produced.'[16]

This is a remarkably unnecessary theoretical construct. The working class is, by any definition, not smaller on a global scale than before but larger. The industrialisation of China, and the rising labour unrest that is accompanying it, should on its own be enough to underline this point. But in any case the statistics make this clear beyond any shadow of doubt. Globally the working class numbers some 2 billion with perhaps another 2 billion semi-proletarian poor around them. Urbanisation, one index of the growth of the working class, has advanced in every corner of the globe. In the world as a whole those living in towns rose from 37 to 45 percent between 1970 and 1995. In the developing countries it rose from 25 to 37 percent and in the least devel-oped countries from 13 to 23 percent in the same period.[17]

In the US there are now some 31 million workers in industry, compared to 10 million in 1900 and 26 million in 1971. In some of the advanced economies, in France, Italy and Germany for instance, neo-liberal social policies have been meeting with sustained union opposition since the 1990s. Even in those countries, notably the US and Britain, where the defeats that labour suffered in the 1980s have not been recouped there is no objective or sociological case for claims that the working class is not the key exploited class in contemporary society. Indeed, in terms of consciousness there are now more people in opinion surveys who define themselves as working class than there were in the 1970s.[18]

Hardt and Negri's redefinition of the working class as the multitude seems rather to be a shallow generalisation based on the fact that in some advanced countries the level of popular rejection of neo-liberalism has taken a form in which the specifically working class struggle is not yet as strong as it was during the last upturn in the 1970s. It also serves them as a reason for rejecting 'centralised forms of revolutionary dictatorship and command' in favour of 'network organisations that displace authority in collaborative relationships'.[19]

The general result of *Empire* and *Multitude* is that the polarity in the modern world is no longer to be seen as between a highly centralised capitalist and imperialist ruling class and the working class, but between the dispersed power of empire and the self-defined democracy of the multitude. To the extent that this attitude could ever produce a practical organisational conclusion it did so in the Italian autonomist movement from which Negri came and which has been reborn in recent years. Its most recent defining moment came in July 2001 in Genoa at the protests at the meeting of the G8. As Alex Callinicos has noted, the Italian state on that day failed to appreciate that its power was dispersed 'everywhere and nowhere' and seemed possessed of the idea that it was concentrated in the form of the carabineri.[20] The soft networks of the autonomists did not prevent the murder of Carlo Gulliani nor the injury and imprisonment of hundreds of other protesters. It was the mass mobilisations of the following day, to an important degree driven by the stand of Rifondazione Comunista, that turned the protests from a rout into a triumphant carnival of resistance.

There is an important point to be drawn from this experience. Successful resistance depends on an accurate appreciation of both the strengths and weakness of the system and of those who oppose it. Neither the 'pro-war left' who have taken the arguments about 'democratic imperialism' or the 'clash of civilisations' at face value, nor those on the left who reflect the triumphalism of those at the helm of the 'one remaining superpower', have been able to provide a suitably accurate account of the balance of the forces as it has unfolded in recent years.

Conclusion

The contemporary capitalist system remains one in which economic competition gives rise to military competition between states. Neither globalisation nor the new imperial order has sufficiently transformed the nature of the system so that divisions between corporations and between states can be suppressed. Nor has it resulted in a system that can manage conflict without recourse to violence. It is unlikely that, over time, such violence will remain outside the metropolitan centres of the system.

Working people and the poor internationally have neither been replaced by a socially indistinct 'multitude' nor lost the capacity to resist the system. The problems that they face in exercising this capacity are not to do with changes in their sociological or economic profile. They arise from the contours of the class struggle in the last 25 years, the theoretical clarity and organisational strength of the left. It is to some of these issues that the final chapter now turns.

7   Resisting imperialism

The rise of the new imperialism has called forth a new anti-imperialism. Beginning with the 1999 anti-capitalist demonstration in Seattle the entire landscape of politics has been transformed by the growth of a worldwide anti-globalisation and anti-war movement. February 15 2003 is its high point so far. On that day simultaneous demonstrations against the coming Iraq war took place in 600 towns and cities on every continent in the world. It is beyond doubt that these demonstrations were the greatest ever globally co-ordinated day of political protest in history. Many of the demonstrations were, like that in London, the single biggest political demonstration in the history of the country.[1] In the first three months of 2003, according to a study by one French sociologist, some 36 million people took part in anti-war protests around the globe.[2]

February 15 does not, however, stand alone as a single moment of protest but forms part of a longer and continuing radical movement. Its precursors were the long line of huge anti-globalisation protests that followed Seattle – Prague, Nice, Gothenburg, Genoa and Florence. And it has been followed by the huge anti-war protests during and since the invasion of Iraq, including those in Turkey, in London during George Bush's state visit in November 2003 and in New York in opposition to the Republican Party convention in the autumn of 2004, the biggest of all the US anti-war demonstrations. In the midst of all this tens of thousands of activists have attended the three European

Social Forums in Florence in 2002, in Paris in 2003 and in London in 2004, while more than 100,000 have attended each of the five World Social Forums hosted by Porto Alegre in Brazil and Mumbai in India.

This movement arose under the impetus of three deeper social processes. The first was the 25 year long neo-liberal offensive that has resulted in greater inequality, cutbacks in welfare provision, privatisation, deregulation, an increase in corporate power and an assault on trade unions. The coming together of organised labour and environmental activists, the celebrated 'teamster-turtle alliance', on the Seattle demonstration foreshadowed the degree to which the generalised nature of the attacks of the last 25 years finally resulted in a united mobilisation across many of the different constituencies affected.

This indeed was the single most important aspect of the movement – its highly generalised nature. There has long been an adage on the left that the breadth of a movement was inversely related to its political depth. Put simply, single issues mobilise large numbers, complex political analyses are narrower in appeal. As the old Russian Marxist, Georgi Plekhanov, put it, agitation is a single idea in front of a mass audience; propaganda is a series of political ideas in front of a small audience. The anti-globalisation movement turned the received wisdom on its head. The movement represented a broad critique of free-market capitalism, an aspiration for an entirely different system-wide set of priorities epitomised by the slogan 'Another world is possible'. Yet the movement had the capacity to mobilise greater numbers than many pre-existing single issue campaigns, trade unions or political parties.

When the anti-war movement arose it inherited this approach. Although nominally about a single issue it was in fact a broad critique of the economic and political imperatives of the new imperialism. The corporate backers of war, the economics of the oil industry, the environmental impact of war, the working of the military-industrial complex, the fate of Palestine, opposition to the oppression of Muslims, the traditional concerns of anti-nuclear campaigners, the history of western colonialism all fitted easily into the anti-war movement, deepening rather than narrowing its appeal.

The generalised nature of the movement was in the first instance a result of the long and generalised nature of the neo-liberal offensive and of the failures of previous partial responses to it. Since the end of the long post-war boom in the mid-1970s, reaching an apogee in the Reagan-Thatcher years, the wave of privatisation, deregulation, welfare cutbacks and attacks on trade unions resulted in the accumulation of bitterness and resentment at the base of society. Trade union responses had been beaten back in the 1980s. Electoral responses that had resulted in an international wave of Social Democratic and Labour victories in the 1990s quickly produced disappointment as the new governments continued the neo-liberal project with only marginal amendment.

In the late 1990s a vacuum existed. The situation was crying out for a radical political response but the traditional single issue campaigns, trade unions and political parties seemed incapable or unwilling to embrace the radicalism necessary for the task. An alternative 'people power' model of protest had arisen on the international stage during the preceding decade but it seemed that it was only for use against authoritarian regimes like those in Eastern Europe, South Africa and Indonesia. But in 1999 and after 'people power' came west.

The second factor facilitating the rise of this movement was the end of the Cold War. The fall of the Berlin Wall had a contradictory effect on the left. Many in the official Communist movement, and many of those in the traditional social democratic parties, the trade unions and third world national liberation movements influenced by state-socialist views of social change, could not but be demoralised by the fall of 'actually existing socialism'. But the end of the Moscow dominated vision of socialism also delivered an opportunity to re-unite the left. Opposition to the common neo-liberal enemy was now the overwhelmingly important issue and divisions over Russia became a merely historical, if still important, question.

Moreover, the disappearance of the Eastern bloc deprived the right wing of a stick with which to beat the left. Had an anti-capitalist movement arisen before 1989 its opponents' very first cry would have been 'so, would you rather live in Russia?' After 1989 this line of argument worked rather better for the left than for the right since integration into the world market caused the Russian economy to decline precipitously. And before 1989 those in an anti-capitalist movement would certainly have immediately divided over whether Russian style central planning was what another world should look like. After 1989 the dividing line in society as well as on the left was between those who were in favour and those who were against resurgent global capitalism.

The third and final social development affecting the rise of the new radical movement was the recasting of the imperial order after the Cold War. The opposition to the first Gulf War was a serious, principled campaign which organised some impressive rallies but it did not break beyond the limits of the traditional left and peace movements. The opposition to the Balkan war did begin to break new ground with a series of well-attended public meetings around the country. But the opposition to the Balkan war was even more important in that it drew together a core of people who would be central to the opposition to the wars in Afghanistan and Iraq. Within this movement they developed a series of analyses and responses to the new imperialism. Crucially these involved an appreciation of the post-Cold War aims of US imperialism, a critique of the 'humanitarian imperialist' justifications of war and an examination of the importance of oil and other energy resources to US security plans.

The founding principles of the anti-war movement

The attack on the twin towers and the Bush administration's response to it transformed the situation. The very first Stop the War Coalition meeting in London, the largest such meeting for a decade, was called in the week after September 11th. Its success proved from an early date that people were just as fearful of the response of the US government to the attack on the twin towers as they were horrified by the attack itself. As the full enormity of the US imperial project unfolded this sentiment spread into a society-wide rejection of the new imperialism, deepening and broadening the already existing anti-globalisation movement as it developed. It is worth examining the key principles on which this unprecedented movement organised.

1. Unity. In the final analysis those who oppose governments only have two fundamental strengths, their numbers and their ability to organise. To make effective use of these strengths unity is essential. The key to unity is to commit the movement to those aims that are essential in any given political situation and to maximise the forces fighting for those aims. The Stop the War Coalition committed itself to the central issue of opposing the attacks on Afghanistan and Iraq and, by extension, the 'war on terror' of which they were a part. It only adopted two other closely related demands. The first was to defend civil liberties since it was obvious from the first that domestic freedoms would also be undermined in the name of the 'war on terror'. The second was to oppose the racist backlash which, it was equally clear, would accompany the preparations for war.

   Around these aims traditional peace campaigners, Labour, Liberal and Green party members, trade unionists, Muslims, socialists, anti-globalisation activists and many others with no previous organisational affiliations could all agree to organise. Attempts to narrow the campaign so that it adopted specifically anti-imperialist objectives, thus potentially excluding pacifists or those simply opposed to this war for particular reasons or, most importantly, those just coming into the movement who had not had the opportunity to become anti-imperialists on principle, were rejected.

2. The movement can be radical as well as broad. Ensuring that the movement was as broad as possible did not preclude a radical approach. While not being anti-imperialist in

declaration, a strong anti-imperialist current of opinion, often commanding majority agreement, was always present. This was not just a question of intellectual argument by anti-imperialists within the broader coalition, although this was vital as well. Critically the agenda of the imperial powers themselves and the instinctive reactions of tens of thousands of activists drove the movement in this direction. The Palestinian issue is a case in point. There had always been pro-Palestinian activists in the Stop the War Coalition, although freedom for Palestine had not been an official policy. But the linking of the Palestinian and Iraq issues by Bush and Blair created the necessity for the anti-war movement to do likewise. The massacre at Jenin fuelled resentment among anti-war activists and made the case put by pro-Palestinian campaigners seem irrefutable.

The same logic can be seen in the attitude of the anti-war movement towards the United Nations in the run up to the attack on Iraq. For many anti-imperialists the attack on Iraq was to be opposed whether or not there was a second UN resolution to justify the invasion. But for many others in the anti-war movement the UN was regarded as a guarantor of legitimacy. In the end it was the blatant manipulation of the UN by the US and Britain, combined with the anti-imperialist argument that the UN is merely the general voice of the imperialist powers, that won a majority to the view that the attack on Iraq was to be opposed with or without a second UN resolution. This majority held through the invasion and continues to oppose the occupation of Iraq despite the fact that this now has UN sanction.

3. The great powers are the main enemy. One of the main justifications of the war is to claim that the governments and armies of small states are a greater threat to peace than the armies of great powers and their allies. The anti-war movement was clear from the beginning that it did not support the dictatorial regime in Iraq, but it also refused to agree with the proposition that such regimes were the greatest

cause of, or the greatest danger in, the newly unstable world of the early 21st century.

A great deal of the energy and argument of the anti-war movement went into demonstrating that 'rogue' and 'failed' states were not some spontaneously arising evil in the world system but largely the product of the preceding policies of the great powers. The economic subjection of poorer countries was traced back to the neo-liberal economic policies of the previous 25 years, the actions of the major states and their international agencies such as the World Bank, the IMF and the WTO.

Neither was the anti-war movement willing to forget the political and military alliances between the western powers and both the Taliban and Saddam Hussein. Islamic militants had been the chosen ally of the US in its battle against the Russian presence in Afghanistan during the Cold War and Saddam Hussein had been armed as a bulwark against the spreading of the influence of the Islamic Revolution in Iran during the 1980s. If the Afghan and Iraqi regimes were the monsters the west now claimed, they were monsters of the west's own creation.

4. Self-determination is the key to liberation. There was never any question that the vast majority of those in the anti-war movement were opponents of Saddam Hussein. Where they differed with the pro-war lobby was in their insistence that the Iraqi people should be the ones who got rid of Saddam.

In support of this argument the anti-war movement pointed to the fact that the pro-war lobby are only in favour of western military action to get rid of totalitarian regimes where its suits their purposes rather than when it suits the purposes of the people suffering under those regimes. There was never any question of military action to get rid of apartheid in South Africa, nor is there now to get rid of the dictatorial regimes in China or Saudi Arabia. The Iraqi and Afghan regimes could have been as dictatorial as they chose if only they had not been weak enough to be attacked with impunity and insufficiently pro-western.

Perhaps the most hypocritical of the pro-war arguments was that which insisted that the Iraqis were too weak to overthrow Saddam themselves. It is true that popular revolutions do not happen to order. They may take years of social development to arise and years of struggle to succeed. But there is nothing that can replace them as an effective agent of democratic change. If the US army invades it takes power. If a popular uprising, however long in coming, takes power then that fact shapes the society that emerges as a result. The fall of apartheid, the overthrow of Suharto in Indonesia, the popular movement in Serbia are merely the most recent testimony to this age old law. It is not necessarily the case that all such popular movements gain everything for which they had hoped. Nor is it true that such risings are free from the attention of western states and corporations. But it is true that the issues are predominantly settled among the people of the country, fought out by domestic political forces, and solutions are not imposed, colonial-style, by other nations' armies.

These then were the general propositions that gained the assent of hundreds of thousands of activists in the anti-war movement and became repeated by millions more in discussions and arguments in the years after September 2001. The fact that within the general movement that came to accept these arguments there was a strong core of anti-imperialists ensured that the movement was very difficult for the pro-war forces to 'knock off course'. The usual stratagems of using the weight of the media, appeals to patriotism, calls for loyalty to troops in battle, denunciations of supposed support for 'dictators and terrorists' were all deployed. But they were relatively ineffective because of the very large central core of activists who were anti-imperialist as well as anti-war.

What does it mean to be anti-imperialist?

The most important anti-imperialist idea is that the drive to war is endemic in the system. Advocates and opponents of the capitalist system are agreed that competition lies at its heart. But competition between rival firms and corporations has always involved the state. Moreover it has fed rivalry and competition between states. Such competition frequently involves the threat or use of force. In this way there is an inevitable propensity for armed conflict to arise. Of course not every state rivalry involves force and not every threat of force results in the use of force. And not every use of force is on the same scale nor does it involve the same loss of life. Nevertheless, the history of the last one hundred years alone is too strewn with the wreckage of industrialised warfare, causing loss of life on a hitherto unimaginable scale, for this simple proposition to lack supporting evidence.

This elementary notion has some political consequences. It inoculates those who hold it against the naïve view that the simple deployment of human reasonableness, either through the medium of enlightened leaders or multilateral institutions, will be enough to banish armed conflict. Systemic problems require systemic answers. This view directs the gaze of those looking for the causes of war away from merely ideological factors, though these too have their proper role to play in any full explanation of war, and towards those structural facets of the system that underpin the drive to military conflict.

A second and equally important notion in the anti-imperialist view of the world is that the system has and continues to develop in an uneven manner, distributing economic and military power differentially among the competing states that make up the system. This means that there are at least two types of imperial conflict. There are those wars which involve military conflict between major, developed industrial powers. And then there are those conflicts between major powers and weaker, less developed states. The First and Second World Wars were clearly conflicts in which major, industrialised states armed with the most advanced weapons of the day fought on both sides. Equally clearly the Vietnam War, the attack on Afghanistan and on Iraq were wars fought between major powers and states incomparably weaker in every indicator of economic and military power.

These two types of war impose different political obligations on those who oppose them, especially if they are in the heartlands of the system. Let us examine the case of conflict between imperial powers first. Karl Liebknecht the great German anti-imperialist of the First World War summarised this obligation in the slogan 'the main enemy is at home'. With this slogan he hoped to ensure that those who were opposing the war would not be drawn into the patriotic fervour then sweeping European countries on all sides of the conflict. Liebknecht's aim was to redraw the main dividing line in society so that it no longer ran between warring nations but between classes, not between nationalities but between governments and those they claimed to represent. If loyalties were not redrawn in this way, if people did not put opposition to the war before loyalty to their government, then there could be no effective resistance to the war because it would always be turned into the safe channel of patriotism.

Those who adopted this approach, Lenin in Russia and John McLean in Britain, were accused of propounding an illogical argument. How, asked their opponents, could the 'main enemy be at home' in every country? But this was precisely the point advanced by the anti-war radicals. The German government, the Russian government, the British government were all and equally responsible for the conflict. And if all the working people in each of these states made it their first priority to defeat the government in their own country then a real internationalism would be possible. Lenin argued, 'We realise that for the working class to be victorious over *all* the robbers we have to start the struggle where we are, in our own country, by making our own rulers the *main* enemy, regardless of the military consequences.'

The opposing point of view was clearly articulated by Fabian Bernard Shaw immediately before the First World War: 'War between country and country is a bad thing, but in the case of such a war any attempt of a general strike to prevent the people defending their country would result in a civil war which was ten times worse than war between nation and nation'. Labour Party leader Arthur Henderson was 'largely in agreement with Mr. Shaw.'

The anti-war socialists replied that only those who have given up any hope of working people being able to intervene in the history of their own society could claim that the only outcome of a war was the victory of one or other of the contending powers. They insisted that a conflict that starts between nation and nation does not have to end that way. It can, in its course, give rise to struggles between the governments of the warring nations and the people of those nations.

In the event it was, of course, revolution in Russia and Germany that halted the First World War. The loss of human life in those revolutions was not, as Shaw predicted, worse than that in the war between nation and nation.

In the second kind of war, that between major powers and subordinate states, the approach of anti-imperialists should be different in important respects. If radicals were simply to carry over the approach adopted in inter-imperialist conflicts like the First World War, the attitude which is equally opposed to governments in all the belligerent powers, they would be treating the most powerful imperial states in the world the same as some of the weakest and most subordinate countries in the world. And such even-handedness would in effect end in support for the more powerful, imperial states. Just imagine if during the Vietnam War anti-war demonstrators had protested equally against the Vietnamese National Liberation Front and the US war machine.

If the anti-colonial movements or states that are opposed to the major powers defeat the imperial powers it weakens the whole imperial system. This is true whether or not those who lead such struggles or stand at the head of such states have this outcome as their conscious aim. Lenin argued that the political complexion of the leaders of small nations – be they nationalist, fundamentalist, dictators or democrats – should not determine whether socialists in the major imperialist countries oppose their own governments in time of war. It is enough that the defeat of the major imperial powers would advance the cause of oppressed people everywhere for socialists to commit themselves to the principle of self-determination for small nations.

It is not a requirement of an anti-imperialist stance that socialists should lend the leaders of national liberation struggles a 'communist colouration', as Lenin put it. In struggles between despotic and undemocratic leaders of small nations and their own working people socialists take sides. We are for the self-organisation of working people, not least because we believe that such self-organisation will lead to a more effective struggle against imperialism. Take the example of Iraq: the illegitimacy of Saddam Hussein's dictatorship meant that on two occasions it failed to mount an effective fight against US imperialism. Yet after the fall of Saddam the Iraqi resistance has mounted one of the most determined struggles for national liberation the US has faced since the Vietnam War.

The only danger for the anti-war movement in adopting this stance is when criticism of the leaders of small nations is elevated to the point where no distinction is made between them and the leaders of the major imperial powers. In each of the recent major wars of the last decade a section of the left has effectively sided with imperialism because it equated undemocratic and authoritarian regimes that were the victims of imperialism with imperialism itself. For Fred Halliday, a long time opponent of imperialism, for instance, Saddam Hussein's Iraq was such an unacceptable regime that it justified the full onslaught of the greatest military powers in the world. For Mark Seddon, editor of *Tribune*, and many others on the left the Milosevic regime justified the imperialist bombing campaign against Serbia. And, as we have seen, many on the left find the Taliban such a uniquely reactionary regime that it justifies the US and British war against Afghanistan.

The most elementary logical distinctions, if nothing else, seem to have been over-ridden in these cases. For instance, one does not have to be a supporter of any of these regimes – indeed one can be politically opposed to them all – to still maintain opposition to imperialist intervention. The basic principle of the right of nations to self-determination requires us to allow the exploited and oppressed people of these nations to settle accounts with their own tyrants. Imperial intervention, as long experience in Africa has taught us, does not help. The left internationally could and did aid such struggles, thus banishing the accusation that respecting the rights of nations to self-determination is to abandon the local populations to the mercy of their dictators.

Those who 'can't wait' for this process of self-determination to unfold demonstrate a patronising lack of patience with the timescale on which an oppressed people form a movement to change their own society and an unwillingness to provide solidarity on terms that such a movement finds acceptable. At worst this is a mere excuse for backing imperial intervention and has been used as such by the imperial governments themselves.

The problem with this approach is not just that those who do the liberating tend to end up doing the ruling afterwards, as we have argued, but that the wider consequence of strengthening imperialism in one corner of the system is that all those struggling for liberation in every other corner of the system then face an emboldened opponent. So even if we accepted the argument that 'liberation' in Iraq might come from the US military, its negative impact would be felt everywhere from Venezuela to Syria.

Social advance is either the result of self-determination or it is nothing. When the great powers became independent modern states it was through just this process. In America it was the long journey of the American people through the War of Independence and the Civil War. In Europe it was a decades long process of revolution and internal political development that produced such democratic rights as we now enjoy. In these processes the American and European peoples certainly benefited from the solidarity of others, from Tom Paine to Karl Marx, from the Lancashire cotton workers who supported the Union in the American Civil War to the Liverpool workers who greeted Garibaldi as one of their own.

Such solidarity had to be delivered in ways determined by or agreed by at least some of those fighting for their own liberation. Thus, in a more recent example, the global anti-apartheid movement acted in concert with the ANC. Likewise the Palestine solidarity movement acts in a common framework with Palestinian liberation groups.

Solidarity arises from below. It predominantly involves united action between non-governmental organisations. It does not preclude state action like the boycotting of goods or the banning of arms sales. But such actions arise from the movement and are not the independent actions of governmental and corporate elites acting for their own purposes.

The left, 'rogue states' and imperialism

The issue of opposing 'dictators' is unlikely to go away both because the US imperial ideology is now much concerned with 'spreading democracy' and because such regimes are likely to multiply in number. The state capitalist model of development is much less common. Anti-colonial struggles have given rise to ruling classes of new nations who now try to carve their own space in the world system by striking deals with the major powers. Such arrangements are, of course, no guarantee that today's imperial ally will not turn into tomorrow's imperial victim – as Saddam Hussein, Slobodan Milosevic and Mullah Omar can all testify. But what this illustrates is that we cannot decide whether or not to oppose imperialism simply on whether or not we find the past or present behaviour of the regime to be progressive.

In the era before the rise of Stalinism this was more clearly understood, at least on the revolutionary left. Writing in the early 1920s George Lukacs commented on the fact the 19th century 'movements for unity of Germany and Italy were the last of these objectively revolutionary struggles' for national liberation. The difference with modern struggles for national liberation, Lukacs observed, is that they are now

> 'no longer merely struggles against their own feudalism and feudal absolutism – that is to say only implicitly progressive – for they are forced into the context of imperialist rivalry between world powers. Their historical

significance, their evaluation, therefore depends on what concrete part they play in the concrete whole.'[3]

It follows that,

> 'Forces that work towards revolution today may very well operate in the reverse direction tomorrow. And it is vital to note that these changes … are determined decisively by the constantly changing relations of the totality of the historical situation and the social forces at work. So that it is no very great paradox to assert that, for instance, Kemel Pasha may represent a revolutionary constellation of forces in certain circumstances whilst a great "workers' party" may be counter-revolutionary.'[4]

Lukacs is generalising from positions developed by Lenin during the First World War. Lenin, for instance, was well aware of the shortcomings of the national bourgeoisie in the oppressed countries:

> 'Not infrequently … we find the bourgeoisie of the oppressed nations **talking** of national revolt, while in practice it enters into reactionary compacts with the bourgeoisie of the oppressor nation behind the backs of, and **against**, its own people. In such cases the criticism of revolutionary Marxists should be directed not against the national movement, but against its degradation, vulgarisation, against the tendency to reduce it to a petty squabble.'[5]

Consequently, Lenin was determinedly opposed to those on the left who refused or qualified their opposition to imperialism on the basis that those facing imperialism did not hold progressive ideas:

> 'To imagine that social revolution is **conceivable** … without revolutionary outbursts by a section of the petty bourgeoisie **with all its prejudices**, without a movement

of the politically non-conscious proletarian and semi-proletarian masses . . . is to **repudiate social revolution** . . . [which] **cannot be** anything other than an outburst of mass struggle on the part of all and sundry oppressed and discontented elements. Inevitably . . . they will bring into the movement their prejudices, their revolutionary fantasies, their weaknesses and errors. But **objectively** they will attack **capital** . . .

The dialectics of history are such that small nations, powerless as an **independent** factor in the struggle against imperialism, play a part as one of the ferments, one of the bacilli, which help the **real** anti-imperialist force, the socialist proletariat, to make its appearance on the scene.'[6]

We do not live in the era of the Russian Revolution but it is still true that whether or not we oppose imperialism is determined by the totality of relations in the system at any given time and not only by the internal character of the regimes that find themselves, however contingently and ineffectively, opposed to imperialism.

Imperialism, anti-imperialism and socialism

Imperialism is an evolving system. Since the very earliest days of capitalism international expansion has been written into its structure. The union with Scotland and the colonisation of Ireland formed one of the first capitalist states, Britain. Both events were decisively shaped by the revolution of the 17th century. And one of Britain's first post-revolutionary wars was with the second major capitalist state of the day, the Dutch Republic. Emerging capitalist states and declining pre-capitalist empires fought for dominance in America, Africa, Asia and the Far East. For two centuries British, Dutch, French, German, Italian and other major powers struggled to conquer the globe, subdue indigenous populations and minor powers.

The apogee was reached in the 20th century as wholly capitalist powers clashed in two world wars and again and again in countless colonial conflicts. Since the second of those world wars formal colonies have largely gained their independence. Oppressed nations have come and gone, fought their battle and joined the international system of states in more or less subordinate ranks. This process began with the American colonies in the 1770s and ran through to the liberation of Ireland and India, among many others, in the 20th century. But that does not mean that the national question has disappeared, merely that it has, like imperialism itself, evolved new forms. The indigenous ruling classes that took the place of their colonial overlords have often struggled to suppress new nationalist forces within their, often artificial, boundaries. So it was, for instance, that the new post-independence Indonesian ruling class fought to suppress the East Timorese. Equally these new ruling classes have struggled with the still ever-present economic and military strength of the major powers. And this returns us to the need, as Lukacs argued, to assess each anti-imperial struggle from the standpoint of the whole contemporary alignment of forces in the imperialist system.

There is however one relatively consistent social position from which this assessment can best be carried out. As their rulers and would-be rulers twist and turn between colonialism and independence, accommodation and belligerence, protectionism and economic liberalisation the inescapable power of the international economy and the weight of the great states bear down on the workers and peasants of these societies. It is here that we come to the one great enduring force opposed to the imperial system throughout its long evolution. Whatever its changing shape – from the primitive accumulation of the slave trade, through the early colonies to the great imperial wars of the 20th century – these classes have stood in opposition to the system. Their struggle has certainly not always been victorious. It has often laid dormant for great lengths of time. But it has, nevertheless, risen again and again to confront both the imperial powers and the capitalist system within which they grew.

Karl Marx made the essential point that no matter how much the spread of capitalist relations may transform the economic structure of what is now called the third world, no matter how many nations attain independence, the fundamental task of human liberation still falls to working people. Writing of British rule in India he argued:

> 'All the English bourgeoisie may be forced to do will nei-
> ther emancipate nor materially mend the social condition
> of the mass of the people ... But what they will not fail to
> do is to lay down the material premises for both. Has the
> bourgeoisie ever done more? Has it ever effected a pro-
> gress without dragging individuals and peoples through
> blood and dirt, through misery and degradation?
>
> The Indians will not reap the fruits of the new elements
> of society scattered among them by the British bourgeoisie
> till in Great Britain itself the now ruling classes have been
> supplanted by the industrial proletariat, or till the Hindus
> themselves shall have grown strong enough to throw off
> the English yoke ...' [7]

The British were eventually driven from India, but the fundamental task that Marx outlined remains unfinished. Since
Marx's day the working class in India and elsewhere in the third
world has grown to be able to take a much more prominent
role in dealing with the inheritors of imperial rule, be they
indigenous bourgeoisies or new foreign powers. The growth of
the international working class has, nevertheless, been a slow
process. Peasants have been, and perhaps still are, a majority of
the world's oppressed and exploited. Various forms of 'extra-
economic' coercion over labour remained a feature of the
system well into the 20th century. In the less industrialised
economies the working class is more differentiated into agricultural and semi-proletarian layers than elsewhere. But for all
this, as one important study shows, 'as the colonial era gave way
to post-colonialism after the Second World War, so the traditional division of labour began to change. A substantial if
uneven, industrial development began in many areas of the
Third World which significantly altered the social and economic

conditions of labour.'[8] This was a new international division of labour that

> 'fundamentally restructured the relations of production in the Third World, with the emergence of a substantial manufacturing sector oriented on towards the world market. The "world market factories" carried out super-exploitation of their mainly female workers, but created the conditions for the emergence of a "classical" confrontation between labour and capital.'[9]

We have seen this long-term economic process of class formation begin to express itself, albeit unevenly, in class consciousness and class organisation. If we think of the unions in countries as distant as South Africa, South Korea, China, Brazil and Indonesia we can see the possibilities. And as part of this process of class organisation political consciousness and political, sometimes overtly socialist, organisations have begun to build.

Conclusion

Resistance to imperialism and capitalism is by no means homogeneous. Even among socialists reformist and revolutionary alternatives exist. And socialism, however defined, is by no means the only or the major set of ideas contending to express resistance to the system. Nationalism and Islamic ideas, to mention only two of the most prominent trends, command the support of many millions of workers, peasants and the poor around the globe.

Nevertheless, socialists do have a better chance than for many generations to build support for their views. Globalisation has created an international working class bigger than at any time in the history of capitalism. But it has failed to create a system that can sustain an acceptable livelihood for or, in many parts of the world, even the very lives of millions of workers. One consequence of this is a renewed drive to war characteristic of the contemporary imperial structure. The fall of Stalinism means that there is no 'external' enemy to blame. This situation has, therefore, created a crisis of confidence in the system. The physical expression of this crisis is the international anti-capitalist and anti-war movement.

It is in this movement that socialists can begin to win a much wider audience for the idea that working people have the power to transform their world. Moreover they can begin to successfully advance the view that the system can be replaced with an international system of co-operative labour so organised that it meets the needs of those who produce social wealth. The alternative to this project is unacceptable. It is that we allow our rulers to continue the routine business of imperialism, the organisation of human misery.

Notes

1 Arms and America

1 See *The Economist*, American Survey, 7 April 1990 and *Business Week*, 'At Ease, disarming Europe', 19 February 1990. For commentary see J Rees, 'The New Imperialism', in A Callinicos, J Rees, M Haynes and C Harman, *Marxism and the New Imperialism* (London, 1994) pp. 78–79.

2 *World Military Expenditure and Arms Transfers* 1996 (July 1997) pp. 49–99. *World Military Expenditures and Arms Transfers*, or *WMEAT*, is an annual originally published by the US Arms Control and Disarmament Agency. It is now published by the Bureau of Verification and Compliance of the US State Department.

3 Graph from *World Military Expenditures and Arms Transfers* (*WMEAT*), see footnote 2 above. While the US spending data in the three editions of *WMEAT* are essentially identical (where they overlap), the estimates of world military spending differ. This results in the three curves being distinct.

4 Data from *World Military Expenditures and Arms Transfers* (*WMEAT*), see footnote 2 above. The numbers shown for spending are in billions of US dollars. They are not adjusted for inflation.

5 Data from *World Military Expenditures and Arms Transfers* (*WMEAT*), see footnote 2 above. The numbers shown for national military spending are in billions of US dollars. They are not adjusted for inflation.

6 See 'Project on Defense Alternatives, Post Cold War US Military Expenditure in the Context of World Spending Trends', www.comw.org/pda/bmemo10.htm#2 The 'threat states' for 1986 include member states of the Warsaw Pact, China, Cuba, Iran, Iraq, Libya, North Korea, Syria, and Vietnam. For 1994 they include Russia, Belarus, China, Cuba, Iran, Iraq, Libya, North Korea, Syria, and Vietnam.

7 S Pelletiere, *America's Oil Wars* (Westport, 2004) p. 110.

8 Ibid., p. 112 and p. 115.

9 H Kissinger, *Diplomacy* (New York, 1994) p. 813. See A Callincos, *The New Mandarins of American Power* (Cambridge, 2003) pp. 57–59 for further commentary.

10 S Pelletiere, op. cit., p. 119.

11 See G Achcar, 'Rasputin plays at chess: how the West blundered into a new cold war' in T Ali (ed), *Masters of the Universe, NATO's Balkan Crusade* (Verso, 2000) pp. 66–72.

12 Ibid., p. 72.

13 Quoted in A Rashid, *Taliban, Oil, Islam and the New Great Game in Central Asia* (I B Tauris, 2000) p. 130.

14 D Johnstone, 'Humanitarian War: making the crime fit the punishment', in T Ali (ed), op. cit., p. 154.

15 G Achcar, op. cit., p. 74.

16 See G Monbiot, 'A Discreet Deal in the Pipeline', *The Guardian*, 15 February 2001.

17 See, 'Bulgaria: AMBO Trans-Balkan Pipeline Agreement Finally Signed', available at www.balkanalysis.com/modules.php?name = News&file = article&sid = 478

18 Letter to President Clinton on Iraq, 26 January 1998, reprinted in M L Sifry and C Cerf, *The Iraq War Reader* (New York, 2003) pp. 199–201.

19 S Pelletiere, op. cit. pp. 122–24.

20 Ibid. pp. 125–27.

21 See M Renner, 'Post-Saddam Iraq: Linchpin of a New Oil Order', in M L Sifry et al., op. cit., p. 582.

22 J Risen, *State of War, the secret history of the CIA and the Bush administration* (New York, 2006) p. 166.

23 'The National Security Strategy of the United States', available on the US government website.

24 M Klare, 'The New Geopolitics', in *Monthly Review*, July/August 2003, p. 55.

2 US economic power in the age of globalisation

1   M. Beaud, *A History of Capitalism 1500–1980* (London, 1984), p. 186 and, for Russia and Britain, B R Mitchell, *European Historical Statistics 1750–1970* (London, 1978), pp. 224–25.

2   M. Beaud, op. cit., p. 186.

3   P Kennedy, *The Rise and Fall of Great Powers* (London, 1989), pp. 454–59.

4   Ibid., pp. 460–61.

5   P Armstrong, A Glyn and J Harrison, *Capitalism Since World War II* (London, 1984), pp. 213–14.

6   M Beaud, op. cit., p. 186.

7   See M Kidron, *Western Capitalism Since the War* (London, 1970), p. 38.

8   P Armstrong et al., op. cit., p. 214.

9   Quoted in D Smith, *Pressure – How America Runs NATO* (London, 1989), p. 55.

10 Quoted in P Sedgwick, 'NATO, The Bomb and Socialism', *Universities and Left Review* No. 7, Autumn 1959, p. 8.

11 Ibid., p. 8.

12 Quoted in P Kennedy, op. cit., p. 503.

13 P Kennedy, op. cit., p. 558.

14 P Armstrong et al., op. cit., p. 219.

15 *World Bank, World Development Report* 1989 (Oxford University Press, 1989) p. 167.

16 P Armstrong et. al., op. cit., pp. 225–26.

17 P Kennedy, op. cit., p. 558.

18 A Bergsen and R Fernandez, 'Who Has the Most Fortune 500 Firms? A Network Analysis of Global Economic Competition, 1956–89', in V Bornschier and C Chase-Dunn, *The Future of Global Conflict* (London, 1999) p. 151.

19 P Kennedy, op. cit., p. 679.

20 Ibid., pp. 554–55.

21 I Wallerstein, 'US Weakness and the Struggle for Hegemony', in *Monthly Review*, July-August 2003, p. 24.

22 Ibid., p. 25.

23 R Brenner, *The Boom and the Bubble, the US in the World Economy* (London, 2002), p. 94.

24 P Gowan, 'US Hegemony Today', in *Monthly Review*, July-August 2003, p. 42.

25 R Brenner, op. cit., pp. 300–301.

26 Ibid., pp. 119–20.

27 Ibid., pp. 124–25

28 Ibid., p. 102.

29 For further discussion see J Rees, 'The New Imperialism', in A Callinicos, C Harman, M Haynes and J Rees, *Marxism and the New Imperialism* (London, 1994) p. 73.

30 See M Haynes, *Russia, Class and Power 1917–2000* (London, 2002) p. 205.

31 Ibid., p. 208.

32 B Kagarlitsky, 'The Russian State in the Age of the American Empire', in L Panitch and C Leys (eds), *The Empire Reloaded* (The Socialist Register, 2005) p. 281.

33 Ibid.

34 Ibid., pp. 282–83.

35 V Mallet and G Dinmore, 'The rivals: Washington's sway in Asia is challenged by China', *Financial Times*, 18 March 2005, p. 19.

36 Ibid.

37 See W Bello, *Dilemmas of Domination, the Unmaking of the American Empire* (New York, 2005) pp. 94–96.

38 V Mallet and G Dinmore, op. cit., p. 19.

39 See the report by *Bloomberg*, 'China's Thirst for Oil Undercuts US Effort to Rein in Iran', (20 December 2004) at www.bloomberg.com/apps/news?pid = 10000103&sid = aGcFtg1NJEMA&refer = US

40 R McGregor and E Alden, 'US running out of patience over China's ballooning trade surplus', *Financial Times*, 15 March 2006.

41 P Gowan, op. cit., p. 46.

42 C Katz, 'Latin America's new "left" governments', in *International Socialism* 107 (London, Summer 2005) p. 146.

43 Ibid.

44 Ibid., p. 152.

45 R Brenner, op. cit., p. 127.

46　Ibid., p. 285.
47　See W Bello, op. cit., p. 79.

3　Oil and empire

1　S Shah, *Crude, the story of oil* (New York, 2004) p. 180.
2　*The Economist*, 27 August 2005, p. 66.
3　S Shah, op. cit., p. 133.
4　*The Economist*, op. cit., p. 11.
5　S Shah, op. cit., pp. 177–78.
6　See G Monbiot, *The Guardian*, 27 September 2005, p. 27.
7　Ibid.
8　M Klare, *Blood and Oil* (London, 2004) p. 23.
9　M Yeomans, *Oil, anatomy of an industry* (The New Press, 2004) p. 6.
10　S Shah, op. cit., pp. 144–45.
11　M Klare, op. cit., p. xxi, and pp. 10–13.
12　Ibid., pp. 32–37.
13　M Yeomans, op. cit., p. 12.
14　P Marshall, *Intifada. Zionism, Imperialism and the Palestinian Resistance* (Bookmarks, 1989) p. 49.
15　J Rose, *Israel: the hijack state. America's Watchdog in the Middle East* (Bookmarks, 2002) pp. 23–24.
16　D Yergin, *The Prize, the epic quest for oil, money and power* (Free Press, 2003) p. 451.
17　Ibid., p. 458.
18　Ibid., p. 468.
19　Ibid., p. 485.
20　Ibid., p. 492.
21　See T Cliff, 'The Struggle in the Middle East' in T Cliff, *International Struggle in the Middle East, Selected Writings*, Volume 1, London, 2001, p. 49.
22　M Yeomans, op. cit., p. 25.
23　Quoted in D Yergin, op. cit., p. 683.
24　See D Yergin, ibid., p. 702.
25　Quoted in M Klare, op. cit., p. 50.
26　M Klare, ibid., p. 87.
27　Quoted in M Klare, ibid., p. 114.
28　Quoted in ibid., p. 114.
29　See ibid., p. 136.
30　Quoted in ibid., p. 155.
31　Ibid., p. 157.
32　See http://www.gravmag.com/oil.html#worldfields
33　Quoted in M Klare, op. cit., p. 78.
34　P Marshall, *Revolution and Counter-Revolution in Iran* (London, 1988) p. 80.

4　Globalisation and inequality

1　M Parvizi Amineh, *Towards the Control of Oil Resources in the Caspian Region* (New York, 1999) pp. 5–6.

2 Ibid., pp. 7–8.
3 Ibid., pp. 6–7.
4 Ibid., p. 11.
5 See C Leys, *Market-Driven Politics* (London, 2001) p. 15.
6 Ibid., p. 41.
7 Ibid.
8 Ibid., pp. 38–39.
9 N Bukharin, *Imperialism and the World Economy* (Bookmarks, 2003) p. 135.
10 For some further remarks on the strengths and weaknesses of Bukharin's analysis see J Rees, 'Nicolai Bukharin and modern imperialism', the foreword to N Bukharin, op. cit., p. 5–6.
11 B Groom, 'As accusations fly between BBC and government, is there a deepening crisis of trust in British public life?', *Financial Times*, 26–27 July 2003, p. 11.
12 Onora O'Neill's Reith lectures, paraphrased in B Groom, ibid.
13 See D Harvey, *A Brief History of Neoliberalism* (Oxford, 2005) p. 16.
14 Quoted in D Harvey, op. cit., pp. 17–19.
15 Office of National Statistics, 'Household Income', available at National Statistics Online, www.statistics.gov.uk
16 D Pilling, 'Engels and the condition of the working class today' in J Lea and G Pilling (eds), *The Condition of Britain, essays on Frederick Engels* (Pluto Press, 1996) p. 19.
17 Office of National Statistics, 'Income Inequality, gap widens slightly from mid-1990s', at National Statisitics Online, www.statistics.gov.uk
18 H Thompson, 'New survey show widespread deprivation in Britain' (27 September 2000) available at www.wsws.org/articles/2000/sep2000/pov-s27_prn.shtml
19 Ibid.
20 R Wachman, 'Top bosses pay doubles in a decade', *The Observer*, 27 July 2003.
21 S Wheelan, 'New data reveal rising poverty under Britain's Labour government', at www.wsws.org/articles/2000/jul2000/pov-j27_prn.shtml
22 Ibid.
23 See C Leys, *Market Driven Politics, neo-liberal democracy and the public interest* (Verso, 2001) pp. 48–49
24 'Simulating the century'. *The Economist*, 6 January 2000.
25 See www.econ.brown.edu/fac/louis_patterman/courses/ec151/chapter_01.doc
26 H P Martin and H Schumann, *The Global Trap* (London, 1997) p. 29.
27 B Sutcliffe, *100 Ways of Seeing an Unequal World* (London, 2001) p. 14.
28 See www.econ.brown.edu/fac/louis_patterman/courses/ec151/chapter_01.doc
29 See 'Undernourishment around the world' and 'Counting the hungry: recent trends in developing countries and countries in transition', www.fao.org/docrep/006/j0083e03.htm
30 D Harvey, op. cit., p. 17.
31 D Sherman and B Garret, 'Why Non-Globalized States Pose a Threat'. This article originally appeared in *Yale Global*. Copyright 2005 University of

Wisconsin-Madison School of Business. Available at http://www.bus.wisc.edu/update/winter03/globalization.asp

32 See N Chomsky, *Rogue States* (London, 2000) p. 102.

33 Ibid.

34 Quoted in H P Martin et al., op. cit., p. 24.

35 D Montgomery, 'For many protesters, Bush isn't the main issue', *The Washington Post*, 20 January 2001, p. A14.

36 'Butskellism', after Tory politician Rab Butler and Labour leader Hugh Gaitskell, designed to illustrate the cross-party, pro-welfare state consensus of the post-war boom.

37 Ofsted is the acronym for the Office for Standards in Education, the watchdog organisation that enforces government education policy.

38 G Evans, 'The working class and New Labour: a parting of the ways?', in *British Social Attitudes, 17th Report, 2000–2001* (National Centre for Social Research, 2000) pp. 52–56.

39 Ibid., p. 52.

40 'Election turnout to slump, poll says', ICM/Guardian poll, 23 January 2001. See http://uk.news.yahoo.com/010123/11/axk43.html

41 *State of the Nation October 2000*, ICM research poll conducted for the Joseph Rowntree Trust, reported in *The Sunday Times*, 21 November 2000, p. 10.

42 Ibid.

43 M Macleod, *Scotland on Sunday*, 5 March 2006.

44 'New economy: myths and reality', *Financial Times*, 13/14 January 2001.

45 'Persisting inequalities underline the poverty challenge for Government', Joseph Rowntree Trust press release, 8 December 1999. See www.jrf.org.uk/pressroom/releases/081299.htm

46 Quoted in ibid.

47 'New economy: myths and reality', *Financial Times*, 13/14 January 2001.

48 Ibid.

5 Their democracy and ours

1 G Rudé, *The French Revolution*, (London 1996) p. 14.

2 K Marx, 'Speech at the Trial of the Rhenish District Committee of Democrats', 8 February 1849, first published in *Neue Rhenische Zeitung* Nos. 231 and 232 (25 and 27 February 1849). A text of this is available in K Marx, *The Revolutions of 1848* (Penguin, 1973) p. 262 but I have used the translation available on the Marx-Engels Archive website: www.marx.org

3 Thomas Jefferson was actually in Paris when the Declaration of the Rights of Man was written. Tom Paine and Lafayette, 'the hero of two continents', joined the revolution, although significantly both were on its moderate wing.

4 B R Mitchell, *European Historical Statistics 1750–1970* (London, 1975) pp. 799–800. The figures for England and Wales are from 1788.

5 Quoted in A Soboul, *Short History of the French Revolution, 1789-99* (Berkeley, 1977), p. 10. This was no exaggeration: only nobles could be Bishops or army officers. Nobles were exempt from taxes which fell most heavily on a peasantry treated as little more than beasts of burden. Some historians have

balked at describing French society before the revolution as feudal because some of the features of the high feudalism of the Middle Ages had already disappeared. But this is to miss the point made so clearly by de Tocqueville at the time: 'Feudalism had remained the most important of our civil institutions even after it had ceased to be a political institution. In this form it aroused still greater hatred, and we should observe that the disappearance of part of the institutions of the Middle Ages only made what survived of them a hundred times more odious'. See A Soboul, op. cit., p. 23.

6 The definitive account of this process is Brian Manning's *The English People and the English Revolution* (Bookmarks, 1991).

7 See Rudé's excellent synopsis of class consciousness in the bourgeois revolution in *Ideology and Popular Protest* (Chapel Hill, 1980) p. 75. The revolution is fundamentally a conflict between 'the "rising" bourgeoisie and the established feudal or aristocratic class that it was seeking to displace from the levers of social and political control'. As George Rudé explains, 'there is more to it than that: in each of these revolutions ... there was also an additional popular element that was also struggling for a place in the sun ... In the English revolution of the seventeenth century, there were not only the leaders of Parliament and the New Model Army, the Presbyterians and the Independents (all broadly representative of the "bourgeois" challenge), but also the Levellers, Diggers and lower class sectaries, who offered some sort of challenge in the name of other, "lower", social groups.'

8 B Levin et al., *Who Built America?* (New York, 1989) p. 132.

9 For an excellent short introduction to the French Revolution see P McGarr, 'The Great French Revolution' in P McGarr and A Callinicos, *Marxism and the Great French Revolution* (International Socialism, 1993).

10 See G Rudé, op. cit., p. 38.

11 Quoted in L Trotsky, *Writings on Britain*, Vol.2 (London, 1974) p. 90.

12 Quoted in A Soboul, op. cit., p. 79.

13 Quoted in ibid., pp. 86–87.

14 G Rudé, op. cit., p. 103.

15 See S R Gardiner, *Oliver Cromwell* (E P Publishing, 1976) pp. 167–68.

16 B. Levine et al., op. cit., p. 163.

17 Quoted in H Zinn, *A People's History of the United States* (Longman, 1980) p. 94.

18 A Soboul, *Understanding the French Revolution* (London, 1998) p. 23.

19 See I Birchall, 'The Babeuf bicentenary: conspiracy or revolutionary party' in *International Socialism* 72, Autumn 1996 pp. 77–93. Also I Birchall, *The Spectre of Babeuf* (London, 1997).

20 Marx and Engels, *The Manifesto of the Communist Party* in Marx, *The Revolutions of 1848* (Penguin, 1973) p. 98. The *Manifesto* was of course written before the outbreak of the revolution.

21 Ibid., p. 97.

22 D Fernbach, introduction to Marx, *Revolutions of 1848*, ibid., p. 38.

23 Marx, *The Bourgeoisie and the Counter-Revolution*, in ibid., pp. 193–94.

24 Marx, *Address of the Central Committee*, in ibid., pp. 329–30.

25 Engels, quoted in H Draper, *Karl Marx's Theory of Revolution*, Vol. II (London, 1978) p. 257.

26 Marx, *Address of the Central Committee*, op. cit., p. 330.

27 A good account of the bourgeois revolutions from above can be found in A Callinicos, 'Bourgeois revolutions and historical materialism' in P McGarr and A Callinicos, op. cit.

28 V I Lenin, *Two Tactics of Social Democracy in the Democratic Revolution*, in *Selected Works* (Moscow, 1975) p. 60.

29 Trotsky's theory is given in full in the Pathfinder Press book *Permanent Revolution*. But perhaps the best account of the theory of combined and uneven development as it applies to Russia is given in the chapter on 'Peculiarities of Russia's Development' in Trotsky's *History of the Russian Revolution*.

30 L Trotsky, *The History of the Russian Revolution* (Pluto Press, 1977) pp. 180–81.

31 Quoted in E H Carr, *The Bolshevik Revolution 1917–1923*, vol. III (London, 1966) p. 53.

32 Quoted in ibid., pp. 17–18.

33 Ibid., p. 59.

34 T Cliff, *Deflected Permanent Revolution* (London, 1986). Originally published in the first series of *International Socialism* (no.12), Spring 1963. Also see T Cliff, *Trotskyism After Trotsky* (London, 1999) chapter 4.

35 Ibid., p. 20.

36 Ibid.

37 Ibid.

38 Ibid., p. 21.

39 J Beinin and Z Lockman, *Workers on the Nile, nationalism, communism, Islam and the Egyptian working class 1882–1954*, Cairo, 1998, p. 11.

40 T Cliff, 'The Struggle in the Middle East', in T Cliff, *International Struggle and the Marxist Tradition, Selected Writings*, Volume 1, pp. 46–47.

41 Ibid., p. 47.

42 Quoted in A Hoogvelt, *Globalisation and the Postcolonial World* (London, 1997) pp. 197–98.

43 Ibid., p. 198.

44 Calculated from figures in B R Mitchell, op. cit., p. 358

45 T Garton Ash, *The Polish Revolution: Solidarity* (London, 1985) p. 17.

46 Ibid., p. 25.

47 See the excellent account in C Barker and K Weber, *Solidarnosc, from Gdansk to Military Reperssion* (International Socialism, 1982).

48 Quoted in ibid., p. 29.

49 The latest English language editon is J Kuron and K Modzelewski, *Solidarnosc: the Missing Link? The Classic Open Letter to the Party* (Bookmarks, 1982) see pp. 72–82 and p. 86.

50 Ibid., p. 56.

51 See C Harman, *Class Struggles in Eastern Europe 1945–83* (London, 1983) pp. 279–80.

52 See interview with Orzechowski in D Pryce-Jones, *The War That Never Was, the fall of the Soviet empire 1985–1991* (London, 1995) p. 213. Pryce-Jones' book combines unreconstructed right-wing Cold War commentary with

genuinely valuable interviews with some of the leading figures in the East
European revolutions.

53 See interview with Jaruzelski in ibid., p. 215.

54 See interview with Orzechowski in ibid., p. 212.

55 J Kuron, 'Overcoming totalitarianism', reprinted in V Tismaneanu, *The Revolutions of 1989* (London, 1999) pp. 200–201.

56 Ibid., p. 199.

57 C Harman, op. cit., p. 297.

58 E Hankiss, 'What the Hungarians saw first' in G Prins (ed.), *Spring in Winter, the 1989 revolutions* (Manchester, 1990) p. 15.

59 Ibid., pp. 25–26.

60 Ibid., p. 26.

61 Ibid., p. 27. 'There are various ways of converting to new power if you are a Kadarist oligarch. … The characteristic oligarchic family in the mid-1980s was the father or grandfather, a party **apparachik**, a high level party or state official; his son a manager of a British/Hungarian joint venture; his son-in-law with a boutique in Vaci Street; his daughter an editor for Hungarian television; his nephew studying at Cambridge or Oxford; his mother-in-law having a small hotel or boarding house on Lake Balaton etc. … These family businesses are absolutely top secret. However, we did discover more than two hundred and fifty businesses belonging to this kind of diversified oligarchic family and there must be several hundred more.'

62 Ibid.

63 Ibid., pp. 30–31.

64 See interview with Kulcsar in D Pryce-Jones, op. cit., pp. 224–25.

65 Ibid., p. 225.

66 Interview with Istvan Horvath, then Hungarian Minister of the Interior, in ibid., p. 232.

67 Honecker quoted in ibid., p. 274 by the then Russian ambassador to East Germany.

68 Quoted in ibid., p. 236.

69 See the account in J Riech, 'Reflections on becoming an East German dissident', in G Prins (ed.), *Spring in Winter*, op. cit., p. 81.

70 Ibid., p. 88.

71 Ibid., pp. 71–72.

72 Ibid., pp. 72–73.

73 J Urban, *Czechoslovakia: the power and politics of humiliation*, in G Prins (ed.), op. cit., p. 116.

74 Ibid., p. 108.

75 The events surrounding the 17 November demonstration and the degree to which they were shaped by a plot to replace Husak have been the subject of two Czechoslovakian government commissions of inquiry. The account in this paragraph is based on evidence cited in G Prins (ed.), ibid., p. 116–17 and in D Pryce-Jones, op. cit., p. 322.

76 Ibid., p. 121–22.

77 Quoted in D Pryce-Jones, op. cit., p. 321.

78 Quoted in G Prins (ed.), op. cit., p. 124.

79 From the transcript of the Political Executive Committee meeting, quoted in D Pryce-Jones, op. cit., p. 341.
80 See ibid., p. 358.
81 Ibid., p. 353.
82 Ibid., p. 350.
83 A Michnik, 'The velvet restoration' in V Tismaneanu, op. cit., p. 248.
84 Ibid., p. 249.
85 J Reich, op. cit., p. 97.
86 J Urban, op. cit., p. 136.
87 M Haynes and R Husan, 'The State and Market in the Transition Economies: Critical Remarks in the Light of Past History and Current Experience', *The Journal of European Economic History*, Volume 27, No. 3 (Banca Di Roma, Winter 1998) pp. 367–68.
88 P Stephens, 'Dark Continent', *Financial Times*, 23 April 1999.
89 J Rees, 'The Socialist Revolution and the Democratic Revolution', in *International Socialism* 83 (London, Summer 1999).
90 Ibid., p. 263. See also D T McKinley, *The ANC and the Liberation Struggle* (London, 1997) p. 6.
91 Quoted in D T McKinley, op. cit., p. 22.
92 Quoted in ibid., p. 34.
93 Quoted in D T McKinley, op. cit., p. 89. Emphasis in the original.
94 Marx, *The Bourgtoisic and the Counter-Revolution*, op. cit., p. 194.
95 A Hoogvelt, op cit., p. 229
96 Duncan Green, quoted in ibid.
97 Ibid., p. 231.
98 'Lula's leap', *The Economist*, 4 March 2006, pp. 57–59.
99 D Plavsic, 'Manufactured Revolutions?', *International Socialism* 107 (London, Summer 2005) pp. 21–30.
100 Ibid., p. 22.
101 Quoted in ibid., p. 26.
102 Ibid., p. 27.

6 War and ideology

1 *Financial Times*, 'The US is going cold on Arab democracy', 15 February 2006
2 S Huntington, *The Clash of Civilisations and the Remaking of the World Order* (London, 1997) pp. 255–58.
3 Samir Amin, for instance, in a speech given to the Socialist Days conference in Cairo, 25 February, 2006, has argued that the Muslim Brotherhood in Egypt is part of the ruling class.
4 S Huntington, op. cit., p. 258.
5 A Beattie, 'Global pain hits poor, distant and the Islamic', *Financial Times*, 15 March 2006, p. 15.
6 A Negri and M Hardt, *Empire*, quoted in E Meiksins Wood, 'A manifesto for global capital?' in G Balakrishnan (ed), *Debating Empire* (London, 2003) p. 64.

7 L Panitch and S Gindin, 'Global Capitalism and American Empire' in *Socialist Register* 2004 (London, 2003) p. 32.
8 Ibid., p. 19.
9 Ibid., p. 23.
10 L Panitch and S Gindin, 'Gems and Baubles in Empire' in G Balakrishnan (ed), op. cit., p. 52–60.
11 E Meiksins Wood, 'A manifesto for global capital?' in G Balakrishnan (ed), op. cit., p. 65.
12 Ibid., p. 69.
13 For an excellent critique of Panitch and Gindin on these points see Alex Callinicos, 'Imperialism and global political economy' in *International Socialism* 108 Autumn 2005, pp. 109–27.
14 L Elliott, 'World gears up for tension as emerging nations threaten to put G7 countries in the back seat', *The Guardian*, 6 March 2006, p. 30.
15 M Hardt and A Negri, *Multitude* (London, 2004) p. xiv.
16 Ibid., p. xv.
17 See C Harman, 'The workers of the world' in *International Socialism* 96, Autumn 2002, pp. 6–9.
18 See for instance B Deer, 'Still struggling after all these years', *New Statesman*, 24 August 1996, pp. 12–14. This shows among other things that in Gallup polls conducted since 1961 the percentage believing that there is a class struggle in Britain has risen from 56 percent to 76 percent in 1996.
19 M Hardt et al., op. cit., p. xvi.
20 A Callinicos, 'Toni Negri in Perspective' in G Balakrishnan (ed), op. cit., pp. 121–43.

7 Resisting imperialism

1 For the best account of the rise of the anti-war movement in Britain see A Murray and L German, *Stop the War, the story of Britain's biggest mass movement* (London, 2005).
2 See Alex Callinicos' column, *Socialist Worker*, 19 March 2005.
3 G Lukacs, *Lenin, a study in the unity of his thought* (London, 1977) p. 46.
4 G Lukacs, *History and Class Consciousness* (London, 1971) p. 311.
5 V I Lenin, *Collected Works*, Vol. 23 (Moscow 1964) p. 61.
6 Ibid., Vol. 22, pp. 355–57.
7 K Marx, quoted in A Brewer, *Marxist Theories of Imperialism, a Critical Survey* (London, 1980) p. 58.
8 R Munck, *The New International Labour Studies* (London, 1988) p. 33.
9 Ibid.

Further reading

This is by no means an exhaustive bibliography, merely some suggestions that the general reader may find of interest. The best overall accounts of the new imperialism are David Harvey's *The New Imperialism* (Oxford, 2003), Walden Bello's *Dilemmas of Domination* (Metropolitan Books, 2005), Tariq Ali's *The Clash of Fundamentalisms* (Verso, 2002), Ellen Meiksins Wood's *Empire of Capital* (Verso, 2003), Michael Mann's *Incoherent Empire* (Verso, 2003) and Alex Callinicos' excellent *The New Mandarins of American Power* (Polity, 2003). Ankie Hoogvelt's *Globalisation and the Post-Colonial World* (Macmillan, 1997) is very valuable. Gabriel Kolko's *The Politics of War* (Pantheon, 1968) is indispensable for understanding the post-war settlement.

The condition of the world economy is clearly and effectively analysed in Chris Harman's *Explaining the Crisis* (Bookmarks, 1984) and Robert Brenner's *The Boom and the Bubble* (Verso, 2002). Peter Gowan's *The Global Gamble* (Verso, 1999) contains many useful insights. David Harvey's *Neoliberalism* (Oxford, 2005) charts the rise of the supporting ideology of the new economic order. John Pilger's *New Rulers of the World* (Verso, 2002) tells us much about the courses through which power runs in our society.

The classical Marxist analysis of imperialism is best approached through Nikolai Bukharin's *Imperialism and the World Economy* (Bookmarks, 2003) and Lenin's *Imperialism, the Highest Stage of Capitalism*. The outstanding study of oil and the Middle East is

Daniel Yergin's *The Prize* (Free Press, 1991) and Michael Klare's *Blood and Oil* (Penguin, 2005) also contains useful information. Brian Lapping's *The End of Empire* (Paladin, 1989) and David Fromkin's *A Peace to End all Peace* (Penguin, 1989) both repay careful reading.

Paul Foot's *The Vote* (Penguin, 2005) is the best study of the evolution of the suffrage and radical politics in Britain. Timothy Garton Ash's *The Polish Revolution: Solidarity* (Coronet, 1983) is, surprisingly given the author's politics, a marvellous history.

The rise of the new mood of resistance can be charted in *The Return of Radicalism* (Pluto, 2000) by Boris Kagarlitsky and *An Anti-Capitalist Manifesto* (Polity, 2003) by Alex Callinicos. An excellent study of the new imperialism and the best account of the anti-war movement in Britain are to be found in Andrew Murray and Lindsey German's *Stop the War* (Bookmarks, 2005).

Index